PRAISE FOR ?

Edmond Schoorel explains the young child's physiology for parents and teachers from a wide perspective, then brings it down to practical details when he writes about the naughty or forgetful child. Diverse topics—such as the birthing process, children's drawings, the physiology of speech and hearing, the physiology of curiosity—are shown in a new light to aid and renew our creativity as educators. This wonderful book has a helpful summary at the end of each chapter and an index. Warmly recommended for everyone who has an interest in young children.

—Christa van Tellingen, M.D.

This book may well become the new study text for Waldorf early childhood educators. It looks deeply into the nature of the fourfold human being and the processes of transformation that characterize child development in the first seven years of life. Dr. Schoorel's book bridges the gap between education and medicine. I highly recommend it to anyone concerned with the healthy growth and development of the very young.

—Rena Osmer, Director of Early Childhood Education,
Rudolf Steiner College

The First Seven Years
Physiology of Childhood

Edmond Schoorel

Rudolf Steiner College Press

The original edition of this book, *De eerste zeven jaar*, was published in The Netherlands. ISBN 90 6238 559 1 © 1998 Edmond Schoorel / Uitgeverij Christofoor, Zeist 1998

This English language edition was translated from the Dutch by Hendrik van Heek in cooperation with Christa van Tellingen M.D. and Dorothy Hinkle-Uhlig. Publication of this book has been made possible by a grant from the Waldorf Curriculum Fund.

Cover photograph of Riely Wilm, by kind permision of Sara and Nick Wilm
Cover design: Claude Julien and Keith Henderson

ISBN 0 945803 68 0

The content of this book represents the view of the author and should not be taken as the official opinion or policy of Rudolf Steiner College or Rudolf Steiner College Press.

Table of Contents

Foreword

by Joan Almon

As a Waldorf kindergarten teacher and educator of teachers, I often wished for a book such as this one. It presents in clear yet imaginative pictures the deeper development of the child as researched initially by Rudolf Steiner and then by countless others, working on the basis of anthroposophy with children around the world. In the first seven years of child development, one sees tremendous similarities in children. In my work as a traveling Waldorf kindergarten teacher, I visited kindergartens in about 25 countries on five continents. I relished the differences among children according to their land of origin, ethnicity, religion, or race, but I was deeply moved by the commonalities that young children display no matter where they are born or into what socioeconomic group. The laws of development are at work in children throughout the world, and they are subtle, rich, and complex. Edmond Schoorel helps make these laws more visible by bringing an esoteric understanding to his descriptions of children's development.

Childhood, as a special stage of human development, is under attack and is often disappearing from the lives of children. Developing a new understanding of child development has become essential, and while the new brain research is impressive and often quite helpful, there is much more that needs to be explored and developed. Such exploration is the task of caring adults—parents, educators, therapists, physicians and others—but a book such as this one, which gives the overall pictures, is a great help.

When I began teaching young children in the early 1970s, there was still an inherent respect for the laws of child development. They may not have been fully understood, but the assumption was that such laws existed and should serve as the foundation for children's education. Things began to change visibly, however, as the demand for hurrying children took hold in the 1970s and 80s. The normal timetable of development no longer sufficed. Children were expected to do more and do it sooner. Despite the warning cries of David Elkind, Jane Healy, Joseph Chilton Pearce and others, the majority of parents, educators, and policy makers did not stop and ask how much stress and strain the children would endure with this sped-up process or what price they would have to pay in the long run. Rather, a mechanistic view of the human being was subtly taking hold, and the idea seemed to be that you could speed up the child's development by applying more gas and putting him on the fast track.

The result has been a growing stress in the lives of children as they strive to satisfy expectations of parents and educators. And with stress and strain come many physical and mental illnesses, which are on the rise among children of all socioeconomic levels. These include depression, hyperactive disorders, and autism, as well as asthma, allergies, obesity, and Type 2 diabetes, formerly called late-onset diabetes but now afflicting children and teens in alarming numbers. There is also growing concern about speech delays, and sleep and eating disorders in childhood. All of this points to the need to more fully penetrate the mysteries of child development and then create appropriate ways to educate and raise children.

One area where I have painfully watched the application of the hurried approach is in the introduction of early academics in the lives of kindergarten and nursery school children. Beginning in the early 1970's, the U.S. began to make major changes in kindergarten education. Basically, the first grade curriculum in writing, reading, and arithmetic was brought into the kindergartens, and over the past three decades the expectation that children would know their letters and be able to do basic reading by the end of kindergarten took hold. The problem is that only a small percentage of children is actually ready for this step at age $5^1/2$ or 6. Yet nearly all children are ready at age seven to focus their attention on the skills needed for writing and reading. What happens to children when we ask them to do too much, too soon?

School districts report that there are some short-term gains among children who are introduced to reading in a consistent way in kindergarten. In first grade they show more ability in this area than children who were not introduced to writing and reading. But these gains do not last. By fourth grade they generally have disappeared, and some reports then show that children who were allowed to play creatively in kindergarten excel over the children who had an academic approach. These gains have been found in physical, social, emotional, and mental development. The effects are especially pronounced among low-income children who can fall seriously behind if they are educated in ways that are not developmentally sound.

After thirty years of making kindergarten an academic experience for children—and now generally doing it for a full day rather than a half day—people recognize that it has not worked. But again, there is no understanding of why it has not worked. Rather than seeing that what has been demanded of children is inconsistent with their own phases of

8

development, policy makers now want to begin introducing academic subjects to ever younger children and want to emphasize early literacy training for three- and four-year-olds. The President and members of Congress seem intent on having young children assessed to see how much they have learned in nursery school and then evaluating their preschool programs accordingly. Again, a few children may be ready for this direct instruction in early print literacy, but the vast majority will suffer, and the rates of illness related to stress and strain will almost certainly increase.

How do we counter these new attempts at what Elkind once called "the miseducation of the child"? There are at least two aspects of child development that need to enter human consciousness if we are to help children grow in healthy ways. One is recognizing what is actually developing in a child at any given time and rejoicing in that stage of development rather than rushing prematurely to the next one. Thus, to understand how a child develops memory and other capacities around age seven, as Schoorel describes in chapter 6, gives a picture that enables one to educate for reading in healthy and appropriate ways.

By themselves, such pictures of childhood phases would be a great help, but there is a deeper level that is also needed. This has to do with the way that children metamorphose and transform as they grow. Physical growth can be measured in quantitative amounts according to how much a child weighs and how tall she is. But to gauge a child's soul and spiritual growth requires the development of a much finer sense of the child. When we feel this deeper pulse we see that some qualities recede and then arise in new and transformed ways, such as when the fantasy life of the kindergarten child begins to recede, making way for imaginative consciousness to arise. A capacity for forming an inner image has awoken in the child. Thus, the six year old will declare with pride, "I can see Grandma whenever I want. I only have to close my eyes." Earlier, she had the capacity for make-believe, but it was not as consciously held or directed. This is but one example of how things transform themselves throughout childhood—and throughout life.

One sees this process of transformation at work in childhood if children have time to bring a process of growth to conclusion. Then it can form seeds for the next stage. Hurrying children can be likened to growing a plant in a hot house. The plant looks wonderful, but it often cannot create viable seeds for the next step in its growth and propagation cycle.

Schoorel's book takes us deeply into both child development and the processes of transformation that characterize human development. It comes at the right moment. We live in a time of great possibilities for anthroposophic insights to come into play in education and child rearing, as in many other spheres of life. Humanity is at a threshold to a higher degree of thinking and spiritual insight and is hungry for ideas that will serve as a foundation for cultural and spiritual renewal. At the same time, there are strong countermovements that would have us view life in highly mechanistic or materialistic terms. The tendency grows stronger every day to reduce our understanding of children's capacities to test scores or to limit the full scope of their sense experiences to that which is captured on a computer screen. Fortunately, most children are born with strong spirits and an intense desire to prevail in the face of adversity. Just now they need all the strength they can muster if their spirits are to survive and thrive. The more we understand them and support them in their healthy growth and development the better—for them and for all of us.

College Park, Maryland, USA   *April 2003*

Preface

This book is written as a travel guide for parents, teachers, and other caregivers of young children. I started to write it as educational material for the training of kindergarten teachers, but—while writing—I thought others might also benefit from this information. I pictured that the insight into the developmental processes of young children would be of help not only for people who work with young children professionally, but also for parents who care for their infants, toddlers, and preschoolers day after day.

The leading thought is that our children are growing up in a time that bears tremendous challenges and is very restless. Parents are facing numerous choices regarding food, clothing, toys, modality of medical treatment, type of school, style of education, use of leisure time, and so on. Many people (family, friends, neighbors, and professionals) want to give good advice. These days parents and educators have to make choices in all kinds of matters related to raising children. Nothing is self-evident and everything is possible. A woman has already had to make choices before giving birth—will it be in bed, in the bathtub, on a bar stool, squatting, or kneeling; will it be in a hospital or at home; will it be with many people present or alone; will the older children be witnessing it or not; will it be with yoga or other relaxing techniques, or just with the classic deep breathing; will it be with anesthesia, with a tranquilizer, with soft music in the background, or in silence? The curious thing is, though, that even when the mother has not made choices beforehand, the delivery will nevertheless happen in a particular way. Afterwards she may become aware of this and ask herself: did it happen the way I wanted it to?

Once the baby arrives, the choices continue to abound. This book does not make these choices for the reader, but it endeavors to shed light on the processes through which the body develops during the first seven years. Knowing these developmental processes, caregivers can choose what they will take from this insight as they take care of young children.

I did make a choice, however, in selecting the concepts I will use to describe the development of the child. These concepts come out of anthroposophy. This has important consequences for the keynote of this travel guide. I am not a social scientist. I am a physician, and I look at children with an eye to their physical well-being. The anthroposophical view of the human being naturally bridges the gap between education and medicine, between therapy and pedagogy. In addition, it is characteristic for the time of childhood that physical and psychological processes interact very strongly. This book is not about education, but about the landscape in which education takes place.

Bilthoven, The Netherlands   *Fall 1998*

Introduction

There is an abundance of literature about child development. Everyone who relates to children can read about the steps in psychological development, such as the sequence of development of cognitive faculties, of emotional life, and of motor skills. But it is not easy to find literature about the biological-physical foundation for this, the physiological prerequisites for this development. This is true for people who are in training for a profession (such as education, psychology, physiotherapy, or nursing), as well as for parents who want to know more about the normal or special development of their child. Almost all of us have a vague notion of the influence physiology has on children's behavior and development. We all know that children become cranky when they are too tired and that they regress to previous stages of development when they are ill. Few of us, however, know why this is so, and we wonder which forces and factors are involved.

This book looks at child development from the point of view of physiology, which focuses on the functioning of the body. The physiology is described with the help of concepts taken from anthroposophy. The facts we find in other literature remain valid, but this specific point of view places them in a different perspective through which we can discover new aspects.

This book is a travel guide in a rather unknown landscape. I will focus on the first seven years of childhood, which normally includes the phase in which the child enters elementary school. The child's first seven years stand out because of the child's vitality and potential for growth during this time. Everything children learn and develop during these seven years is transient. Children learn to think, but only to develop a capacity and not because they need to apply it. They learn to walk, but only for pleasure and not because they need to go where life takes them. Children learn to play, but only for the fun of it, so that later they may be able to play the challenges of life. It is characteristic of the first seven years that they are germinal and that they are very precious. This unique quality may get lost when parents, educators, and other caregivers think that young children have to learn because they need the content of this knowledge later in life. If this book helps you to be enthusiastic about this unique and precious time of childhood, it has fulfilled its main purpose.

This book will show that it is a typically human trait to keep faculties *in a germinal state*. I think it is of great help to use anthroposophical concepts in describing this typically human trait. Concepts such as "life," "keeping in a germinal state," "development," and "thinking" can be clarified by the anthroposophical concept of the *ether body*. This book will use anthroposophical concepts regularly. As it is written also for readers who are not familiar with the anthroposophical vocabulary, the most important of those concepts will be explained in the following section. I will give a short characterization of these concepts, which describes exactly what is meant but also leaves space for individual application. These concepts may help the reader to become acquainted with another way of looking at the human being.

The most important anthroposophical concepts used in this book are those of the twofold, threefold, and fourfold nature of the human being.

Twofold nature of the human being

If I want to describe which aspects of the human being are related to the past and which to the future, I could use the concept *twofold*. Let me give an example. If you ask, where does the baby come from? you may receive two answers. One is "from the cabbage patch"; the other is "delivered by the stork." The cabbage is a picture of vital growth forces, of substance, of heredity, and of the past. These are prerequisites for the child to come to earth. The stork is a picture of heavenly forces that carry the child to earth. These are forces that enable something new to develop, through which each child bears a promise. Because the child comes from heaven, he or she has a future. Because the child on earth has entered into a body that is subject to natural laws, he or she is connected to the past.

We also notice this twofold nature when we observe the human being at night and again in the day. Sleeping is connected to building up, recovery, and growth; being awake is connected to consciousness, tiredness, and breaking down. Night processes are a necessity for us to stay healthy and to remain who we are. Without enough sleep, we get confused. We need daytime processes to go through experiences by which we can develop. We will become different from who we were. A person who never quite wakes up and lives his or her life rather dreamily runs the risk of acting as an automaton.

14

From the point of view of destiny, we can describe this twofold nature of the human being as follows: because of the past, we have limitations—our life is predetermined; because of the future, we have the possibility of making decisions about our life in freedom of choice.

Threefold nature of the human being

1. We can use the concept *threefold* when we look at the human body as it appears in space. We can distinguish the upper pole, the middle region, and the lower pole of the human body.

In the upper pole, the senses and the brain dominate. It is also referred to as the nerve-sense organization.

In the middle region, also known as the rhythmic organization, the rhythmically working organs are located, such as the heart and the lungs.

In the lower pole, we find organs that are functional in metabolism and in movement, such as the liver, the intestines, and the muscles. It is also known as the metabolic-limb organization.

2. Like the human body, the human soul also has a threefold nature. The threefold nature of the human soul manifests in: 1) thinking, or making mental images, 2) feeling, or expressing emotions, and 3) willing, or acting.

These three main soul activities can be related to the three regions of the human body. The upper pole—the nerve-sense region—is related to thinking and making mental images. The middle region—the rhythmic area—is related to feeling and expressing emotions. The lower pole—the metabolic-limb region—is related to willing and acting.

We can distinguish the three regions of the body and the corresponding soul functions, but we can not isolate them. Sense perception occurs in all parts of the body, as do feeling and willing. The point is where the three soul functions and the three bodily organizations have their bases. I could formulate it in this way: wherever there is sense perception—even in the big toe—the upper pole is present; wherever there is feeling—even in the head—the middle region is active; wherever there is willing, the lower pole is at work.

15

When we look at the different body parts, we can observe that the threefold nature penetrates the entire body. Looking at the arm, we may observe that the upper arm is mainly connected to strength, the lower arm to feeling, and the hand to sensing. Looking at the hand, we may observe that the wrist has to do with the will, the palm with feeling, and the fingers with sensitive touching. Looking at the finger, we find the signature of the threefold nature in the proximal phalanx, middle phalanx, and distal phalanx. Even when we look at the nail, we notice a growing zone, a sensitive middle area, and a free part with which we can touch in a sensory way. When we look at a face, we experience the forehead as being the most *head*—the upper pole. The middle of the face with the eyes, ears, and nose—serving perception and respiration—represents the middle region. The jaws have a relation to the lower pole—the digestive process starts there. Of the jaws, the immovable upper jaw is more upper pole; the movable lower jaw is lower pole. The cheeks and tongue in between the jaws are related to emotions (middle region). In the jaw, we find incisors (making the first acquaintance with the food—a sensing quality), eye teeth, and molars (grinding the food—a willing quality). The covering layer of the tooth—the enamel—is more upper pole; the root of the tooth represents the lower pole, and the neck of the tooth represents the sensitive middle region. We can look for this layering of the body's threefold nature in every organ.

3. Each of the three bodily organizations has its own special relationship to the outer world and to the inner world.

The upper and lower poles form a polarity, with the middle region in between.

The upper pole will take in the outer world through observation and thinking, and internalize it without changing it.

The lower pole, through metabolism, will destroy the outer world—food—and use it for building up the body. With our limbs we take hold of the outer world and change it.

Upper pole:—the outer world penetrates into the inner world. Lower pole:—human activity changes the outer world.

Our breathing shows how the rhythmic region holds the middle between the two polarities. A part of the outer world is internalized by inhaling, and subsequently a part of the inner world is given to the outer world by exhaling.

The fourfold nature of the human being

I will now describe the fourfold nature of the human being, and I will use, more or less figuratively, the word body for each of the four aspects. They are: the physical body, the ether body, the astral body, and the I-body or I-organization. These four bodies are also called the four members of the human body.

The physical body of the human being requires space. The space taken by one physical body is not available for another physical body. This is true for all things and beings that have a physical body—minerals, plants, animals, and humans.

The ether body maintains life in the human being, animal, or plant. It comprises all life functions such as breathing, biochemical processes, and regeneration. The word "ether body" is therefore synonymous with the word "life body." Processes require time; therefore the ether body is also referred to as "the time body". The ether body also has formative properties; from that point of view it is known as "the formative body."

When the ether body has receded from the physical body, formed matter such as a piece of wood or a seashell remains. It is dead. When this happens to the human body, the remains are the physical body in the proper sense of the word. As a corpse (derived from the Latin word for body) it starts to decompose.

We are allowed to use the word "body" in the concept "ether body," because we are referring to an organization of functions and properties that has a certain continuity and can be recognized. The ether body is normally not visible to human eyes because, unlike the physical body, it is not composed of matter. We do, however, perceive the activity of the ether body within the physical body. This activity comprises all life processes in the body. Biorhythms, heartbeat, brainwaves, the daily rhythms of organic functions, and the female menstrual cycle are all examples of the activity of the ether body. In addition such aspects as the way a person is shaping his or her life; the way he or she usually deals with situations; his or her habits; they all speak the language of the ether body too.

The astral body is the bearer of abilities. Thus we notice that not only space and time (physical body and ether body) are organized in the human being, but also "quality".

Behavior; the ability to think, to feel, and to will; sympathy and antipathy; the ability to have wishes, desires, or passions; all are embedded in the framework of the human astral body. It provides the human being with the ability to experience pain, joy, sadness, sensations, and memories. Human beings experience the world on the stage of their astral bodies. This stage is experienced as an inner world—the bodily foundation of the soul. As humans, animals also have an astral body and they too have an inner world out of which their impulses for movement are generated.

We do not see the astral body with our normal eyes. We do see, however, the activity of the astral body within the physical body. This activity uses the inner organs such as the heart, liver, lungs, and kidneys as its instruments. The nerves also are part of this. We need these impulse conductors to be able to move and perceive. At night the human being is not conscious because the astral body is not within the living body, but is in the spiritual world. At night the astral body moves among the stars, one could say.
The I-body or I-organization is the fourth member of the fourfold human body. The astral body and the I-organization are referred to as the higher members of the human body. They are closely related, as we may see when a person is falling asleep or waking up. The I-organization—the bodily bearer of self-consciousness—takes the astral body along when one falls asleep (they leave the -living- body behind) and again when one wakes up (they come back into the -living- body).

The I-organization is a recognizable system of intentions, directions, and goals, through which the human being can say "I" to him- or her-self. It becomes visible when the human being acts not only out of wishes, desires, or education, but also makes conscious choices. The warmth of sincere enthusiasm and of true ideals is a tool of the I-organization. With this tool, the human being can come to self-consciousness and self-realization.

The I-organization is the bodily foundation of the human I. The human I is a spiritual being, eternal, and on the way to learning how it can do good out of free choice. When the human being dies, the fourfold body is left behind, and the I follows its way toward the next incarnation.

If we could "peel off" the fourfold human body from the top down, we could say the following:

- without the I-organization, the human being has no goals and no
   future;

- without the astral body, he or she has no consciousness and
    would be asleep;
- without the ether body, the human being is dead;
- without the physical body, he or she is a pure spiritual being on
    the road between two earthly lives.

This book will sometimes refer to spiritual beings that are not humans. Some of these belong to the earth and are connected to the elements—earth, water, air, and fire. They are known as elemental beings. Others belong "above" the earth, in the spiritual world. From them the earth and its development, which includes human evolution, have come forward. These higher spiritual beings are known as hierarchical beings or "angels". Over all of them rules the Trinity—the Father-god as the Creator and as the guardian of His creation, the Son-god as Lord of the present, and the Spirit-god as the One who sends impulses from out of the future.

If you would like to know more about spiritual beings, I can recommend books and lectures by Rudolf Steiner. This book will occasionally give explanations about them as far as is needed for a proper understanding of its content.

1 The Importance of the First Seven Years for the Rest of Life

The subject of this book is the physiology of children during their first seven years, which approximately spans the time from birth till the change of teeth. In the first chapter, this seven-year period is considered in relation to subsequent developmental phases. Before adulthood, the body develops in three phases of approximately seven years each. During these phases, the physical body, the ether body, and the astral body go through a developmental process. As we are used to speaking of the birth of the physical body, so we can speak of the births of the other members of the human body—the birth of the ether body, the birth of the astral body, and the birth of the I-organization.

The first part of this chapter describes these birth processes as "making oneself appear," which is being born into an outer world. This raises the question whether and when the four members of the human body are also involved in an activity that is directed inward, in the opposite direction. "Being born into an inner world" is the subject of the second part of this chapter. The birth of the physical body and everything related to it can be used to understand the birth processes of the other bodies. The third part of this chapter depicts the birth of the physical body as making oneself appear outwardly and an internalizing of functions as well.

What children experience during their first seven years is of great importance for their biographies. The last part of this chapter will discuss this.

Births of the ether body, the astral body, and the I-organization

The births of the four bodies—the carrier of one's individuality—occur during the first twenty-one years of life. At each birth another body becomes visible. The physical body is born one year before the child's first birthday, the ether body is "born" at about the age of seven, the astral body at about the age of fourteen, and the I-organization at about the age of twenty-one. This shows a discontinuous development. During a limited period of time a certain step of development is taken and then completed. This is a signature of the working of developmental laws. The human body develops in the first twenty-one years in three large steps marked respectively by the birth of the physical body, the change of teeth, the change of voice, and reaching adulthood.

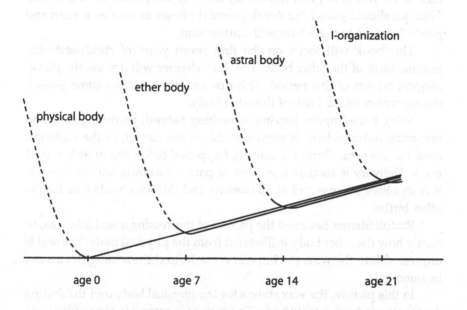

Fig. 1 *Bodily development during the first 21 years is not a continuous process. The dotted line indicates the phase of not yet being born; the solid line indicates the state of having been born.*

The development of the child's faculties and capacities does not proceed in a regular continuous process of differentiation. The permanent teeth will appear only once and then this phase is closed off. At that same time, children receive the faculty of thinking only once, and that is what they have to work with for the rest of their lives. We will later see that the power of thought is related to the teeth.

The same type of developmental process is active in learning to walk and to speak. There is a time in which children acquire these abilities spontaneously—learning to walk around the age of one and learning to speak around the age of two. If, for one reason or another, the human being has to learn this (again) at a later age, it will be very hard and sometimes even impossible.

The same principle also holds true for acquiring the ability to propagate and reach the state of adulthood. One phase of development ends—a tool for further development is given—and it now depends on the person how he or she will use that tool for continuing development. When we realize that these phases of development are once-only occurrences, we will gain great respect for the way the phases are organized. Thus we should guard the developmental phases as well as we can and guide the child to the future with enthusiasm.

This book will focus on the first seven years of childhood—the gradual birth of the ether body. The third chapter will discuss the physiological aspects of this period. This first chapter describes some general characteristics of the birth of the ether body.

Being born implies leaving something behind, becoming free, and becoming independent. A picture of this is the cutting of the umbilical cord. But the actual birth has already happened before the umbilical cord is cut. Delivery is usually a process of pain, resistance, and hard work. It is an active process, not at all passive, and this also holds true for the other births.

Rudolf Steiner has used the picture of impressing a seal into wax, to clarify how the ether body is liberated from the physical body. The seal is impressed into the wax, the imprint is made, and the sealing device can be removed.

In this picture, the wax stands for the physical body and the sealing device stands for the ether body. The picture is correct in many ways—in both situations there is an active process of connecting and disconnecting, there is material that is used, there is a result that cannot easily be changed any more, and there is a human being involved. However, the picture also deviates from reality. During the process of impressing the seal, the sealing device does not change; the ether body of the child, however, goes through a significant metamorphosis during the seven years of its making the imprint.

During the birth process of the ether body, two events happen simultaneously. The ether body works on the physical body, which changes through this. At the same time the ether body is changing also, adapting itself to the physical body. These two aspects of the birth of the ether body are interrelated. The stronger the imprint that the ether body makes on the physical body, the more the ether body itself will change and the more easily it can liberate itself from the physical body. Later in this book, we will discuss these two sides of the birth process as two sides of each process of development—on the one hand working the material, on the other hand undergoing development. Figure 2 shows this in a diagram. The higher body, as yet unborn, works on the lower body that has been born.

This principle holds true also for the subsequent phases of life. Between the ages of seven and fourteen, the astral body works on the young ether body and, in doing so, prepares for its own birth at the age of fourteen. Between the ages of fourteen and twenty-one, the I-organization guides the young astral body and, by doing so, it learns to prepare the young person for entering adulthood.

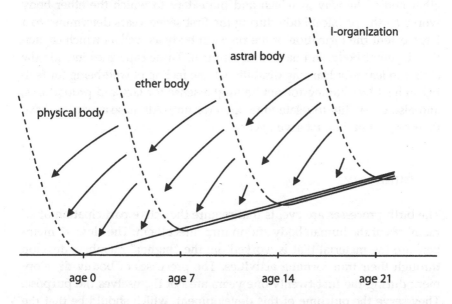

Fig. 2 The physiological principle behind the births of the four bodies. In each seven-year period, the body that has just been born is worked upon by the next higher body as yet unborn. For the higher body, this activity of transforming the lower body is a prerequisite of its own birth.

The four members of the human body (the four bodies) connect in a hierarchical order. The physical body submits itself to transformation by the ether body, the ether body does so in relation to the astral body, and so on. We can see this beautifully in pedagogy. Teaching the child good habits such as drinking and eating properly in order to stay healthy (properties of the ether body), requires that the adults give the right example or use rewards and punishments (measures from the realm of behavior—the realm of the astral body). The same principle works in self-education. When we want to educate our physical body, we call in the help of our ether body. For instance, if we want to lose weight, we will change our eating habits.

The physiological basis of this principle becomes manifest in the birth processes. This principle is the foundation of the so-called "pedagogical law." This law states that a member of the human being is educated by the next higher member. Similarly to the way the astral body of the teacher works on the ether body of the child, so—with the help of the environment—the unborn astral body of the child works on the child's ether body. The way in which and the extent to which the ether body works on the physical body during the first seven years determines to a large extent the formation of the physical body as well as which capacities the ether body will have after its birth. These capacities include the ability to learn (or learning disabilities), the feeling of well-being (or feeling unhealthy), having (or not having) a sense for tact and proportions, and also the ability to relate to religion (or not). All these capacities have their origins in the first seven years.

Summary

The birth processes are events that require the active participation of all members of the human body and in turn affect them. The "lower" members are the material that is worked on; the "higher" members develop through their transforming activities. The processes of bodily development during the first twenty-one years are not themselves the purpose. They serve the outcome of this development, which should be that the adult human being is able to make decisions independently, healthily, and out of free choice.

Seen from this point of view, we could select the following mottoes for each stage of the first twenty-one years. For the first seven years the motto could be *making the physical body one's own*; for the second seven years, *cultivating one's ether body*; for the third seven years, *mastering and tuning one's astral body*.

Inner births of the four bodies

When do the members of the human body begin to work? Do they start at conception, at birth, or do they start gradually over the years? To be specific:

— Physical body. When can the physical body be observed as matter in space?

—Ether body. When are children capable of maintaining their own life?

—Astral body. When do children know the effects of their behavior?

—I-organization. When is the child aware of the reality that his or her existence makes a difference?

Answering the question may be the easiest for the ether body. The answer is: it is the time when children themselves start to take care of their life processes, such as breathing, digestion, warmth, metabolism—which is when the physical body is born. Within minutes, life processes are internalized. Before this time, the mother took care of all this; as of this moment the child does it him- or herself. Thus this is the beginning—an inner birth. The outer birth of the ether body occurs at the age of seven, signalled by the appearance of the permanent teeth.

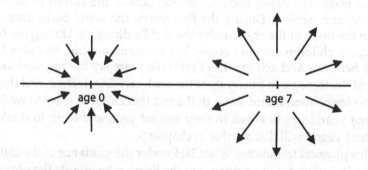

Fig. 3 The births of the ether body. Inner birth occurs at physical birth, outer birth when the change of teeth begins.

How is it with the other members of the body? When is the physical body born into the inner world? The question, when were you born? refers to the outer birth of the physical body, which coincides with the inner birth of the ether body. But the physical body must also have started somewhere at some time! It started during the first month of pregnancy. Some mothers are aware of this moment. They experience the transition from not having had their period to being pregnant. This is when the being who wants to be born connects to the growing fertilized egg cell. Seen from the spiritual world, this is a decision of this being—to come to earth in about eight months.

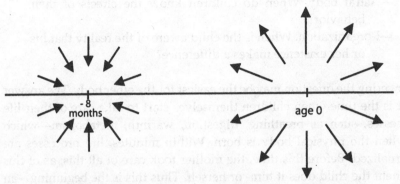

Fig. 4 The births of the physical body. Inner birth occurs shortly after conception, outer birth a year before the child's first birthday.

The inner birth of the astral body does not coincide with the birth of the physical body. The astral body is, among others, the carrier of desires, emotions, and egoism. During the first years, the astral body does not work in the body of the child under the child's direction. During the first three years, children are not egoistic but innocent, neutral, and objective in their behavior and actions. The first three years lay the physical foundation of the three main functions of the soul—willing, feeling, and thinking. This foundation is laid through the fact that children learn to walk in their first year, learn to speak in their second year, and learn to think in their third year. I will discuss this in chapter 5.

This physical foundation is not laid under the guidance of the child's astral body, but under the guidance of the Being who guards the physical carrier of the soul, knowing the human soul and its origin—the Being of Christ. Because of these three protected years, the soul will in principle be capable of doing good, feeling truth, and thinking freely again in each incarnation. After these three years, the child him- or herself is given the guidance over the astral body. That is to say, the environment of the child (family, school, friends, etc.) participates in this guidance, because the astral body is not yet born into the outer world.

Thus at about the age of three, the astral body is born into the inner world. Around that time, children are aware of their I; they can express verbally their wishes and thoughts, and, for most people, remembering oneself can go back to this time. When the astral body is born into the outer world, at the age of fourteen, the process of self-realization begins, the training of one's individual soul capacities.

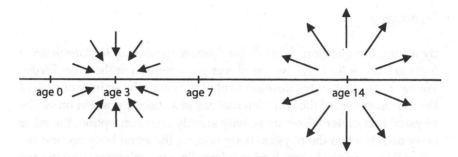

Fig. 5 The births of the astral body: Inner birth occurs around the age of three, when memory begins. Outer birth occurs around the age of fourteen, when the voice changes.

The births of the I-organization, both inner and outer, fall outside the scope of this book. Nevertheless I want to mention them. The I lives in warmth. The warmth-organization is a good measure for the degree to which the I takes hold of the physiology of the body. The I also lives in encounters. The relationship of human beings to their environment is also a measure for the degree to which the activities of the I have been internalized. In these two areas, a remarkable change takes place in the child around the age of ten—warmth is no longer directed from the head, as is the case with young children, but from the abdomen. For the first time now, the child goes through the experience of not being part of the outer world. About ten years later, when the I is born into the outer world and the human being reaches adulthood, it will become apparent how the person then actually deals with warmth and encounters.

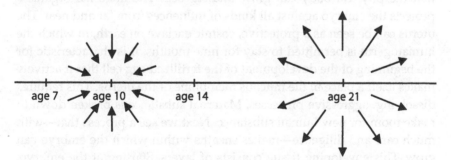

Fig. 6 The births of the I-organization: Inner birth occurs around the age of ten, when children start to experience themselves as distinct from their environment. Outer birth occurs around the age of twenty-one, when human beings start to shape their lives independently.

Summary

By asking the question, *when do the different members of the human being begin to work in the body?* we can direct our attention to the inner births. We have seen that, in the development of the child, the activity of each of the four members of the body internalizes at a specific point in time. The physical body internalizes its activity shortly after conception, the ether body does it when the physical body is born, the astral body around the age of three, and the I-organization internalizes its activity around the age of ten. This is the general rule. However, because these moments of birth can vary to a certain extent, each child has his or her own variation.

In this book I will use the word *birth*, as is common, in the sense of being born into an outer world.

Physical birth as a picture

We have seen that the developing child goes through a number of births. Now we will research whether an understanding of physical birth may pave the way for an understanding of the births of the other bodies. For that purpose, we will have to look at prenatal development—the months during which the physical body is prepared for birth.

First of all, the embryo needs conditions that support its development. Its environment must be receptive, sheltering, and caring in order that the physical body can grow undisturbed. The maternal organism protects the embryo against all kinds of influences from far and near. The uterus can be seen as a protective, cosmic enclave on earth, in which the human germ is permitted to stay for nine months. It is characteristic for the beginning of the development of the fertilized egg cell that it actively makes itself a place in the mucous membrane of the uterus. This requires dissolving, aggressive processes. Maternal substance is broken down to make room for new human substance. Next we see a process that—with much care and diligence—makes sheaths within which the embryo can grow. This enveloping tissue consists of layers. Starting at the embryo, the first layer consists of amniotic fluid; the membrane of the amnion forms the second layer, and the third layer is the chorion, which is connected to the placenta. All of this, including the placenta, is the tissue of the child! Within these sheaths, the physical body is built. The physical body develops with a strong emphasis on the formation of the head. The various organs of the body are not immediately located at their ultimate positions; they often follow a complicated route before they arrive at their destinations. The inner organs are formed by invagination and evagination of basic simple tube-shaped structures. Each organ has its own pace of development. Many organs are physically completed long before birth. The state of development of the lungs determines when it is time for the physical birth. When the lung has developed to the state that it can fill itself with air and hold the air, the child can be born. There are also many organs that are not completed at physical birth. These will mature after birth.

We all know, but many of us tend to forget, that the umbilical cord connects the embryo to its own periphery. This periphery is nurtured and carried by the maternal organism, but the child interconnects the center and the periphery of his or her own organism through the umbilical cord.

The most remarkable of all changes that occur at birth is that the child becomes visible. Of course, the child was there beforehand, and the mother especially notices the child's presence, often months before birth. To other people it was obvious that the mother was pregnant, but the child was invisible. At birth the child makes his or her appearance for the first time. Sonography and similar techniques do not alter this fact. It is a characteristic property of the physical body before birth that it exists invisible to physical eyes. Only at birth does it make its appearance, and what then appears is a surprise. People have expected the child, but his or her appearance is unexpected. At birth, babies fill their lungs with air for the first time, and after a few minutes they carry out the exchange of gasses that the mothers did for them up to this time. After the first inhaling, the first exhaling occurs, and often children make themselves heard at this occasion. As the child starts to control the exchange of gasses—control respiration—so also will he or she gradually take on other life functions. Children need to keep themselves warm, digest their food, care for their blood circulation, and enable the building up and growth of their organs and their bodies. Before birth, the sheaths took care of all this. At birth, the layers of the enveloping tissue—the sheaths—lose their functions and the child internalizes these functions. The moment of birth is critical. We notice this especially when there are birth defects, for instance, of the heart. Before birth, such a defect is generally not noticed. The defect was there, but the periphery of the embryo took care of the organ's life functions through the mother.

We can describe the changes of the physical organs at birth in the following way. Before birth, these organs grow and are formed, but they do not yet function. After birth, these organs continue to grow and to be formed, but they also have to function. In due course, this functioning is practiced, and it will reach maximum capacity after weeks, months, or years.

At birth, the child enters the field of gravity. This is literally so, because as of this time, the child has weight. Before birth, the child weighed nothing, or—to say it differently—he or she was outside the field of gravity. Of course, the mother became heavier. Only at birth does the child encounter the laws of three-dimensional space. We will discuss this in more detail in the chapter about the sense organs.

The birth process is not only accompanied by joy and happiness, but also by effort, pain, and suffering. In most situations, the mother is not alone during labor and delivery. People close to her and medically trained professionals assist her. When they do the right thing, they create conditions for mother and child in which the birth process can go forward without impediments. Intervention is hardly ever necessary, but if it is necessary, it should not be postponed.

The direction in which the child is born also speaks its own language. In most cases, the head comes first, that is to say, the back of the head (the occiput). With a twisting motion, the other parts of the body then follow. However, there are also many instances where, rather than the head, the coccyx comes out first. In principle, this should be considered a problematic variation.

There are laws that determine the time at which physical birth should take place. A main factor determining this time is the degree of maturity of the lungs. These laws are not applied rigidly. There are variations of acceleration and deceleration. A premature birth is often caused by some defect of the child, or it can be caused by a mother's strong adverse reaction to the pregnancy. This adverse reaction can show in her developing high blood pressure, for instance. Sometimes an emotional shock or her being physically overburdened can cause premature birth. The child that is born prematurely requires special attention and care.

Children that are born past their due dates will only suffer damage when they are born several weeks late. It is often difficult to find the cause for such a delay. Sometimes the birth canal is too narrow; sometimes the mother is too tense. It is certainly not true that a premature birth indicates that the child has physical strength, nor that a late birth is beneficial for the constitution of the child. It is, however, true that each child will do best when allowed to be born at his or her specific time and at his or her specific pace.

These phenomena of physical birth enable us to get acquainted with the other births. Their processes are similar to a large extent. They only happen less visibly.

30

Effect of the first seven years
on following life phases

Everything that happens during the first twenty-one years is a preparation. Twenty-one years of preparation enable a person to lead a life that is, or is not, mentally healthy and spiritually balanced. You can read more about this in literature about biographical laws.

I will discuss physical, mental, and spiritual fields of activity for children during their first seven years. To do this, I need to say something about the development that takes place in the second and third twenty-one year periods—the ages 21–42 and 42–63.

In the Introduction, I described the threefold nature of the human being that we encounter in the structure of the physical body and in the main functions of the human soul. The upper pole, the middle region, and the lower pole of the human body correspond to thinking, feeling, and willing. In this chapter, I will mention still another threefold nature of the human being—body, soul, and spirit.

Using the word *body* in this context, I am referring to all four bodies —members—of the human being. The I-organization has a special position, different from the other three bodies. When the I-organization is born at the age of twenty-one, a new phase of twenty-one years begins. The development of the other three bodies is then more or less completed, and from then on human beings start to focus on the development of their own capacities. In doing so, they develop their own personalities. The I-organization is the physical basis on which the I can unfold. In this context, the I stands for the personality that evolves in three phases—the phase of the sentient soul (age 21–28), of the mind and heart soul (age 28–35), and of the consciousness soul (age 35–42).

The development of the I-organization is determined by the development of the I as it manifests itself in the human soul. Thus, we can speak of three phases of bodily development (physical, etheric, and astral body) and of three phases of soul development (sentient, mind/heart, and consciousness soul).

After the age of forty-two, there are again three phases of seven years each, in which spiritual capacities can be developed. The first six 7-year phases are given by nature. They occur with everyone. After the age of forty-two, it is up to each individual whether or not to try to develop his or her spiritual capacities. The capacities of the spiritual human being are not given by nature and they cannot be taken for granted. They are there as a goal for the human being who wants to strive towards cleansing the soul from ignoble motives, towards leading his or her life in a way that it does not harm others, and towards taking care of the body so that it can become a temple of God. In anthroposophy, these three higher capacities are known as spirit-self, life-spirit, and spirit-man. Together they form the higher I. The nine phases of seven years are related to one another as indicated in figure 7.

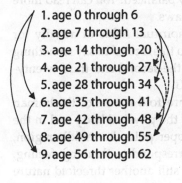

1. age 0 through 6	completion of the physical body
2. age 7 through 13	completion of the ether body
3. age 14 through 20	completion of the astral body
4. age 21 through 27	development of the sentient soul
5. age 28 through 34	development of the mind and heart soul
6. age 35 through 41	development of the consciousness soul
7. age 42 through 48	capacities governed by one's own spirit-self
8. age 49 through 55	capacities governed by one's own life spirit
9. age 56 through 62	capacities governed by one's own spirit-man

Fig. 7 The seven-year phases and the relationships among them.

The development of the physical body during the first seven years of childhood forms the basis for the sixth period of seven years—the phase of the consciousness soul. Directly and indirectly, via the consciousness soul, the first period of seven years is also the basis for the ninth—the phase of the capacities governed by spirit-man.

The consciousness soul is the most objective of our soul capacities. It enables us to find a relation to the world that is not biased by our bodily desires and wishes, our intellect, our mood, and our preferences or antipathies. The physical body sets the limitations that the consciousness soul will encounter. The degree of perfection that the consciousness soul can reach during the sixth period of seven years depends on the degree of perfection that the physical body has reached during the first seven years. The "space" of the physical body determines the degree of freedom of the soul.

The way this space is used depends to a large extent on what happens in the four intermediate phases. Much can be made impossible when physical space is wasted, but also much can be compensated for when there are physical limitations.

Here are some examples. During the first seven years, children's diseases and other illnesses that come with fever have the task of giving the physical body resistance. I will discuss this in the sixth chapter.

When children successfully have gone through a number of diseases that come with fever, more than just their immune systems has been trained. Thirty years later they will reap the benefit. As adults, they will be able to develop their own visions and insights independent of family, culture, tradition, habits, and sympathies or antipathies.

If children have been content with their physical bodies and have never been ill, they may experience their physical instruments as uncooperative and unruly during the consciousness soul development phase. It may then be a hindrance for them to find an independent vision in their personal circumstances and in the challenges of their time.

During the time of the consciousness soul, the "free space" will be different for a person who, as a child, has had the opportunity to play, climb, run, and sometimes carry heavy loads (in a free space for physical development), compared to a person who has grown up with sophisticated toys and was always taken to and from home by car.

When you, the reader of this book, have already gone through the phase of 35–42 years of age yourself, you might check whether you recognize this correlation in your own development. You can look back to the harvest of the first seven years in regard to the autonomy of your soul.

I will be brief on the ninth phase of life, because I have not yet experienced it myself. This is the phase during which the spiritual fruits of one's own life may become available, and the seed for the next incarnation begins to be formed. During this phase, we are harvesting that part of our physical existence that we have been able to lift up to a spiritual level. In the course of life, a person encounters the limitations of physical existence again and again. This can be, for instance, a physical handicap, poverty, difficult life situations, or problems at work. Each of us will deal with this differently. Some people get caught in it; others will flee from it. When we avoid these two extremes and manage to perceive daily life as a picture of a spiritual reality, the ninth phase of life can bring us much wisdom and strength for the future. It is as if mundane daily life becomes transparent. It feels good to be in the company of a person who possesses this mature wisdom.

So far, I have described metamorphoses of the physical body. We can do the same for the ether body. During the first seven years, the ether body forms itself by working on the physical body. The fruits of this practicing remain present as capacities during our whole further life. They include the capacity to stand up against influences from the outer world, to create a buffer between one's own inner world and the outer world, to have powers of resistance and transformation—in short—the basis of health.

I see health as the capacity to safeguard the integrity of the body. If we have acquired this capacity during the first seven years, it will be there for life as a basis for health, safety, and ease. More specific metamorphoses of the ether body will show themselves during the fifth and eighth 7-year periods—the phases of the heart and mind soul, and of the working with one's own life-spirit. The basis for this is laid in the second period of seven years, during which the capacities of the ether body mature.

The first seven years influence later phases of development in three ways. Firstly, the physical development of the first seven years is the basis on which all later developments are built. As a building is not more sturdy than its foundation, the later developments of the human being are not stronger than the foundation laid during the first seven years. Secondly, the first seven years have a direct influence on the development of the consciousness soul. The restrictions and possibilities of the physical body determine the degree of autonomy that the soul can acquire between the ages of thirty-five and forty-two. Thirdly, what has been acquired during the first seven years and during the phase of the consciousness soul will determine what is possible during the ninth phase of life. This has to do with whether and how the human being can attain wisdom and a healthy spirituality between the ages of fifty-six and sixty-three.

2 Pictures of the Ether Body

Before focusing on the development of the child's ether body in the next chapter, I want to introduce the concepts of *ether body* and *ether forces*. Ether forces are invisible to our physical eyes, but they exist and they are active. We can become acquainted with them if we look at the effects of their activity. When ether forces work into physical substance, we can see their imprint in the forms and pictures that arise. I want to describe three such pictures—the plant, the human teeth, and children's drawings. The plant is an expression of formative etheric forces, and it gives us a reference with which to grasp the concept of the ether body. The teeth are not just instruments to chew with, but they are also perfect pictures of the formative forces of the human ether body. Children's drawings are made by children's hands, which during their first years are guided mainly by their ether body; therefore, children's drawings can be fruitfully studied to understand the processes of the ether body.

In this second chapter, I want to acquaint you with the activity of ether forces and with the concept of the ether body, as a useful preparation for understanding the development of the ether body of the young child, which I will discuss in the third chapter.

The plant as a picture

The annual plant gives a clear picture of what the ether body of plants can accomplish. The same ether processes occur in perennial plants, but with them, certain parts of the plant—such as the stem or the rhizome—do not die during the winter.

Development of the annual plant

The seed that has been buried in the soil during the winter will generate a root and, subsequently, two cotyledons in springtime. These were already present in the seed and can develop under the influence of warmth, light, and moisture with the help of nourishment available in the seed. The root directs itself vertically towards the earth's center, and in contrast, the cotyledons take a position that is more or less horizontal. Thus we have met the two sides of the plant—the parts that are oriented along a vertical axis (stem and root) and the parts that are oriented horizontally (leaves). From these two parts, the horizontal and the vertical, the whole plant will develop—root system, stem and leaf, flower and stamens, ovary and receptacle, fruit and seed. I will first describe the formation of root, stem, and leaf of the annual plant and after that the formation of flower, fruit, and seed.

Root-, stem-, and leaf-formation

Vertical parts of the plant

The root will continue to grow and usually will branch out into an extensive network of pale, whitish, grayish, brownish, or sometimes colorful roots that will have the tendency to become woody. The direction of growth will adapt to local conditions such as rocks. Often the extensive network of the root system will become shaped like a globe, but nevertheless its direction of growth will be towards the center of the earth (a positive geotropic direction). The roots must keep growing to continue being functional. The apex of the root will secrete matter to dissolve substances in the soil, which—with water—will be taken up as nutrients by the plant. Through its root system, the plant reacts to the properties of the soil. In some plants, the color of their leaves or flowers may show whether the soil is more acid or more alkaline. The root systems of adjacent plants may grow into one another and often this close contact leads to the exchange of substances. We know that trees in a forest are related through their root systems. If one tree is infected with a harmful substance, this substance will also enter other trees.

Above the ground, the stem will develop away from the earth's center (a negative geotropic direction). It will also grow toward the light, but principally it grows away from the earth. Beyond the earth's atmosphere, where there is no gravity, plants cannot orient themselves along the vertical axis from earth's center toward the periphery. There they grow either toward the light, or, when they are kept in the dark, they grow in every possible direction (the total of all possibilities, of course, forming a globe). The stem is built up out of two parts—the nodes and the part between the nodes, the internodes. During the growing process, the internodes will become long when there is little light and will stay short when there is a lot of light. Just like the root, the stem will grow best in the dark. You can prove this for yourself with the following experiment: let one potato sprout in the dark and another on the windowsill, and notice the difference over time (see figure 8).

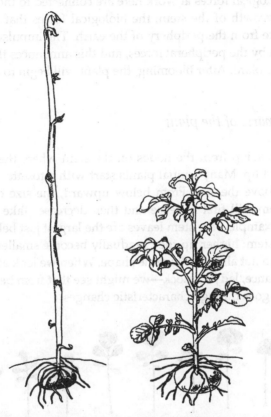

Fig. 8 *The effect of darkness and light on the growth of potato sprouts (From Thomas Göbel, Die Pflanzenidee als Organon angewandt auf die Rosenverwandten Europas, Niefern-Öchselbronn 1988.)*

The growing-point of the stem is located at its apex, and therefore there is theoretically no end to the growth of the plant. Some climbing plants can grow several yards a year, and a certain type of bamboo can grow twelve inches overnight. When the plant starts to flower at the end of the stem, its lengthwise growth will come to a halt. Plants either grow or bloom. When they bloom, the end of the stem will not be a growing-point, but a receptacle where, at a later stage, fruit formation can begin. After the blooming has come to an end, the stem might still grow farther. We can see this phenomenon clearly in poppies where the seedpods often extend several inches above the flowers that are still blooming.

The stem develops in an alternation—growth of the internode and growth dammed up in the node. Darkness is favorable to growth of the stem; the biological forces at work here are connected to the earth. Light inhibits the growth of the stem; the biological forces that are active in light originate from the periphery of the earth. The impulse to bloom is set in motion by the peripheral forces, and this announces the end of the growth of the plant. After blooming, the plant will begin to die.

Horizontal parts of the plant

The leaves develop from the nodes on the stem where the growth has been dammed up. Many annual plants start with a rosette of closely set leaves just above the soil. From below upward, the size of the leaves along the stem will first increase and then decrease. Take the stinging nettle as an example—the stem leaves are the largest just below the mid-point of the stem; higher up they gradually become smaller. The leaves of the plant do not all have the same shape. When we look at some crucifers—for instance, lady's smock—we might see that from below upward the leaf form goes through characteristic changes.

Fig. 9 Metamorphosis of the leaf of a crucifer, the hairy bitter cress (Cardamine hirsuta L.). (From Thomas Göbel, Erdengeist und Landschaftsseele. Gestaltwirkungen geistiger Wesen im Pflanzenreich und in der Mistel, Dornach 1994.)

Compared to the size of the leaf, the stalk of the lower leaves is relatively long. Higher up along the stem of the plant, the surface area of the leaves increases; still higher up along the stem, the surface area of the leaves decreases again, because indentations begin to become more pronounced. Near the top of the stem, the indentations disappear, and the leaf that remains at the end of the stem is small and pointed (see figure 9). These metamorphoses are characteristic not only for the crucifers but for all annual plants and for many perennial plants. The metamorphosis

38

goes through four stages—forming a stalk, forming a surface area, forming indentations, and becoming small and pointed. Each single leaf will grow toward its predestined shape, but over time, the plant as a whole will show the different forms of the leaves.

The single leaf will attain its definite form in four stages of metamorphosis. It will start pointy, then it will differentiate, then it will become fuller and broader, and finally the stalk will elongate. These metamorphoses are, of course, most pronounced in the leaves that are close to the base of the stem. These are the same metamorphoses the whole plant goes through, but in the reverse order (see figure 10).

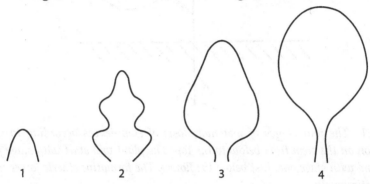

Fig. 10 The four stages of metamorphosis of the single stem-leaf. The earlier stages are depicted out of proportion, for the sake of clarity. The leaf will go through these four stages consecutively. The formative etheric forces work continuously.

If we compare the two phenomena—the developmental stages in the leaf formation of the plant as a whole (figure 9) and the developmental stages of the single leaf (figure 10)—we might gain an understanding of how the formative etheric forces of the plant work on its horizontal parts, the leaves.

The formative forces of the plant will either generate a single leaf, which over time will reach its definite shape in four stages, or they will generate one leaf after another with different shapes that, seen together, show the four stages of metamorphosis in the leaves of the plant as a whole. The first process works continuously—the leaf starts young, grows to the full, and then dies off. The second process works discontinuously—at the lower stem the plant shows an "old" appearance and higher along the stem it will gradually become "young."

The single stem-leaf will show a process of aging (see figure 10). In contrast and as a matter of necessity, the development of the horizontal parts of the plant as a whole will show a rejuvenating process (see figures 9 and 11).

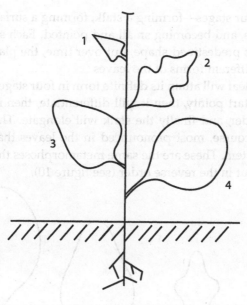

Fig. 11 The four stages of metamorphosis of stem-leaves according to their position on the stem from below to the top. The plant will start with stage four and end with stage one, just below the flower. The formative etheric forces work discontinuously.

Formative principles of the ether body

The forces that form the plant are in fact ether forces. The plant consists of a physical body and an ether body. The forces in the plant's ether body are the only ones capable of giving form to the plant.

The following law rules the formation of the horizontal parts of the plant. In forming the shape of the single leaf, the ether body of the plant is bound to the plant's physical body, which results in a process of aging. In receding from the single leaf, and inducing from one node to the next —rhythmically—the formation of leaf after leaf, the ether body is working within its own dynamics, which results in a process of rejuvenation.

In the biological forces working in the vertical parts of the plant, the plant's ether body is working either from the periphery or from the earth. I described how light and darkness are correlated respectively to inhibiting and stimulating growth. The cosmic ether forces bring death to the vertical parts of the plant's organization, whereas the ether forces from the earth bestow life on them.

Summary

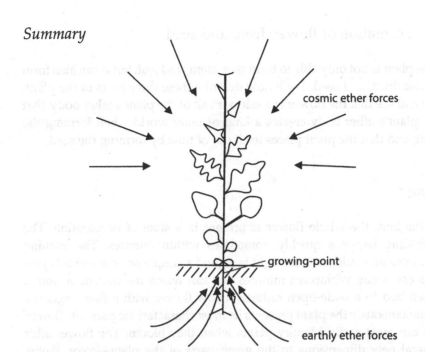

cosmic ether forces

growing-point

earthly ether forces

Fig. 12 The horizontal and vertical parts of the plant are placed in a field where the cosmic and earthly ether forces interact. The earthly ether forces work from below as far upward as the lower stem-leaves. The cosmic ether forces work from above down and are responsible for the metamorphoses of the shape of the leaves.

We can make the following diagram:

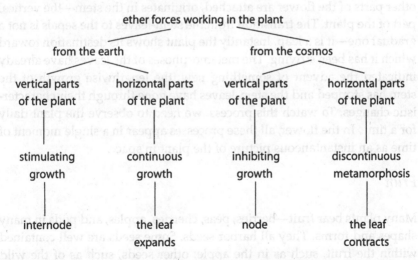

Fig. 13 Diagram of the working of earthly and cosmic ether forces on plant growth.

Formation of flower, fruit, and seed

The plant is not only able to form root, stem, and leaf, but it can also form flower, fruit, and seed. I will now describe these three parts of the plant. We will see that the flower is a self-portrait of the plant's ether body, that the plant's ether body creates a kind of inner world when forming the fruit, and that the plant places itself out of time by forming the seed.

Flower

In the bud, the whole flower is present in a state of preparation. The unfolding happens quickly, sometimes within minutes. The evening primrose on a midsummer night is a good example of how fast this process can occur. Within ten minutes you can watch the transition from a green bud to a wide-open radiant yellow flower with a fine fragrance. Instantaneously the plant presents its most characteristic part—its flower. We can most easily identify plants when they bloom. The flower adds several new dimensions to the green parts of the plant—color, flavor, nectar, and pollen. Insects, butterflies, and birds are attracted, and along with the wind, these animals secure pollination, which in turn enables the plant to generate fruit and seed. The life span of the flower is often quite limited, and within a few hours or days it withers and falls away.

The flower originates in the horizontal parts of the plant. This is so for the sepals, petals, stamens, and pistil. Only the receptacle, to which all other parts of the flower are attached, originates in the stem—the vertical part of the plant. The transition from the stem-leaves to the sepals is not a gradual one—it is a leap. Instantly the plant shows its destination toward which it has been striving. The metamorphoses of the leaves have already indicated the advent of something new; the lengthwise growth of the stem has stopped and the stem-leaves have gone through their characteristic changes. To watch this process, we need to observe the plant daily for a time. In the flower, all these processes appear in a single moment of time as an instantaneous picture of the plant in space.

Fruit

Many plants bear fruit—berries, peas, cherries, apples, and pods in many shapes and forms. They all harbor seeds. Some seeds are well contained within the fruit, such as in the apple; other seeds, such as of the wild geranium, will be thrown out at some moment by the plant itself.

Not all plants bear fruit. The dandelion, for instance, creates downy seed heads. Comparatively speaking, we could call the globe of the seed heads the fruit of the dandelion.

When fruits contain flesh (as with berries and apples), they are likely to be eaten by animals. The flesh is digested, but often the seeds are not digested and are thus excreted; in this way, animals can help propagate plants.

The vertical and the horizontal parts of the plant integrate to form the fruit. Before the stage of blooming, as well as during the flowering, the horizontal and the vertical parts of the plant exclude one another and do not integrate.

The flower is a leap from one formative principle to the next. The fruit, which is characterized by the integration of the horizontal and vertical parts of the plant, is a leap toward a further formative principle. Blooming gives a mirror-image; fruiting creates an inner space, and within that space—which is sometimes filled with air (such as in the apple, poppy, and rattlegrass)—the seeds develop.

Seed

When the flower is pollinated, the pollen penetrates through stigma and style into the ovary. A complicated process of cell division in the ovary creates the cells that will form the seed. Seeds contain the following elements—the coat (which shields the seed's content from the outer world and provides nourishment for the later seedling), the cotyledons, the radicle, and the growing-point. After the seed has developed—usually within the protective cover of the fruit—development comes to a halt and a resting phase begins. The seed ends its resting phase when humidity and warmth initiate the germination process. Dry seeds can maintain their capacity to germinate for years. Grain found in Egyptian tombs has been brought to germination even after thousands of years. Seeds secure the propagation of plant species. As long as plants grow, bloom, and generate seed, they will continue to exist. Seeds are also eaten by birds and other animals, and by human beings. Grain supplies humanity with an important means of nutrition.

The phenomenon that seeds have a resting phase in their development signals a formative principle that is essentially different from the two I described earlier. Pollen penetrating the style indicates that cosmic formative forces take hold of earthly substance that the plant has made available for seed formation. As long as the seed, generated through this process, is still connected to the plant, it has a spatial orientation opposite to that of the plant. The plant orients its growing-point to the cosmos, its root to the earth. Within the seed, the reverse is the case—the radicle (the embryonic root) is directed *upward* and the growing point is oriented *downward*. The forces of growth are held back, because the orientation of the forces within the seed is neutralized by the opposite orientation of the identical forces in the plant. The formative principle of the seed is based on the fact that not only the substances of the horizontal and vertical parts of the plant permeate one another, but also, in addition, the whole is brought into a state of rest. This state of rest depends on the fact that the forces from cosmos and earth within the plant neutralize the same forces within the seed. The reversed orientation of the seed (compared to that of the plant with which the seed is connected) is a picture of this.

Thus, when the seed transcends the laws that rule the processes of plant growth, it steps out of time and enters a sphere that we could refer to as *eternity*.

Formative principles of the ether body

We have met three formative principles of the ether body of the plant when we looked at the development of the root, stem, and leaf. We met additional formative principles when we focused on the development of the flower, fruit, and seed.

When the ether body of the plant creates the flower, it does not stay in its own realm of rhythm and time, but it steps into the timelessness of the instant, into space. In doing so, the ether body—where it verges on the plant's astral body—gives a picture of qualities of the plant's astral body.[1] The plant does not internalize its astral body. If it did so, it would become an animal. It can, however, present its self-portrait to beings with an incarnated astral body, such as the insects and butterflies that come to drink nectar and assist in pollination. Human beings can delight in the flowers that plants display. The slogan, "Say it with flowers," indicates that human beings can be touched by flowers and that also the human astral body can open up to the flowers' color, fragrance, and beauty.

In fruit formation, we meet another formative principle of the plant's ether body. The formation of an inner world with the help of the principle of penetration is actually an astral principle that is part of the development of animals, which have an incarnated astral body. The plant does not go that far, but fruit formation is a first step in that direction. The ether body creates an organ that is "fleshy," the fruit-pulp. Animals such as birds, mice, and squirrels eat the fruits, which enter their digestive tract. This is the proper place for what is akin to the astral body.

In seed formation, we meet still another formative principle of the ether body of the plant. In the seed, the plant has reduced itself to minimal visibility. Through the seed, the *I* of the plant—eternal as it is—can create a new plant on the earth over and over again. The seed can have a quality of rest, because the forces that would initiate growth have been neutralized. We will see later that the human being has an orientation between the cosmos and the earth, which is similar to that of the seed—the root pole above, the growth pole below. In seed formation, the ether body of the plant creates an organ that fits the *I*-activity of the plant. The ability not to let a developmental process evolve, but to hold it as a potential, is typical for the human being.

Summary

The next diagram shows the ether body of the plant as formative forces in time.

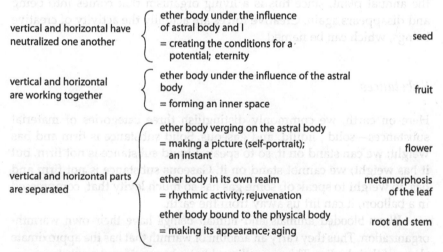

Fig. 14 The ether body of the plant as formative forces in time.

The annual plant that germinates, grows, blooms, and generates fruit and seed has five different possibilities to form its organs. Three of these ways to form an organ are typical for the plant, which—as we know—has an ether body and a physical body as it makes its appearance on earth. Where the ether body is bound to the physical body, it generates single organs (root, leaf, or flower) and makes them grow. These organs will age and die after a while. Where the ether body is free, it works in leaf formation and initiates the characteristic metamorphoses of the leaves. The stem-leaves, in their form quality, become younger the farther they are situated from the bottom of the stem. Where the ether body verges on the astral body, it gives a picture of the plant in the flower. This is a process of here and now. The formative process of the plant that leads to fruit formation shows properties of the plant's astral body. Fruit formation leads to an inner space. The formative process of the plant that leads to seed formation shows properties of the plant's I. The formative ether forces neutralize one another and thereby create a state of rest within which the plant can form an enclave outside of time.

Substances, elements, types of ether and elemental beings

At the end of this section on the plant as a picture of the working of ether forces, I will introduce some concepts that you may not yet be familiar with. These concepts are "substance," "element," "type of ether," and "elemental being." We can look at material substance as the end result of the working of creative forces. This working is especially visible in the annual plant, since this is a living organism that comes into being and disappears again. Creative forces are actually the activity of creative beings, which can be named.

Substances

Here on earth, we commonly distinguish three categories of material substances—solid , liquid, and gaseous. Solid substance is firm and has weight; we can stand on it, so to speak. Liquid substance is not firm, but it has weight; we cannot stand on it. Gaseous substance is not firm and has no weight to speak of; some gas has so much levity that, compressed in a balloon, it can lift us away from the earth.

Warm-blooded animals and human beings have their own warmth-organization. Thus they carry an amount of warmth that has the approximate shape of their bodies. This warmth could also be considered a substance.

The concept of "substance" can also be used for realities in the non-material world. When we speak of spiritual substance, soul substance, or ether substance, we do not use the word *substance* as a metaphor. When discussing children's drawings later in this chapter, I will distinguish between the substance of children's drawings and the form this substance is given. Thoughts are the substance of a train of thought; psychological themes are the substance of a novel; pictures and moods are the substance of a dream.

The plant consists mainly of solid and liquid substances. There is also some gaseous substance involved. If plants have hollow cavities, these may contain small quantities of air; this trapped air is not a substance of the plant. However, the oxygen released by the plant and the carbon dioxide taken up by the plant are part of the plant process. These gaseous substances envelop the plant, which builds itself up from the carbon of carbon dioxide and gives off oxygen to the surrounding air. The plant does not have its own warmth substance.

Elements

The concept of "element" is related to the concept of "material substance," but these concepts are not identical. The *earth* element works in all that is solid. The *water* element works in all that is liquid. The *air* element works in all that is gaseous. In all movement, the *warmth* element is active. The elements manifest in the physical-chemical world, but they themselves are not material. They are physical realities, but they are not a physical-chemical substance.

The earth element is subject to the laws of three-dimensional space, as is any material substance. The water element is subject to the laws of two-dimensional space (width and length), as is the plane. Whenever a substance has the tendency to form a plane, we can attribute this tendency to the working of the water element. The laws of one-dimensional space (length) rule the air element, as they do the line. Whenever a substance has the tendency to form rays, we can attribute this tendency to the working of the air element. The warmth element has no dimensions; warmth works from outside of space and time, and it will bring something into movement at a single point.

For centuries the "doctrine of the elements" has influenced human thinking about nature and about the human being. A balanced mixture of the elements—in the right proportions—meant health; illness was an indication of a disturbance in the harmonious combination of the elements.

Ether types

Each element in the physical world corresponds to one type of ether in the ether world. Thus there are four types of ether:

> *life ether*, corresponding to the earth element;
> *chemical ether*, corresponding to the water element;
> *light ether*, corresponding to the air element; and
> *warmth ether*, corresponding to the warmth element.

The four types of ether work in the physical world through the four elements, or stated otherwise, each type of ether has its corresponding element, which is the medium through which it works.

I will now give a brief description of the activities of the four types of ether. Each type of ether works in rhythmic alternation between two polarities. Ether does not work in one steadfast direction but always works rhythmically between opposites.

Life ether
When we look at the cross section of a tree trunk, we can see the rhythmic working of the life ether in the annual rings. Over and over again, a phase of growth is followed by a phase of lignification. The life ether makes the trunk the essence of the tree's appearance, whereas physically the trunk is the most lifeless part of the tree and the most woody. (In the third chapter we will see that the life ether also constitutes the human skeleton, which is the most hardened and lifeless part of the human body. At the same time, the skeleton contains the bone marrow—a source of life, a place where the blood is generated.) The life ether encompasses the polarity of life and death processes. Goethe said, "Nature invented death to attain an abundance of life." I think he was referring to the life ether when he wrote this.

Chemical ether
By assimilating carbon dioxide, the plant is engaged in chemical processes needed for its own life as well as for the life of its environment. Light processes in the plant break down water into energy and oxygen. The energy is used to build up plant substance from carbon dioxide, and the split-off oxygen is given over to the environment. Human beings and animals need this oxygen to live. (In the third chapter we will see that the hemoglobin of the blood can bind significant quantities of oxygen and dispose of it later. As in the plant, so in the human body this process requires the presence of fluids. Oxygen is taken up—in the lungs—or given off—in the tissues—depending on the composition of the surrounding fluids.)

The chemical ether works between the polarities of binding and loosening the bonds. Binding leads to a larger unity, while loosening the bonds leads to a splitting off from the whole.

Light ether
When the plant unfolds its flower, it shows how the light ether has worked in it. The fleeting beauty of the flower, showing the plant species in an instant, is the product of light ether at work. (In a later chapter we will meet the working of the light ether in memory. Both in remember-

ing and in forgetting, the light ether is at work. Memory pictures have a fleeting existence, just as flowers do.)

The light ether works between making something appear and making it disappear. We can observe the activity of the light ether in all that becomes visible or recognizable and in all that volatilizes or disappears.

Warmth ether

The plant seed ripens in the warmth of the sun, and at the same time the life processes within the seed are reduced to an absolute minimum. Seed has its task in the future; it protects the species from extinction. (In human physiology we notice the same process when, with the help of the warmth ether, our thinking can penetrate into the heart of the matter; this we will see in a later chapter.)

Warming up and cooling down are the polar functions of the warmth ether. Warming up leads to expansion, and it creates space. Cooling down leads to contraction, coming into itself.

Elemental beings

Behind any force is a being that employs it. What I have called ether activity is in fact the working of etheric beings. With the plant, these beings can be named. Fairy tales mention them frequently—gnomes, fairies, and fire beings. Some adults and many children can perceive and describe them. They are not composed of material substance, as is the plaster figure in the yard, but of etheric substance. They are not visible to our physical eyes, but they work in and for the physical world. It is their task to care for the earth and all that lives on it. The activity of each type of ether is the daily work of a category of elemental beings. Their traditional names are related to the elements they work with:

> earth beings—gnomes, dwarfs
> water beings—nymphs, undines
> air beings—fairies, sylphs
> warmth beings—salamanders

Summary

We looked at the plant as a visible ether formation, or said differently, as the visible activity of elemental beings. In its connection to the substances of the earth and in its responsiveness to the working of the ethers from out of the cosmos, the plant gives a picture of the mediating quality of the etheric.

We may conclude this part of the chapter with the following diagram.

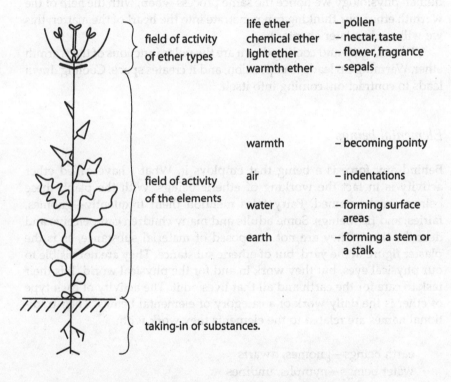

field of activity of ether types	life ether	– pollen
	chemical ether	– nectar, taste
	light ether	– flower, fragrance
	warmth ether	– sepals
field of activity of the elements	warmth	– becoming pointy
	air	– indentations
	water	– forming surface areas
	earth	– forming a stem or a stalk
taking-in of substances.		

Fig. 15   The visible plant between cosmic and earthly influences.

Now we must carry our understanding of the plant as a visible ether formation, when, in the following chapters, we seek to understand the development of the child between birth and the age of seven.

Human teeth as a picture

In this part of the chapter, I will proceed from describing the organs of a living organism, such as the plant, to describing organs of a living and ensouled organism. I want to lay out the picture character of the teeth, to further our understanding of the concepts of etheric forces and ether body. I will hardly pay attention to the fact that the teeth are also instruments for biting and chewing, for dividing and reducing food substance. The structures and functions of all the organs of ensouled beings, the animals and we humans, express properties of the soul and its instrument, the astral body. The long whiskers of mice indicate their sensitivity. The fact that bulls do not have whiskers, but have horns tells something about the bulls' thrusting force. Elephants do not have horns, but tusks, which indicates that something other than the thrusting force is of importance to these animals. What could this be? Let us compare elephant tusks to crocodile teeth. The teeth of the crocodile point backward, the tusks of the elephant curve forward. The crocodile has an astral body that moves between extreme rest and extreme movement. One moment it is lying in the water like a tree trunk; the next moment, in a flash, it catches its prey between its jaws. The elephant would never do this. Its tusks do not present a picture of catching, but of sensing and connecting. It can touch in a sensitive and subtle way with its trunk. The teeth also express this quality of the elephant's astral body. When we look at human teeth from this point of view, we will discover that we cannot find anything that is significant. This is so, because human teeth express properties of the ether body rather than of the astral body. They actually present quite a true picture of the human ether body. I want to elaborate on some aspects of this picture character of the human teeth. We will see how the working of etheric forces can be understood by observing successively the form of the individual tooth, the set of teeth as a totality, the threefold nature of the teeth, the change of teeth, and the teeth as a boundary.

There is a danger in describing the teeth in this way. The danger is that people may use it as an alternative to palmistry. "Show me your palms and I will tell you who you are and what will happen to you." People could do the same with teeth. We can avoid this danger if we keep in mind that humans are different from animals, because we are not only predetermined beings but also, and above all, free beings. In spite of, or even because of, his or her physical limitations, the human being can truly become him- or herself.

51

Human teeth: a picture of the working of ether forces

In this section I will discuss the statement: the human teeth are a picture of the human ether body. Organs are pictures of qualities of the astral body. We can observe this best in animals, because they do not have an I-organization, which also is active in organ formation. A full description of the teeth of many animal species would illustrate this observation. However, I will limit myself here to a few remarks.

The teeth are classified as three types—incisors, canines, and molars. In rodents, the incisors are most developed; in predators, the canines; and in ruminants, the molars. In these animals, the movements of the lower jaw in relation to the upper jaw have adapted to their specialization. Rodents have specialized in vertical movement of the lower jaw. A squirrel or a hamster eating seeds shows rapid little movements by which the seeds are cut into small pieces. Predators make quick catching movements with their jaws. Compare a dog's eating with a hamster's eating. The hamster eats with rapid little movements of its jaws, taking a long time and spilling a lot of food. The dog demonstrates the "catch—bite—swallow" phenomenon and does not leave the smallest particle of meat in the bowl. Cows chew with slow grinding movements of their molars. The joints of their jaws are structured so as to support the horizontal movements of the lower jaw.

The human teeth strike a balance among these three specializations. None of the three tooth types—incisor, canine, or molar—is more developed than the other two. All three movements—cutting, catching, and grinding—are possible, but only to a modest extent. The human teeth do not show specialization. This makes it unlikely that they express a characteristic property of the astral body. What do they show instead?

This must be either the ether body or the I-organization. These two along with the astral body, are responsible for the formation of the physical body.

We can recognize the formative activity of the I-organization by the absence of specialization, as mentioned above. The appearance of a *vertical orientation* is another phenomenon that indicates activity of the I-organization. The vertical posture of the human being is the clearest expression of this. We can observe this also in the human face. Forehead, cheeks, and mouth are in one vertical line. In animals this is not the case; the forehead recedes, and a snout or beak protrudes. The I-organization works in the human teeth by preventing specialization and emphasizing a tendency to a vertical orientation.

The fact that the birth of the ether body coincides with the beginning of the change of teeth already suggests a relationship between the ether body and the teeth in human beings. There are more indications for this. Looking at plants, we have seen that the ether body of the plant portrays itself in the flower. The life forces have receded from the flower to a large extent. This is what makes the flower so transient and allows it to be a picture. The flower phenomenon shows that the ether body is capable of creating pictures when it draws life forces away from the material substance of the physical body. However, this needs preparation. First the green, growing plant is created; blooming can only occur afterward. In plants, the impulse to bloom comes from cosmic ether forces that inhibit growth. The being of the plant is portrayed in the flower; the ether body facilitates this process as a mediator.

The formation of the teeth goes through a similar process. Children are born without teeth. In their first year children grow tremendously. Towards the end of the first year, the growth rate diminishes and the first teeth will erupt. When the ether forces of the head are born—after a little more than three years—the set of baby teeth is complete. (I will elaborate on this in the third chapter.)

The teeth are part of the skeleton, which is the least vital part of the body. In the skeleton, the teeth have a special position. Nowhere else is bone tissue visibly exposed, and no other tissue heals with such difficulty as does tooth bone (dentin). The set of teeth as a totality represents a picture. It is more than a number of adjoining teeth and molars, just as the flower is more than a number of petals. The set of teeth is like a flower. The teeth are generated by the formative force of the ether body when it is largely receding, after it has first built up the physical body. Because of this receding of the ether body, the teeth have a picture quality, and they are also vulnerable.

Summary

Human beings do not only form baby teeth; they will also form permanent teeth between the ages of six and twelve. I will elaborate on this later in this section.

I have asked the question, what are the human teeth a picture of? I hinted at the answer when I described the influence of the I-organization on tooth formation. I can summarize this section of the chapter by being more explicit. The ether body is a mediator in the process of tooth formation; it portrays in ether form that which is "superior" to it. Due to the activity of the astral body, the etheric forms in the mouth do not become flowers, but organs with a digestive function. The activity of the I-organization makes the teeth a picture of the human ether forces.

Form of the individual tooth

The form of a tooth is large or small, simple or complex. A simple molar has four cusps of equal size. A complex molar may have six cusps, which make us think of a mountain landscape with valleys, ravines, and mountains of different heights. Also the incisors and canines are small or large, simple or complex in shape. As a rule, the shape of large teeth is more simple and the shape of small teeth more complex.

Within the polarity of *matter* (or substance) on the one hand and *shaping* (or formative force) on the other hand, each tooth develops its own characteristic form. Its substance originates in the metabolic pole; its formative forces originate in the nerve-sense pole. These two processes of tooth formation can be given the names of two substances—magnesium and fluoride.[2] A large tooth that erupts early indicates a predominance of the magnesium process. A tiny tooth that erupts late indicates a strong working of the fluoride process.

The magnesium process delivers the power with which the teeth are pushed out of the hard jawbone. The fluoride process not only shapes the tooth; it also causes the hardening of the tooth enamel—the outer layer of the tooth.

Calcium turns the teeth into bone and makes them the hardest bone of the body. The physical presence of calcium enables us to see on x-ray the earliest beginning of tooth development in the jaws.

The tooth is the result of the cooperation between the magnesium forces of the lower pole and the fluoride forces of the upper pole. The former provides the substance, the latter the shape.

The set of teeth as a whole

The teeth of the upper and lower jaw are closely arranged in an arched curvature. The arch of the upper jaw is a semicircle in the front, whereas the arch of the lower jaw is more angular. The two arches come together in such a way that the teeth of the upper jaw protrude a little beyond those of the lower jaw. When we clench our teeth, the teeth of the upper jaw touch the teeth of the lower jaw all along the line.

When we compare the set of baby teeth with the set of permanent teeth, we will notice that the front part of the arch does not change position or curvature. See figure 16.

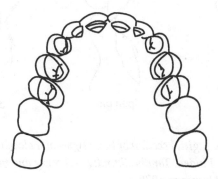

Fig. 16 The baby teeth projected on the permanent teeth, at about ⅔ of the actual size. The front part of the arch keeps about the same size before and after the change of teeth. (From Prof. Dr. F.P.G.M. van der Linden, Tandheelkundige scholing and nascholing. Deel 1, Gebitsontwikkeling, Nijmegen 1979.)

Dentition is not completed immediately. Babies are born without teeth. In the second half of the first year the first teeth erupt—first lower, then upper, starting in front in the middle and going to the sides. At the age of three, the toddler has a complete set of upper and lower teeth.

With the onset of the change of teeth, the set does not remain complete. For years, children will have one or more gaps in the arches. Some children take a long time to fill all the empty places. There are also children whose permanent teeth do not first push out the baby teeth but erupt behind them.

The way the teeth of the lower jaw and those of the upper jaw fit together is called occlusion. Dentistry classifies a number of malocclusions; the three most common of these I will mention here:

> When the incisors of the lower jaw do not reach as far forward as those of the upper jaw, the bite is called distal.

> When an opening remains in front when the molars are clenched together, the bite is called open.

> When the incisors of the upper jaw reach over those of the lower jaw, the bite is called deep. Sometimes children may bite with the lower teeth in the gum of the upper jaw.

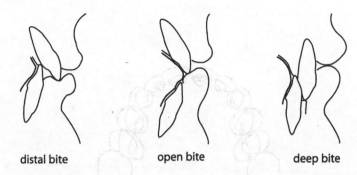

distal bite   open bite   deep bite

Fig. 17   Diagram of a sagittal section of three types of malocclusion. (From Prof. Dr. F.P.G.M. van der Linden, Tandheelkundige scholing and nascholing. Deel 1, Gebitsontwikkeling, Nijmegen 1979.)

Usually children keep their mouth closed. Then the closed lips hide the teeth. Teeth are visible bone; they are nonetheless usually hidden. If children have difficulties breathing through their nose, they often keep their mouth open. Then the teeth are visible, especially if, in addition, the upper lip is short. Teeth of the lower jaw are usually visible only if certain muscles of the mouth are extremely weak.

Of course, we can also show our teeth more or less consciously. When we laugh or grimace, we bare our teeth. We can bare our teeth on purpose, if we want to make an impression on someone and show our strength. Perfect teeth are worth looking at.

Currently, many of us spend a lot of money and energy on dental adjustments. When the occlusion or the alignment is off, dentists and orthodontists can do a great deal. However, the harmony we then see is not only the work of the child's ether body but is also technically produced.

All these phenomena give a picture of the forces that have formed the teeth. I will now reflect upon these forces a little more.

The upper and lower jaw can be regarded as the limbs of the head. In the Introduction, I described the threefold nature of the human body, and from that description it is not hard to arrive at the observation we just made. The joint of the lower jaw corresponds to the hip joint; the jaw corresponds to the upper and lower part of the leg; the chin to the foot; and the teeth to the toes. We have five toes on each foot and the child has five teeth on either side. Permanent dentition adds three molars on either side. I will come back to this later in this section.

The same correspondence holds true for the upper jaw. Only the jaw joint is missing; the upper jaw is fixed to other skull bones.

The lower jaw represents the ether forces of the lower pole, the upper jaw those of the upper pole. When all is right and the occlusion is normal, the ether forces of the upper pole dominate over those of the lower pole. When the bite is distal, the ether forces of the metabolic region have not been strong enough. When the bite is open, the upper and the lower pole have not made good contact. When the bite is deep, the formative forces of the upper pole have been too strong in relation to the forces of the lower pole.

Our arms are designed to take hold of the world, to change the world. They have a radial structure—their bones are like rays, from center to periphery increasing in number: one bone in each upper arm, two bones in each lower arm, and five fingers on each hand. The legs have the same radial structure. In the jaws (the limbs of the head), however, this radial limb structure has been subordinated to the spherical shape of the skull.

The part of the jaw that, at the age of three, has delivered the baby teeth, has used up its growth forces to such an extent that it does not change after that. Then, the completed baby teeth are the picture of ether forces that now have become available for creating pictures. That is to say, they are those ether forces that can be withdrawn from the task of building up the physical body and made available to the soul for the capacity of creating pictures—thoughts and mental pictures. We can see that the thinking of the young child is of a preliminary nature by the fact that children lose their baby teeth. Only after the change of teeth do children begin to acquire the capacity to make individualized mental pictures. For years, this will still show gaps, like the empty places in the set of teeth. An orderly row of teeth with proper space for each tooth can be a picture of the picture-forming ether forces that enable the thinking to be orderly and composed. The absence of sufficient space for all of the teeth is a hindrance to thinking. The lack of space can be caused either by the large size of the teeth or by the small size of the jaw. As we have seen before, the size of a tooth is determined by the ratio between the magnesium forces and the fluoride forces. The size of the upper and lower jaw respectively is related to the strength of the ether forces of the upper and the lower pole.

When we expose our teeth, we actually show our ether body, or rather, the picture of it. When we "bare our teeth," we do this on purpose to show our strength and be impressive. When we laugh, we do not mind exposing ourselves, because we feel safe in the situation. If breathing through the nose is inhibited or the upper lip is too short, we have a physiological problem. It forces us to expose our inner world to the outer world unconsciously, and thus we have a problem with boundaries.

The set of teeth in its totality gives a picture of the ether forces of the metabolic-limb pole. The upper jaw represents its upper pole quality—the formative forces. The lower jaw represents its lower pole quality—the metabolic forces. In the relation between upper and lower jaw, we can observe the relation between the upper pole and the lower pole of the human body.

Threefold nature of the teeth

The threefold nature of the teeth manifests in two ways. I have described the upper and lower jaw as representing the upper and lower pole. We can see the middle region only when the teeth are being used. The incisors cut the food material into pieces, the canines and first molars reduce the size of the pieces further, and the molars grind the food up still further. To do this properly, the upper and lower jaws have to cooperate. Food allows us to observe the function of the middle region of the set of teeth. Through the rhythmic movements of chewing, the outer world is adapted to the conditions of the inner world in order that the digestive process can work further on the food. I will elaborate on this in the third chapter when discussing the life functions.

The threefold nature of the teeth also becomes manifest in the classification of incisor, canine, and molar, as representing respectively the upper pole, middle region, and lower pole of the human body. In observing rodents, predators, and ruminants, we saw tooth specialization. Human beings do not specialize. However, the function of each of the three types of teeth is different. With our incisors, we make our first acquaintance with the food; we determine its consistency. Partly based on this experience, we decide whether we will continue eating, using our canines, front molars, or back molars. The teeth have a very sensitive touch. We can discern a hair much more easily between our teeth than between our thumb and index finger. We also need our teeth when we articulate in speaking. We can notice this especially when we pronounce the s, t, or d. We use our molars when we need force, for instance to crack a nut or to chew. This shows their relation to the lower pole. Our canines are modest. In shape, they are midway between sharp incisors and broad molars. I assume that they do not have a specific function in the process of chewing. Some people have robust canines, and others have tiny ones. In some people, the canines look somewhat like incisors, and in other people, they look more like molars. They form an area of transition.

When the incisors dominate (buckteeth), the body shows a disposition to predominance of the upper pole. However, there has to be enough "magnesium process" to provide the substance for these teeth; otherwise they will be strong, but will remain small.

When the molars are big and heavy, the body shows a disposition to predominance of the lower pole. However, if the "fluoride process" is strong also, the molars will be short and broad, and erupt late.

When we see a predominance of one of the three—incisor, canine, or molar—we may say that the upper pole, the middle region, or the lower pole of that human being has the disposition to dominate. That is to say: the ether forces engaged in the formation of the respective types of teeth are dominant in the corresponding parts of the human body. However, we must also pay attention to the influence of the formative principles in each individual tooth—the magnesium-fluoride ratio.

Change of teeth

Most children are proud when they lose their first tooth. It proves that they are growing up. There are no other organs that make room for new organs in such a drastic way. We also could look at it as if the new organs force the old ones to go. A lost baby tooth is a treasure. In some cultures, children receive money for each tooth they lose, and the lost tooth may be saved in a small box or even be made into a pendant.

What makes the change of teeth so special? What exactly happens? Are we able to understand its picture character? These questions form the subject matter of the following subsection.

At birth, the upper and lower jaw already contain a first germination center out of which the permanent teeth will develop. This development takes place from infancy till almost the end of grade school. The change of teeth starts at about the age of six when the first permanent molars erupt, posterior to the second baby molar. Before that, the jaw has grown lengthwise to provide space. After the four first molars have erupted, the actual change of teeth begins. The baby teeth become loose because their roots are resorbed. The permanent teeth take their place. The change follows the same order in which the baby teeth and molars have erupted. At about the age of ten, the canines are changed and at the age of twelve, the fourth molars erupt behind the third molars, which had come six years earlier.[3] At last, at about the age of nineteen, the wisdom teeth erupt if the jaw has space left for them. The germination of the wisdom teeth occurs around the age of seven.

The numbers in figure 18 help us to understand the ether body. They show when the ether body makes an imprint in the upper pole of the human body, when it starts to be personalized, when it starts to be born, and when its birth is completed.

	germination	eruption	loosening
baby teeth	5 months	7 months	7 years
baby molars	5 months	13 months	11 years
permanent incisors	3 to 4 months	7 years	
permanent canines	1½ years	10 years	
third molars	at birth	6½ years	
fourth molars	3 years	11½ – 12 years	
wisdom teeth	7 years	19 years	

Fig. 18   Timing of tooth and molar eruption.

There are several developmental areas in which some capacity is first acquired and then replaced by a new one. In speech development, we have the transient phase of babbling. This is international; it belongs to being human. The development of motor skills shows the transient phase of the walk reflex and other inborn patterns of movement. These patterns are the same for all human beings. They need to disappear and make room for the child's own movements. We can look at the set of baby teeth in the same way. It is a transient phase. It is built up with care and has a function in the process of becoming human. After that, it is disposed of with care and replaced by the set of permanent teeth, which is individualized. The baby teeth, babbling, and the primitive reflexes can be likened to the gifts that the good fairy has given at the child's birth. They may be used as a model, as an example. The set of teeth of the young child is the model of the ether forces that the child received at birth. With the birth of the physical body, the ether forces are born into the inner world, as described in the first chapter. At the age of three, the complete set of baby teeth is born into the outer world. This means that, at least to some extent, the ether forces in the upper pole have been released from the task of building the physical body. At the age of three, children can have imaginations and thoughts with the forces, which, until then, they used for building up and shaping the head. The thinking of young children is as transient as their baby teeth. This thinking is also the gift from a good fairy, and it has to grow and mature before it can be used for abstract thinking or utilitarian thoughts.

In the meantime, the development of the child goes on. The ether body works into the physical body from above downward, and also recedes in the same order (see chapter 3). When the ether body has penetrated the lower part of the physical body and has transformed the lower pole as its last activity, the ether forces, which have become individualized in the process, are now released from their task of building the physical body. We may say, "the ether body is born." The first sign of the birth of the ether body is the eruption of new molars, for which there was no example in the teeth of the young child. Children's first new molars show what the children have accomplished in their activity of working on their physical bodies and transforming them. This then sets the stage for the change of teeth. In the course of this process, the children can start to use their own power of thinking—they can start to shape their own thoughts and memories. The general human model does not include an example for the formation and birth of the third, fourth, and fifth molar. It is a process of the individual human being who, in a sense, steps out of the cosmic order. I think this may again change in the future. It could be possible that human beings will have fewer teeth in the future if humanity moves closer to the cosmic order, or, in contrast, that they will have more teeth if humanity moves farther away from the cosmic order. This is a process that takes time—many generations or incarnations.

To summarize: the appearance of the full set of baby teeth is a picture of the ether forces, which were given to the child at birth, becoming free. These ether forces are like a model, on the basis of which the child forms his or her individual ether body. The result of this process of ether body transformation becomes visible in the permanent teeth.

Teeth as a boundary within the ether body

I already mentioned the function of the teeth as a boundary between the inner and outer world. When we show our teeth, we show our inner world. I would like to mention some other aspects of the boundary character of the teeth.

Anyone who has had the experience of feeding a child knows that the teeth can become an invincible fortress when the child clenches them. You enter dangerous terrain, as you may be told by anyone who has tried to open the child's mouth with a finger and was subsequently bitten. When a child clenches his or her teeth, the child is telling you "I do not want this," or "I will not take this from you." Consequently, the child makes it clear that he or she has an inner world and that he or she wants to be the ruler over it, at least with regard to food. This may be a nuisance at the dinner table, but seen from a developmental point of view, it is an important step forward.

When someone has not been able to express something, he or she may say, "I could not get it out of my mouth." The ancient Greeks would have said, "it could not pass the arcade of my teeth." This may sound more or less the same, but there is a big difference. The outline of the lips is the most outward boundary of the mouth. The teeth lie inside of that, and they are the next to last boundary. "Pass the arcade of my teeth" could also be stated as "cross the border of my ether body." In an abstract way we could say, "the thoughts that were formed within my ether body could not leave me." This expression indicates that the teeth are not only a factual physical barrier, but also the picture of a factual etheric boundary. The teeth form the boundary that thoughts must come to before they can be spoken.

The teeth are also a boundary for our tongue. When we try to speak with our tongue between our teeth, we will lisp. When we stick out our tongue towards someone, we indicate that we do not care about the boundary formed by our teeth. The same holds true for children who suck their thumb or fingers. This indicates that they do not want to be independent or feel their limits. Instead, for a moment, they let go of the boundary of their ether body and dream away or fall asleep.

These examples also confirm that "the arcade of my teeth" is a true picture of a narrow boundary between the inner and outer world—a boundary within the ether body that has to be understood as such and taken seriously.

Summary

Each tooth, as well as the entire set of teeth, has a picture character. We owe it to our I-organization that our teeth are not specialized. This is the reason that the teeth present a true picture of the human ether forces. If the teeth were specialized, they would give a picture of astral forces, as we have learned. The form of each tooth arises out of the interaction between the magnesium forces from the lower pole and the fluoride forces from the upper pole. The formation of the teeth in the upper and lower jaw arises out of the forces from the upper and the lower pole, respectively. Their relation is pictured in the occlusion. The upper pole, middle region, and lower pole are also portrayed in the incisors, canines, and molars. Altogether, the teeth are a boundary between the inner and outer world—a boundary within the ether body. The baby teeth being replaced by the permanent teeth portrays the replacement of the given model by an individual variant of the ether forces. The power of thinking —as transformed ether forces—goes through a similar metamorphosis.

The child's drawing as a picture

It is obvious that children, when they draw, don't draw the reality but rather a picture of the reality, and thus children's drawings are similar to all other products of a creative process. Every piece of art has an "as if" character and it is good to probe what lies behind this "as if." The same holds true for children's drawings, which, however, should be called creations rather than pieces of art. This part of the chapter aims at describing why children's drawings have an "as if" character. We will see that, in their drawings, children do not copy something, but rather present a picture of something. I will describe the direction of the processes that the child depicts. There are two directions. One process moves from below upward and the other moves in the opposite direction, from above downward. The various elements in the drawing—especially the house, the tree, and the human figure—can show something about the creative source out of which the child draws. As it is with other developmental steps, the changes in the child's drawings over the years show a general lawfulness in the way each child makes his or her variations. The general lawfulness is related to the birth of the ether body, the individual variation to the child's developing personality.

A sketch of the development of drawings made by children up to the age of seven

There comes a moment when the two-year-old child makes his or her first scribbles on paper, thanks to an increased control of body movement. Before this moment, the child has worked hard to attain this control by crawling, climbing, grasping, walking, and so on. The first scribbles are mostly just lines going back and forth, often in various colors one on top of the other. In the beginning, the child hardly—if at all—pays attention to what he or she is doing. Only slowly will he or she start to direct the movements of the hand by controlling them with the eyes, and then the chaotic movements on the paper make way for more or less orderly lines or circles. The lines start to intersect each other and may form a true cross. The circles initially are open, but at a certain moment they will be closed with much diligence. Often the child puts an extra accent within the circle or near to it. Before the child arrives at a single accent, there is a period during which "it rains dots."

In the second phase, the child will draw separate picture elements on paper. While drawing, the child gives them a meaning that can change, often within a short time. A scribble, in which an adult can see nothing, indicates a house, the sun, the vacuum cleaner, or a cat. The child is working on ordering the content of what he or she perceives. The child gives things a name in response to the creative stream that is appearing on the paper in movement and in form.

Fig. 19 The scribbles become circles and spirals.

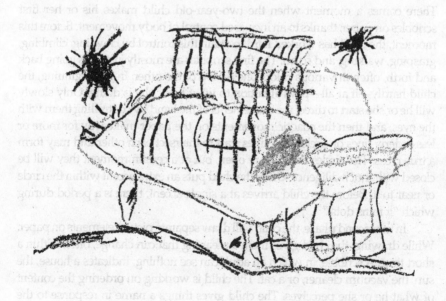

Fig. 20 The scribbles are gaining meaning; there are many rhythmic elements.

Fig. 21 Brightly colored patterns in geometrical forms.

Gradually more and more rhythmic elements repeat themselves in the drawing, which signals the transition to the third phase. The child now draws brightly colored patterns in geometrical forms and seems never to tire of putting this colorful rhythmic wealth on paper. He or she is glad to give these drawings away. Up to and including this rhythmic phase, children's drawings are more or less similar, and it is not easy to recognize whether a drawing has been made this month or last month, by this child or by another. As the child is developing those drawings (scribbles, circles, dots, lines, figures, colored patterns), he or she will also make drawings that "look like something."

The first human figures are composed of a circle with rays and a face. Then come the "head-legs," followed by various phases of adding a torso, arms and legs, hands and feet, fingers and toes, and hair. During the phase of the colored rhythmic patterns, the human figures have a distinct torso, but no waist yet.

The houses are usually developed out of colored patterns in which "archetypal houses" initially are hidden. Only later, houses with straight walls and a pointed roof will appear, followed by the square with a triangle. The house starts to have windows and a door; often there is a (round) window in the triangle of the roof; the chimney will almost always be leaning to the side, but with smoke coming out of it. Then the attention will turn toward the inside of the house as the child knows it. In the Netherlands we may then see tables, chairs, a lamp, the staircase, and even flowers on the table. After the rhythmic phase, walls will hide the inside of the house. The windows receive bars; the window ledges have flowers. The door will move to the outside of the house for a while, wide open at the side of the house, and adjacent structures may also appear.

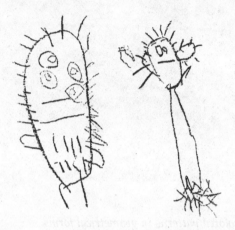

Fig. 22 "Head-legs."

Fig. 23 Houses.

Initially the tree looks similar to the human figure—a globe with two lines or one line. During the rhythmic phase, the "fir tree" appears in children's drawings. Only afterwards come the crown of the tree and branches. This goes through a development from a few lines to a distinct crown with branches, leaves, and fruit. At the end of the seven-year period, the tree is complete. It then will show branches, a trunk, and roots.

This tripartition can then be noticed in the drawings as a whole as well. There is the sky with clouds, birds, the sun, butterflies, and airplanes. On the earth we see grass, plants, and animals. In the space in between, human life evolves.

Fig. 24 Tripartition in children's drawings.

The sun will also go through a development in children's drawing. As soon as the child is able to draw a sun, the sun will appear in almost every drawing. At first it is a circle with rays, hardly distinguishable from the first human figure; often there is more than one sun in the drawing. In the next phase, the sun is depicted at the upper edge of the paper, one sun right above the human figure. During the rhythmic phase, we often find the sun in a corner with long rays all over the paper. Then the sun will move towards the middle of the paper, often as a semicircle below the sky or from behind clouds. There are children who, in this phase, do not draw the sun at the top of the paper but rather as a goldish yellowish atmosphere over the whole drawing from a center somewhere above the paper.

Many children will combine color composition and figure drawing for a short time in the second half of the rhythmic phase. Somewhere in the middle of colored geometrical forms, a scene will appear, such as a little house with a tree and a human figure. After that, drawing colors will become less frequent, and drawing figures will come more to the fore. For a long time, however, children can fall back to earlier patterns of just colors, rainbows, or window curtains; this may occur, for instance, when the child is tired.

At the age of seven, the child can make a drawing of what he or she intends to. "Mom, I'm going to draw a Christmas tree for Grandma." While drawing, this intent may disappear out of the child's consciousness, and he or she then draws trees, a little house, and a dog. "Look what I made, Mom!" "Didn't you want to draw a Christmas tree for Grandma?" "Yes, I will do that now!" Even if children know what they are drawing, all kinds of creative elements enter into the picture. Decorations, fragments of a story, and their own inventions can all find a place in the drawing.

The picture character of children's drawings

When given the opportunity, all children will draw and thus show their creative potential. Animals do not make drawings; they only do what is necessary and what their instinct commands. First I will describe the processes that underlie children's drawings, and then I will describe the symbolism of the various picture elements.

Processes

We can distinguish three phases in the drawings children make during their first seven years. The first is the phase of scribbling. Out of the pleasure of moving, and out of the more or less controlled movements of arm and hand, lines and figures appear on paper. They are tokens of the dynamics of the child who is drawing. From the way the lines are drawn, we can learn about the dynamics of each child. Is the drawing feeble or strong, spare or full, monotonous or colorful, soft or sharp in outline?

This is the kind of question we can ask when we see drawings by this age group. The answers will tell us something about the dynamics and vitality of the lower pole.

The second phase is rhythmic. The drawings show the rhythm of the middle region of the human body that does not become tired. Grass, smoke, ladders, and other rhythmic elements belong to this phase. The drawing of figures is still subject to repetition. Colored geometrical surfaces show another side of this rhythmic phase. Rather than distinct figures, life is made visible as it unconsciously streams in its fullness and colorfulness.

In the third phase, children can direct their hands to such an extent that they can draw what they intend to. The child creates an image of a house and starts to draw this. He or she does not copy a house from memory; inwardly the child creates a picture of a house, and that is what he or she will draw.

The sequence of movement dynamics, rhythm, and making mental pictures, indicates a developmental direction from below upward. The metabolic-limb pole dominates the first phase; the rhythmic region of heart and lungs dominates the second phase; and the nerve-sense pole dominates the third.

We can also find the reverse direction—from above downward—in children's drawings. To be exact, we have to say that there are four phases of development. The three already mentioned are preceded by a phase in which the child does not yet draw. In this zero phase, all energy is being used for growth and development. The movements are as yet uncontrolled and chaotic. Order and rest is brought into this from above downward. In the third chapter I will elaborate on this. A still head is a prerequisite for coordination between eye and hand. Sitting firm and stable is a prerequisite for the free movement of the arm. When all of the forces available for growth and development of the head are no longer needed, the head can come to rest, and it can control movement to such an extent that it can direct the arm. Then the first phase of drawing can begin.

After controlling the head, the child then takes hold of the rhythmic region. The life functions that are concentrated in pulse and breathing become partially free. As we have seen before with the head, the rhythmic region now no longer needs all of the forces for growth and development. However, this will not lead to rest as with the head, but to feelings that arise half consciously, rhythmically streaming and pulsating in colorful pictures. This is shown in the second phase of children's drawings.

Lastly, the child starts to master the lower pole. The forces of growth and development that become free now will serve neither the stillness of the head nor the wealth of feelings, but rather the direction of the child's will. The child can now start to draw what he or she intends to. The child will be learning, and at first will not always succeed.

This is the second direction of the developmental process, and it goes from above downward. The first process provides the material for the drawing. The second process takes hold of this material and makes the substance visible. For every drawing and for each element of the drawing, we can ask ourselves the questions: What comes from the process that is going from below upward; what is the material for the drawing? and What comes from the process that is going from above downward; how is this material made visible? To answer the first question, we can look at a finished drawing. In answering the second question, we need to see how the drawing is made.

The material given by the lower pole is, of course, different from that coming from the upper pole or the middle region. During the first phase of drawing, the ether body in the lower pole is still totally devoted to its task of nurturing and developing the physical body. When the ether body has linked itself to the physical body, ether forces arise that work continuously. I mentioned this when discussing the plant. The developing single leaf goes through a continuous process from simple to complex, from warmth form to earth form. (See also figure 15.) We can see a parallel process in children's drawings, as they go from one form to another, from simple to intricate, in a continuous developmental process.

Children's drawings also show a discontinuous process, whenever a new form or a new element appears that cannot be derived out of the previous ones.

Returning to the theme of this section—the ether material that is used in children's drawings—we come to the second phase. In this phase, the ether body of the middle region is releasing itself from its connection with the physical body. Through this, it enters into a looser and freer relation to the physical body, and it can now receive impulses from above, from the astral body. Thus, the ether body acquires the capacity to make pictures, which is comparable to the plant's ether body making its self-portrait in the flower. The material for the second phase of children's drawings does indeed have this picture character.

In the third phase, the ether body of the head has already been released from its organic activities for some time. The free ether body provides memory pictures, thoughts, and mental pictures as material for the drawing. Corresponding to the character of the upper pole, the material has contours, boundaries, and symmetry.

We can come to the following diagram:

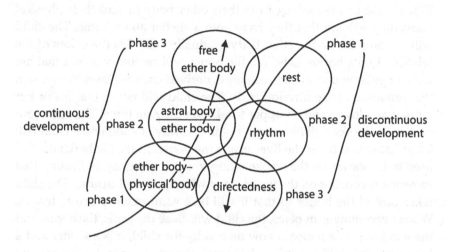

Fig. 25 Developmental aspects of children's drawings.

The house, tree, human figure, and sun as pictures of the child's body

There are three pictorial elements that are researched and described by everyone who studies children's drawings—the house, the tree, and the human figure. They are the basic elements of children's drawings. I will add the sun to these, because the sun is also present in almost every drawing. It is self-evident that the child expresses something essentially different in each of these four pictorial elements. Everything the child draws during the first seven years has ether substance as its material. I described this in the previous section. Thus the child is always drawing his or her ether body, irrespective of whether he or she depicts a house, a tree, a sun, or a human figure. Obviously the child can look out from his or her ether body in various directions. Looking in one direction, children will see their own house; looking in another direction, children will see their own tree; in a third direction, they will see their own human form, and in the fourth direction, their own sun.

Though it cannot be proven, it seems very likely that the child is drawing views of his or her physical body, ether body, astral body, and I-organization, respectively.

House

When children are looking from their ether body toward their physical body, they will see that they have both a shelter and a home. The child will see how his or her ether body gradually solidifies the colors of the rainbow into a house. Later on, the house will receive contours that are more angular and more mathematical, derived from the laws that govern the formation of the physical body. The child will notice that his or her house has a lower and an upper level, later on even three. The open connection to the sky will disappear, but in one way or another the child will let us know that he or she lives inside the house. In the Netherlands, this used to be shown by the smoke rising from the chimney, indicating that someone is cooking on the wood stove where a fire is burning. The child takes care of the house so that it will be a comfortable place to live in. When everything is in place, the child will close the walls, the doors, and the windows. The house is now owned by the child; it is a shelter and a home. But the child can still look through the windows to the outer world and the child can go in and out through the door.

Fig. 26 A house, a tree, a human figure, and a sun.

72

Tree

Looking toward the ether body means looking at vital forces and life processes. The child will discover that there are two types of life processes. The one connects the child to the outer world—the cosmos and the earth; the other helps the child grow and makes him or her strong, nurturing the child's inner world. Initially these two types are not yet separated, but are still concentrated around the main stream through which the vital forces of the child are unfolding from below upward. Up there is as yet an unknown area. The child feels a limit, as if his or her tree ends there. But later the child will discover that higher up in the tree a treasure of wealth and vitality is hidden that wants to be looked at. Flowers, fruit, and birds—it is quite busy up there. The child will scout out every corner of this newly discovered area of life forces, and he or she will extend his or her branches into it. Also at the lower end of the tree something is happening. The trunk will become more firm and it will connect to the earth with strong roots. His or her tree will not be blown over! Through its roots, the tree will take nourishment and strength from the earth; in its crown, it will show what it has to offer. The sun is shining, ladders are placed against the trunk, and the fruit is ready to be picked.

Human figure

When children look from their ether body toward their astral body, they will see themselves as a human being in development. At first they will notice that there is an inner world as well as an outer world and that they can fill their inner world with impressions from the outer world, acquired by listening, looking, tasting, and touching. They will develop large ears from listening, big eyes from looking, a big mouth from tasting, and numerous feelers from touching. Their human figure can even do more. It can stand upright, there is an above and a below, the figure can walk without falling over, and it can keep its balance. Their human figure also has sensations in its stomach; these need to be attended to. They will notice that their human figure can go somewhere and that it has arms and legs to catch, to eat, to rejoice, to run, and to kick. When children have discovered their thinking, feeling, and willing, they will notice that they are naked when they do not wear clothes. They will discover all kind of moods in their human figure, and they will try to express these in all kinds of hats and clothing. Often he is a prince and she is a princess, but sometimes she is a poor girl or a proud mother. Sometimes there are so many moods that the human figure is drawn three times on the same sheet.

Fig. 27 The human figure.

Sun

When children look toward their I-organization, they see something that is far away. The child's I-organization will only connect with the other bodies at the age of ten, and it will not start to work from the inside till much later. For the time being, the children will see their sun when looking in the direction of their own I-organization. Children observe now what has brought them to earth and what is guiding and protecting them day by day. Their own sun is superior to good and evil—also to the good and evil, the weal and woe of their own being. When the child feels well, his or her sun will shine on his or her ether body. If the child does not feel well, it seems as if the sun no longer has the strength to radiate.

With these four descriptions, I have tried to indicate the symbolic value of the house, tree, human figure, and sun. We can look at them as true pictures of the four members of the child's body, as the child perceives them.

General and personal

In reading the previous sections about the development of children's drawings, you may have realized that your child or one of your children did not follow the described order. It may very well be that only one child made the classic drawings at the classic time. Children will skip phases, catch up at a later time, do them in one single day, or mix them together. In a single drawing, trees from different phases may appear. With a younger sibling, an older toddler may still draw "curtains," and so on.

Right from the very first scribble, it is self-evident that each child has his or her own style and pace, his or her own picture language and themes. The individual character of the child shows itself in the way the child handles the material. Some children work fast and superficially; others work slowly and thoroughly. Some stay in one phase for a long time and then suddenly leap forward; others change phases several times in the course of a few months. We can compare it to learning to walk—the end result is more or less the same for all children, but the way each of them arrives there is quite different.

This book can only attempt to give a general outline and cannot be specific about individual children.

Summary

When we compare the picture character of children's drawings to the picture character of the plant and to that of the teeth, we can say the following:

The plant shows the ether body as it works on and with the physical body. Pictures arise that show the impact of time. In the flower, time has come to a halt, as it were. Therefore, the flower is the most distinct picture of the totality of the ether body.

The human teeth, too, show a picture of the totality of the human ether body. The ether body, under the guidance of the astral body, is forming organs. The I-organization prevents specialization by the astral body, and, therefore, the ether body can come to the fore. The teeth are a still life of the polarity between the upper and lower pole in the ether body.

In children's drawings, the child him- or herself is involved as a creative force. Day by day, the child follows the activities of his or her ether body when drawing. These activities express themselves as pictures through the shapes, the colors, the spatial distribution, as well as the pictorial elements of the drawing. As children develop, all aspects of their drawings go through a development. During the first seven years, the ether body is the field in which everything occurs. The ether body forms the physical body (the house), nurtures the life forces (the tree), lets itself be influenced by the astral body (the human figure), and feels that it receives impulses from the I-organization (the sun). The development of children's drawings demonstrates two processes working in opposite directions. From below upward, material for the drawing is furnished. From above downward, the child receives the restfulness, the rhythm, and the purposefulness to form the material.

3 Birth of the Ether Body

The physiology of the human body during the first seven years of childhood evolves around the central theme of the birth of the ether body. First I want to make some introductory remarks about the birthing process and connect this to the first chapter which described physical birth. Next I want to give some examples of how organisms work. An organism is a living structure in which all functional activities are attuned. The ether body is responsible for this attunement.

Then I will discuss the four types of ether, which constitute the substance of the ether body, and the seven life processes, which constitute the tools of the ether body. I will describe them as they appear in metabolism.

The chapter will end with a description of the birth process of the ether body. In the upper pole of the human being, the four types of ether arrange themselves differently from the way they do in the lower pole. This different arrangement is essential for a child's development. The influence of the upper and lower poles upon one another awakens and develops certain capacities that the child needs. The direction of the birth process is from above downward, similar to all birth processes. Thus the order in which children receive their capacities from the ether body is also from above downward.

Being born—
emancipation and endowment

Emancipation

Birth starts a process of emancipation. This becomes obvious when we look at the physical birth. Before birth, the baby is dependent on the layers that envelop the embryo (amniotic fluid, sheaths, and placenta) and on the mother who provides space for this cover and cares for it. After birth, not needing this covering anymore, the baby takes over its functions for him- or herself, as I have described in the first chapter. From the moment of birth onward, the physical body is independent, but the child is not yet independent. That will take another twenty or so years. From the moment of birth onward, the child's physical body is exposed to the physical environment, to gravity, temperature, and light, and the child must deal with these phenomena. The mother can help for a while, but in principle, children must be able to manage by themselves. They must learn to close their eyes against bright light, to stand up against gravity, and to dress against the cold.

A similar emancipation occurs when the ether body is born. The child's ether body is emancipated from the child's own sheaths as well as from those provided by the "mother." Physical pregnancy involves one mother. In the ether world, not only the physical mother but also other people provide the sheaths of the etheric pregnancy, which lasts for about seven years. I call the caring, sheltering environment of the child "the mother." Infants or toddlers without a "mother" will be malnourished, figuratively speaking. This shows that the young child is completely dependent on the environment to stay alive. In the course of the first seven years, the child gradually becomes less dependent in this respect, and when the permanent teeth break through at the age of seven, they become an image of the newly acquired independence. Before the birth of the ether body, the child was still dependent not only on his or her own ether sheaths but also on those from the "mother." After the birth of the ether body, children have to establish their own relationships to the laws of the ether world, which are the laws of the four types of ether: the life ether, the chemical ether, the light ether, and the warmth ether. Children must then maintain their own ether forces—the laws of their own organisms—over and against the laws of the ether world outside. For example, young children can be sensitive to the weather. When there is a storm, young children tend to behave chaotically, but from the age of seven onward, they must learn to overcome this. They must be able to be calm inwardly, even in the midst of a tempest outside. Education includes teaching children to become independent of the influences from the outer ether world. In the sixth chapter (subsection on the physiology of forgetting and remembering), I will call this "consolidating." There I will explain this in relationship to memory.

We can say that with the outer birth of the ether body an inner world is born. The child must be able to protect the personal inner world against the outer world. From age seven onward, the outer world should no longer be allowed to enter the child's inner world unchanged. The child must be able to recognize what is foreign, what comes from outside, and then to either adapt this to his or her own body or otherwise reject it. The function of the life processes is to distinguish between the inner and the outer world. Thus the life processes are very important for the birth of the ether body.

Endowment

There is another aspect of the birth process. Birth is the beginning of a path that we tread until we die. We each use our individual body to walk this path. At birth we receive our personal physical body and that is *it* for this life. When our personal ether body is born, we receive it to use it. When something is given to me, I can use it the way I want to. However, I will be honoring the donor by treating the gift with care. The four bodies we receive are a gift bestowed by heredity, and each individual must decide how to care for these bodies. We receive our physical body as a means to tread our path on earth. We receive our ether body as an opportunity to create an etheric enclave on earth. Within this enclave each human being can build up a personal inner world with his or her own thoughts, imaginations, and memories.

Attuning activity of the ether body

Wound healing

The entire ether body comes into action in wound healing even when the wound is small. A scratch that has been bleeding will form a scab as a provisional protection. The spot will become red and warm as a sign of increased activity. Blood cells are brought in to clean the wounded area and ward off infection. Proteins are provided for building up new skin tissue while tissue cells in the wounded area divide rapidly and connective tissue is formed to firmly link the newly formed cells together. The right amount of elastic fibers is deposited in the connective tissue to bridge the gap of the wound. The wound closes from the edges inward. When that is accomplished, cell division stops and the scab falls off. Then the skin, which consists of several strictly ordered layers, will be repaired according to its inner architecture. The layering is restored, and skin organs such as sweat glands and hair roots are newly formed. After some time, even the original typical skin lines will be there again.

When we picture to ourselves the enormous complexity of this ordinary process, we should be impressed by the activity of the ether body. The ether body activates and terminates processes at specific times to reach a distinct goal. In this example, the ultimate goal is skin repair, and this goal determines the sequence of the phenomena described above.

The last step in wound healing is the restoration of the human form, but the process of wound healing actually also begins with a provisional restoring of the human form when the scab initially covers the wound.

The wound needs to be cleaned and materials for the repair need to be provided, all of which prepares for the necessary tissue growth. There must be a defense against bacteria. Dead cells and other superfluous material (such as the scab) must be disposed of. This complicated process must be controlled by making the right choices—which part of the whole process should start when and where, which materials need to be provided, and what needs to be disposed of?

Organ formation

In embryonic development, the liver starts as a tiny protrusion of the intestine. A few cells start on their own, separate from the other cells, and start to multiply. Soon there is more than one type of cell, as the cells differentiate into cells that will become proper liver cells, cells that will become ducts in the liver, and cells that will line the blood vessels in the liver. Small islets of growing blood cells develop and the connection between these blood cells and the surrounding blood vessels is carefully prepared. A distinct bile system also develops in the liver—bile forming cells, bile ducts, and the gallbladder that connects to the intestines.

Who tells the few original liver cells to start this process? Who makes the choices, who is responsible for the differentiation, and who makes sure everything is attuned? The answer is—the ether body. The design of the human liver is contained in the ether body—not only the design of the liver itself but also the design of the entire network in which the liver is embedded and which the liver uses to connect with the blood circulation and with all other organs. The ether body contains many such blueprints and can make them available as activity goals. On its way to a certain goal, every cell will obey these blueprints. The blueprint of the liver is not static but is always changing over time. The liver in the sixth week of pregnancy is something quite different from the liver in the tenth week of pregnancy. In the tenth week, the cells have differentiated more, and they have settled in their definite places.

After the human being is born and the liver is fully developed, it may happen that a part of the liver is lost through an accident, an infection, or for another reason. Then the blueprint of the liver is activated again. The ether body provides the processes, substances, and movements that will repair the liver.

In fact, what is valid for an organ (I have taken the liver only as an example) also applies to the single cell. The cell is a complex entity with a cell membrane, nucleus, cytoplasm, and several cell organelles, which provide for the metabolic activity in the cell. To keep even one cell alive, the ether body contains the concept of "cell" and the blueprint of the cell. The concept includes the distinction between inner and outer, and the blueprint of metabolism, respiration, and setting boundaries (nucleus). Thus, even in the single cell, we encounter one of the fundamental principles underlying the structure of all parts of the human body—its threefold nature.

A kindergarten class

A class of young children is an organism. This organism works from the moment the children start the day till the moment after school when each one has digested the day's experiences.

In the morning, everywhere in the city young children are washed and dressed. Often they need some encouragement to finish their breakfast. All is geared towards being at school on time. The teacher is waiting to receive the children. The children hang up their coats, take what they need, and run into the classroom. They may first have to form a line and shake hands with the teacher one by one. Some may be crying and clinging to their mothers. Often the classroom is rather small for the number of children. Then the day starts. Who will play with whom? Who are the observers? Who takes initiative? A new child comes in; one of the older children gives the newcomer a tour. "That's the way we do it" is very important in kindergarten. The teacher tells a story—for a moment the children are silent and sit quietly. Then some children will make a drawing, others will build something, and still others will help the teacher to set the table for snack time. Cleaning the room, washing hands, and finding a place at the table may follow next. It is nice at the table; some children are silent, others are speaking loudly. At the end of the morning, the children are tired. After coming home, some have to rest before they can play outside. At night they dream about their experiences.

The processes that happen in the kindergarten originate in a design. It is not only the teacher who creates the design, it is also the school, the school system, the parents, and tradition. Therefore the class is limited in size, there are criteria for admission, there are rules for social behavior, there is a program, etc. Each child brings something from the outer world into the classroom. Nonetheless, they all obey the rules of the class. They have to learn to drop some habits to be accepted in the class. Each child brings something that is unique and that becomes a part of the whole. It enriches the class, and the class grows because of it. The class is more than the sum of all the individual children. The children as a class are often able to deal unexpectedly well with new situations. It is the structure of the organism of the class that makes this possible.

Who decides whether or not the group will accept a child? Who sets the rules? Who creates the atmosphere? The answer is again—the ether body of the class.

This ether body is different for each class, even within one school. Outsiders who visit kindergarten classes often notice quite different styles. Many styles can be healthy, but they all must obey the etheric laws. These include: each single part has an influence on the whole; every detail should adjust itself to the whole; there must be equilibrium between maintaining form and adjusting to changing circumstances. If you asked, how can this ever work? you might look at the examples in the chapter on pictures of the ether body. There we describe the ether body as a form-giving entity that works between the polarities of substance and form, aiming at proper development, and using time processes. An experienced teacher can tell you how it seems to work.

These three examples illustrate the fact that the ether body of each organism works out of the totality into the details, and out of the future into the present. It works through different processes, the life processes, which are mutually dependent on one another and often work in succession. These life processes are discussed beginning on page 84.

Substances and processes of the ether body

In this part of the chapter, I will present the four types of ether as the substance of the ether body. As a potter works with clay, so does an organism work with the four types of ether. Life ether, for instance, will enable an organism to do quite different things from those that warmth ether allows it to accomplish.

The seven life processes constitute a system of potentials that can generate processes everywhere in the organism. Whenever the internal life of an organism needs to be built up with materials from outside, or instead, needs to be protected from them, the life processes will become active. I will discuss the seven life processes by focusing on digestion and metabolism.

The four types of ether in the human body

In the second chapter, I already described the four types of ether. Each of them works within a polarity.

Warmth ether:	warming up—cooling down
Light ether:	making appear—making disappear
Chemical ether:	creating bonds—disconnecting bonds
Life ether:	bringing to life—leading to death

There are no other types of ether than these four. Thus the ether body consists of these four polar activities. Examples follow:

Life ether—bringing to life and leading to death

Cell growth and cell death
In bone formation, bone cells need to multiply. However, after a while the cells need to be disposed of for the bone to grow further.

Immunity
When infection is imminent, the body starts to produce many new cells and protective agents. In the battle against the intruder, not only must the intruding entities die, but also the defending cells, the protective agents, and the body's own tissue.

Chemical ether—creating bonds and disconnecting bonds

Blood clotting
The blood continuously maintains an unstable equilibrium between dissolving and clotting. When needed, blood components (such as fibrin) can be linked to one another, but after a while, a clot will be dissolved and its components disconnected.

Calcium metabolism
With the help of vitamin D, the blood can take up calcium from food. As growing bone develops from cartilage, it takes up the calcium out of the blood. When the organism faces a shortage of calcium, this will be taken out of the bones and given off to the blood again.

Light ether—making appear and making disappear

Bone formation
Through the influence of light, vitamin D is formed in the skin, which in turn influences the growing bone so that the skeleton will develop normally. The inner structure of each bone is dependent on the direction of the mechanical forces to which it is exposed. When the direction of forces shifts—for instance, when the child starts to stand without support—the former inner bone structure is replaced by a new one.

Hypertrophy and atrophy
A muscle that is used a great deal becomes bigger and heavier (hypertrophy). A muscle that is no longer used (for instance, because of nerve damage) will wither away (atrophy).

Warmth ether—warming up and cooling down

Thyroid activity
When thyroid activity is low, it will make a person feel cold. When the thyroid is highly active, a person will feel warm. A person with low thyroid activity will gain weight, even when eating very little. A person with high thyroid activity will lose weight, even when eating heavily.

Fever
A child with a high fever will lose weight and will not digest food properly. When the fever is gone, the child usually likes to eat again and often can digest things he or she could not digest previously.

In the second chapter, we have seen that teeth truly are a picture of the ether body. Thus we can see the working of the four types of ether clearly in the form of the individual tooth. The life ether—mainly in its life repelling quality— shows its force in the working of fluoride. We can see the influence of the chemical ether in the structure and layering of the crown. The working of magnesium—which makes the tooth erupt and grow—shows the working of the light ether. Through the warmth ether, the teeth—especially the incisors—can be sharp. Baby teeth show more warmth ether activity than permanent teeth do, generally speaking.

The seven life processes in the human body

The ether body transforms the outer world into an inner world in seven steps. These steps (which actually are processes) are taken simultaneously but must be described sequentially.

Figure 28 presents a table to assist in further reading. Three of the seven life processes are directed toward the outer world, three are directed inward, and one process creates the balance.

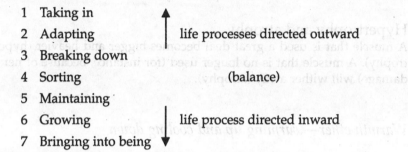

1 Taking in
2 Adapting   life processes directed outward
3 Breaking down
4 Sorting   (balance)
5 Maintaining
6 Growing   life process directed inward
7 Bringing into being

Fig. 28 The life processes.

We may ask, what about other processes necessary for life, such as: hormonal activity of the thyroid, pancreas, or adrenals; blood circulation (the heartbeat is the ultimate sign of life); and chewing food? We can indeed make a long list of activities within the human body that are necessary for life. All these activities, as long as they are related to either the breaking down of substances from the outer world or the building up of substances in the inner world, can be incorporated into the concept of the seven life processes. It is important to understand that, in this context, the concept of *substance* does not only include matter, but also nonmaterial phenomena such as air, light, a scientific formula, and the content of a lecture.

In discussing these seven life processes, I will start with the fourth—the *central* process, continue with the three processes that are directed outward, and end with the three processes that are directed inward. There will also be a special section on the evolution of the seven life processes in time, under the heading *the birth of the life processes.*

Sorting: The central life process

The task of the life processes is to maintain the inner world of an organism. The process of *sorting* plays a central role in this task.

Physiological activity in the human body occurs between rather narrow boundaries. Body temperature will usually be 97–100 °F (36–38 °C), in extreme situations 84–105 °F (28–42 °C). Adult height will usually be between 5 and 6½ feet (150–200 cm), of course with exceptions. Every aspect of the inner world of an organism has limitations known as *normal values*, and within these norms, the ether body contributes to the development of the organism. It is necessary that everywhere in the human organism a "too much" be excreted and a "too little" be replenished.

In his description of the *central* life process, Rudolf Steiner used the German word *Sonderung*, the meaning of which includes both segregating (or eliminating) and integrating (or assimilating). I will use the word "sorting" to describe this process. The process of sorting radiates through all other life processes. In other words—the other life processes adjust themselves to the coordinating task of this central process that tries to maintain equilibrium between all life processes. The process of sorting leads to visible excretions such as the stool, urine, sweat, and saliva as well as internal secretions of hormones into the blood stream and digestive juices into the intestines. There is another aspect as well. Assimilation (integration) and elimination (segregation) occur as a result of choices that were made, of which we are normally not conscious. The body asks continuously, does this or that belong, or does it not belong? Can I take it up and assimilate it, or do I need to keep it away and protect myself against it? This is the central question of immunology—the physiological defense against what is "alien" and the protection of what belongs to one's own body. It is important to understand that the life process of sorting creates the physiological foundation of the bodily identity, the biological self.

In illness, part of the biological self is not functioning. In inflammation, an infectious process may have entered the body from outside. In tumor growth, a process takes place inside the body, a process that works from within, over which the life process of sorting is not strong enough to gain control. With an autoimmune deficiency, the physical defense is directed against one's own body. This takes the rug out from under the feet of physical existence.

Taking in: The first life process

Taking in is the first step in the interaction of the seven life processes with the substances from the outer world. This first life process allows some substances to enter the organism. These substances can be material or nonmaterial.

The first thing the newborn takes in is air. Life starts with the first inhaling and ends with the last exhaling. Rudolf Steiner has called the first life process *Atmung* (breathing), which he used in a figurative sense. I will call it "taking in," to emphasize that it extends well beyond the intake of air. Nutrition also belongs to this process of taking in. To be fed, children must be willing to open their mouths to allow the intake. We know how tight little children can close their mouths when they do not want to open them. The tastiness of food can facilitate the activity of all life processes, beginning with the taking in.

The breathing process makes us acutely aware how dependent on the outer world the physiology of the human body is.

In the body, the life processes use oxygen, which we take in from the air outside of us. In the tissues, oxygen binds with carbon. This bond converts the carbon into carbon dioxide that must be given off again. Physiologically, the human being is quite open and given over to the outer world when breathing. Nothing from the outer world, however, is permitted to enter the inner world of the body unless it is changed. Thus, in breathing, an effective protection is a necessity. We cannot protect ourselves by closing our nostrils; day and night they are open, as our ears are. The first life process gives this protection in an active way. The stimulating life force of the oxygen from the outside air is met by our inner vitality, and the excess living carbon is given off to the outer air as carbon dioxide.

The physiological processes involved in controlling the exchange of gasses occur on three levels—in the tissues, in the lungs, and in the kidneys (see figure 29). The metabolic processes in the tissues utilize oxygen (taken in through the lungs) and produce carbon dioxide (excreted through the kidneys and the lungs). Carbon dioxide production is increased in situations such as physical labor, mental activity, and fever. Therefore, the tissues are in constant danger of acidification; the ether body, however, cannot function in an acid environment. Both the kidney (as a digestive organ) and the lung (as an organ of the middle region) can excrete carbon dioxide and thereby reduce the level of acidity. The kidney, of course, does not take in oxygen as the lung does. There is no linear correlation between the excretion of carbon dioxide and the intake of oxygen through the lungs. Increasing the rate of respiration results in a decrease of the level of carbon dioxide in the blood, but not in a comparative increase of the level of oxygen in the blood; the oxygen level reaches its maximum rather quickly.

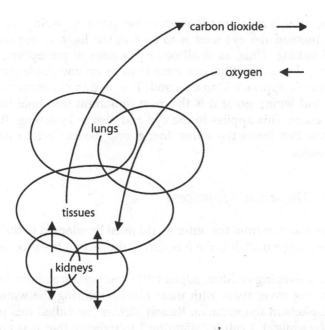

carbon dioxide ⟶

oxygen ⟵

lungs

tissues

kidneys

Fig. 29 The metabolism of gasses in the human body. Oxygen is taken in by the lungs. Carbon dioxide is generated in the tissues and excreted by the kidneys and lungs.

The rhythm of breathing gives the protection that breathing needs. The function of breathing, as such, is the exchange of gasses; we can observe this in the lungs. The *rhythm* of breathing, however, has a different task. The breathing rhythm assists the first life process, the taking in.

The exchange of gasses pertains not only to oxygen and carbon dioxide but also to nitrogen and hydrogen. Nitrogen is a component of all proteins in our body and hydrogen is necessary in all processes of energy transfer.

Carbon   —bearer of life
Oxygen   —bringer of life
Nitrogen —substance of ensouled life
Hydrogen —bridge to the warmth processes

Each organ has its own way of taking in the outer world—of "breathing." The breathing of the eye takes care that the eye is not blinded when it takes in light. What can the eye do to prevent being blinded by the light? Contracting the pupils will diminish the amount of light entering the eye.

Closing the eyes is much more effective but prevents seeing! The most important method the eye uses is to look at the light source intermittently by blinking. Thus, as in all other processes of perception, vision is a rhythmical process. If the eye were to focus on one single point, the image would disappear within a second. The rhythm of connecting with the object and letting go of it is the most important threshold between inner and outer. This applies to the eye and also to breathing. It is the rhythm itself that forms the active, living, and flexible barrier between inner and outer.

Adapting: The second life process

A substance taken in from the outer world must be adapted to the conditions of the inner world. It is the function of the second life process to do just that.

We help sleeping children adjust to the temperature of the environment when we cover them with more blankets during the winter and take off blankets in the summer. Rudolf Steiner has called this process *Wärmung* (warming). I call it "adapting," to indicate that it is not only a matter of adjusting to temperature but that it is a matter of accommodating and preparing for all kinds of further processing. We must chew our bread, moisten it, and warm it up before it is ready for the digestive process. Inhaled air must be moistened and warmed up before the lungs can deal with it. Warmth is an essential medium in many accommodating processes.

It is the task of the second life process to provide a differentiated warmth organism in the human body. All organs have a different temperature, and each organ has, as well, a differentiated warmth organization. In addition, each organ has a warmth pattern that fluctuates between day and night, between our being awake or sleeping. The life process of adapting must be able to ward off heat and chill from the outside, as well as enable the body to generate and give off warmth.

Warmth is actually not homogeneous. When we talked about the exchange of gasses, we distinguished carbon dioxide, oxygen, nitrogen, and hydrogen, composing a fourfold air organization. We can also describe four levels of the warmth organization.

At the physical level of biochemistry warmth is regulated especially with the help of phosphorus and hydrogen.

What we know in ourselves as feeling warm or cold cannot be equated to energy transfer at the level of the cells, but can be understood as occurring on another level. Our feeling warm or cold is more or less independent of the energy transfer in cells.

There is a third level. Our movements generate warmth when we start to move actively, either unconsciously as in one's teeth chattering or consciously as in pacing up and down. Emotions also work at this level. We blush with shame, tremble with fear, are scared stiff, and so on.

The highest level of warmth in the human being is enthusiasm, the capacity to warm up to something. When we adults have an ideal—and in the child this can be wanting something dearly—then obstacles can be quickly removed and new ways found.

The table below lists the four levels of warmth on the left and examples for each of them on the right.

energy transfer	— phosphorus and hydrogen
feeling warm/feeling cold	— warmth organism
warmth of soul	— love/hate
idealism	— enthusiasm/indifference

The processes of the fourfold warmth organization are strongly interrelated. The most physical level also reflects any activity at the other three levels. We all know that warmth of soul has an effect on the physical warmth processes in everyone, especially in children. I will now focus on the physical level of warmth.

Of all the organs, the liver and muscles are the primary generators of warmth. In these organs, biochemical reactions, which are metaphorically called combustion processes, set warmth free to serve the functioning of the awake and active human being. In the muscles, these exothermic reactions serve outwardly directed human activity. In the liver, these exothermic reactions serve that part of human metabolism necessary for daytime activity (catabolic processes). From late afternoon till early morning, the pattern of biochemical reactions in the liver shifts away from exothermic (catabolic) reactions to assimilation (anabolic) processes, which require warmth. However, the exothermic liver reactions do not cease entirely at the end of the day; they linger on during the night. The moment they come to an end, the human being must wake up so that daytime activity can resume. The bloodstream distributes warmth throughout the body to all organs. The miraculous distribution-structure of the blood vessels achieves warmth differentiation in the organs. The distribution-system of the blood vessels is designed in such a way that there are connections between blood vessels—anastomoses—and in this way the blood supply to a certain area can be regulated with precision. Even when the blood supply seems to be constant, anastomoses appear to open and close rhythmically.

The skin's blood supply and the activity of sweating (an elimination which belongs to the *central* life process) enable the skin to hold warmth or give it off within certain limits. Through radiation and evaporation, the skin (the endpoint of a process that started in the liver and the muscles) gives off considerable quantities of warmth. The skin is a complex organ, and one of its functions, the one described here, is to be an open and active boundary for the warmth processes, the function of *adapting*.

The warmth and chill from the outer world are not permitted to enter the inner world unchanged. When we cool off passively, as a rock does, we catch a cold. When we are heated up passively, we get burned. Therefore a healthy warmth organization includes protective reactions. When heat affects the body from outside, for instance through a hot-water bottle, the body will respond by generating inner warmth—warmth is mobilized. When cold affects the body from outside, the body has two ways to react. Either it takes warmth away from the skin surface to maintain the inner body temperature, or it mobilizes warmth to neutralize the cold. Warmth mobilization occurs in fever. The function of a fever is to adapt what has been taken in from an alien outer world to the requirements of the inner world.

Compared to warm-blooded animals (which are naturally adapted to their milieu through their fur coat or feathers) or to cold-blooded animals (which barely need a separate warmth organization), the human being is rather helpless in dealing with outside temperatures. However, the human being does use clothing to adapt to outside temperatures. Clothing and nutrition are two areas where culture has taken on some physiological functions.

The warmth process, or the process of adapting, mitigates the impact of the outer world so that the inner world can receive it. This applies to all areas of human physiology. I will give two examples—the eye and digestive organs.

In the eye, the light must be modified in such a way that the eye can handle it. Therefore we have the ingenious set-up of lens, vitreous body, and the function of accommodation. Through this the light is transformed, and it attains a quality the inner world can deal with.

The second life process modifies nutrition, bringing food to the right consistency and temperature. All solids have to be liquefied. Nutriments in a liquid state need to be brought to the right temperature; what is too cold has to be heated up, and what is too warm has to be cooled down. Since mother's milk is liquid and has the right temperature, the baby can consume and digest it without much activity from the life process of adapting.

90

Breaking down: The third life process

The third function of the life processes is to change the substance that has entered the organism from outside so thoroughly that no trace of its alien origin is left.

Human beings have to breathe; they also have to feed themselves. At present, we, as human beings, cannot nourish our inner world on our own. We need food from the outer world. We need to take it in and destroy it to receive forces for building up the substances of our inner world. Human beings are very different from one another in this respect. One person needs a lot, the other very little; both can be normal from a physiological point of view. In special situations, earthly nutrition is hardly needed. There are descriptions of saints who through intensive meditation were able to maintain their body and stay alive while eating hardly anything. Normally human beings have to deal not only with air and temperature, but also with material substances from the outer world—food. Air is taken far into the body; warmth or cold needs to be assimilated; food must be broken down. The inner world cannot tolerate a nutrient that keeps any of its original properties. The process of digestion aims at destruction, systematic analysis, annihilation, and "de-creation" of substance. The destruction is not a purpose in itself, but is meant to serve life. There we touch on a close relationship with the life process of maintaining. I will go into that later. The life process of breaking down aims not only at meeting nutriments, taken from living sources in such a way that the material substance of the food disappears, but also at awakening something. The awakening of a specific force is the main purpose of this life process. The destruction process encounters the force that lived in the substance that has become food. Only after this force has been neutralized can the food substance disappear. In nutrition, the human life process of breaking down encounters beings of the elemental creative world.

In the second chapter, I described how plants are built up by ether forces that are activities of what I called elemental beings. When food derived from plants is digested, these elemental beings are set free. Yet they should not be free within the human body, and the human ether forces have to stand up against the ether forces of the plant. This is the battle of digestion. This battle strengthens the ether forces of the human being. In the process of digestion the elemental beings that were captured in the food are taken up by the ether body of the human being. They are no longer bound to the plant, nor are they free anymore, but they are taken over by the structure of the human ether body.

Many substances from the plant kingdom, the world of animals, and the mineral kingdom are suitable for human digestion. Yet there are

91

also some that cannot be digested—which can be different for different people. A person's digestive strength is complemented in the outer world by a counter-image—that is this person's nutriments. This means that the person can destroy food in such a way that nothing living remains of it. Only human beings are capable of doing this. When animals eat something, it is not digested as thoroughly. This is why we can use animal excrement, but not human excrement, for manure.

The organs that accomplish this process of destruction are the digestive organs. They make use of digestive juices that go after the different nutritive substances with a high degree of purpose, efficiency, and strength. There are enzymes that split up the carbohydrates, proteins, and lipids—hydrolyze them and de-conjugate them. This happens in the mouth, the stomach, and the small and large intestines. From this point of view, the whole gastrointestinal tract is outer world. Only after something has been digested completely can the inner world create an individualized substance in place of the original material.

Everything that has not gone through the entire process of breaking down remains outer world, for instance the salicylic acid in the blood from aspirin. Substances such as aspirin do not become part of the human body but are excreted. Something similar occurs with food allergies. When children do not break down the food completely, the undigested parts do not become part of their organism. The allergic reaction is an effort to excrete what could not be metabolized.

Rudolf Steiner called the third life process *Ernährung* (nutrition). He was not referring to the process of building up an inner world, but he was looking at the process of breaking down substances from the outer world. The third life process forms a bridge between created nature and the creative individual inner world. This bridge is given by nature and exists naturally but must nonetheless be actively developed. Young children cannot digest some food that they will be able to digest a few years later.

We need energy to destroy. When we are tired or ill, we cannot digest as well. A sick person needs food that can be easily digested. When the vitality comes back, the appetite also comes back.

Breaking down is the third step that every organism has to take when it is taking in substances from the outer world. The eye has to destroy the light; otherwise the light would cause damage to the eye. Rhodopsin is used for this destruction. It enters into a photochemical reaction with the light and makes it disappear.

Also in the examples beginning on page 78, we can find the life process of breaking down. As a wound heals, cells and substances that are no longer useful are broken down. In organ formation, cells have to be cleared away continuously so that new cells can fulfill new tasks. In the kindergarten class, old habits need to disappear so that new ways of doing things can develop. Each new child affects the balance of the class so that the class has to change to receive the newcomer. The newcomer has to change too. Perhaps he or she has to let go of certain habits. The central life process (sorting) is always the one that calls for making choices that fit the new concept. The third life process guides the decisions regarding what has to disappear. From the aspect of time, we can see the future working in this life process, inasmuch as this life process prepares the body for what will come next.

The next three life processes are *maintaining, growing,* and *bringing into being.* These three work closely together. Their purpose is to maintain and care for the living human body. They have their main task during embryonic development and in the first seven years of childhood. When the ether body is born, these three life processes will start to serve memory and thought. They then maintain and care for a healthy and coherent mental life. After the birth of the ether body, taking in, adapting, and breaking down keep their activities more connected to the physical body than the last three life processes do.

The three life processes directed outward work together in pairs with the three life processes directed inward. I will discuss the latter (numbers 5, 6, 7) in their connection to the former (numbers 3, 2, 1).

(4) sorting

(3) breaking down————— maintaining (5)

(2) adapting ————————— growing (6)

(1) taking in————————bringing into being (7)

Fig. 30 Connections between the life processes.

Maintaining: The fifth life process

The digested food enters the phase of *maintaining* or building up the body after and only as far as it has been broken down. There we see the close relation between the third (breaking down) and the fifth life process. The purpose of maintaining is to help the body recover from fatigue, damage, and breakdown.

93

Breaking down is a process that is actively directed toward the outer world. Maintaining actively builds up the substances of the inner world. Breaking down occurs mostly during the day when we are awake. Maintaining occurs especially at night when we are asleep. During the day we take in food and other material and immaterial substances from the outer world, all of which need to be broken down. At night, when we are unconscious, we have to recover from the toil of the day. The life process of maintaining accomplishes this night activity. Since our activities and experiences differ each day, we ourselves develop each day, and therefore the process of maintaining must be able to restore the body somewhat differently each night. This life process does not work with impulses from the future (as the third life process—breaking down—does), but it adapts the past to the present; it does not, however, conserve the past.

Where do the building materials for the maintaining process come from? To answer this question we need to look more closely at the relation between the third (breaking down) and the fifth life process.

I have described how the process of digestion breaks down substances from the outer world and de-creates them. Matter disappears; creative power appears. Matter does not simply disappear from the earth. In a process that is complementary to the disappearance of matter, the fifth life process creates new substance. This newly created substance is original and has never existed on earth before. It is highly individualized. The third life process made creative power appear, and thus it enables the fifth life process to materialize substance. From this source streams human substance, as yet undifferentiated. Then—still guided by the fifth life process—a process of differentiation starts, and the newly created substance is tailored to the organ that needs it. Undifferentiated protein becomes liver protein; undifferentiated lipid becomes phospholipid for the nerve cell membrane. In physiology, this is known as assimilation. Assimilation is the process of taking in nutrients and using them to build up the organism for recovery and growth. In college we are usually given a simplistic model, without much explanation of how the proteins, carbohydrates, and lipids from the food are later to be found in the body as human lipids, human proteins, and human carbohydrates.

The third and fifth life processes have to interact in order that the breaking down delivers the energy that enables the maintaining process to form the right substance. The process of digestion creates the conditions for the process of maintaining to work, by providing it with the forces it needs. When these forces are not used, there is unused power of creation; when the digestion does not function well, the source of new human substance dries up. Between these two polar processes (the third and the fifth), the central life process (sorting) is at work. Choices have to be made to separate what belongs to the organism from what does not belong. Seen from the middle, both breaking down and maintaining are the executors that make the choices reality. These choices fit into the plan that the human being has made for him- or herself. This plan contains blueprints for the human organs and functions. The blueprints are basically the same for all of humanity, but they allow for infinite individual variations. Heredity and the individual's karmic past determine the variations.

Where in the body does maintaining occur? To find the proper organs for it, we have to look at assimilation processes. Where does human substance come into being? It starts in the walls of the intestines, which have a surface the size of a soccer field, and are one of the boundaries between inner and outer world. In the walls of the intestines, the outer world that is disappearing meets the newly appearing inner world.

After this, more steps need to be taken to build up the human substance that is appropriate. The substance must be individualized (because each individual has his or her own protein); it must be adapted to the organ in which it has to function; it must be living substance; and it must fit the physical body. To say it differently—the new substance must fit the I-organization, the astral body, the ether body, and the physical body of the human being.

Anthroposophy talks about the four protein-forming organs—the heart, kidney, liver, and lung. These organs need to be looked at from a broader point of view rather than just from their physical and physiological appearances. The "heart" is everywhere where substance is the carrier of the I; the "kidney" is everywhere where substance is taken hold of by the astral body; the "liver" is everywhere where substance is used by the ether body; and the "lungs" are related to the substance of the physical body. These four organs are the physical focal points of the four steps, just mentioned, that the process of maintaining takes in forming new substance.

Looking at hormones, the adrenal glands play a central role in the process of maintaining. The hormones of the adrenal cortex protect against excessive breakdown and assist in the process of assimilation in a powerful way. We can see the function of the adrenal glands as part of the organ system of the kidneys, which serves the astral body.[4]

In the previously given example of physiological processes in the eye, the process of maintaining includes the production of rhodopsin, which replaces what is used up in the photochemical reaction. The fifth life process is a night process, but it also needs to be active during the day. This is necessary not only for the eye, but also for making mental pictures. In the inner world, light is re-created so that it can be perceived later as a mental image. Yet the last two life processes (the sixth—growing, and the seventh—bringing into being) are also needed to build up the complete mental image, which can then be perceived by the soul. We can find the recuperating quality of the maintenance process also in the examples beginning on page 78 (wound healing, organ formation, and the kindergarten class).

Growing: The sixth life process

An organism not only needs to be maintained, but it also needs to grow. The second life process (adapting) adapts the substances of the outer world to the bodily conditions. The sixth life process makes the digested substances fit the inner world. This is the task of growing. Growth is the signature of a young organism, eager to live. Human beings, animals, and plants grow when they are young. Growth is one of the important characteristics of life. However, it is not the ultimate characteristic, because a living organism can stop growing. Growth is a phase of development. An organism must be able, while growing, to adapt to new situations. Growing, therefore, includes differentiation as a preparation for a new situation.

Plants oscillate between vegetative phases (when their substance increases) and generative phases (when flowers and seeds form). Animals will grow until they reach adulthood. Once an animal is full-grown and can function as required by the species, the forces of growth are used to maintain the proper physiology of the organs. Some lower animals such as polyps keep the faculty for growth. Severed parts can be replaced (growing and maintaining) and new offspring can be created (growing and bringing into being).

In plants, we can easily see the influence of environmental factors on growth. A dandelion in the flatlands looks different from a dandelion in the mountains. The factors that regulate plant growth—such as type of soil, temperature, length of day, and light—work primarily from the outside. These same factors also work on the human being, but primarily from the inside. However, in young children the yet unborn ether body is wide open towards the periphery, and therefore, factors of the outer world still have a strong influence on their growth. Too little warmth and affection, for instance, may restrict the growth of children.

The phase of growth in the human being includes the embryonic stage and the first eighteen years of life. After that, the soul can use the forces of growth because the body does not need them anymore. Soul-growth is unlimited. Thoughts can always be deeper, feelings can always be broader, and our actions can always have a higher moral quality. The body keeps its faculty of growth for situations such as wounds, fractures, or the need to use different muscles in a new profession.

Growing always goes together with maintaining and bringing into being. We may nonetheless look at them separately.

We can measure growth—length, circumference, and weight. We use growth curves and normative values. These are averages for a segment of the population. They hide, however, what we can see in the individual child. Each child reveals that growth is not steady but occurs in phases. In children, growth proceeds alternating between growth in length and growth in width, stretching and filling out. This alternation, leading to a steady growth rhythm, belongs to the activity of the ether body, in this case—the life process of growing.

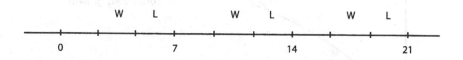

Fig. 31 The first third of each of the initial three seven-year periods shows an accent on growth of the head, the second third on growth in width (W), and the last third on growth in length (L).

Growth of the limbs makes us taller; growth of the trunk fills us out. After each phase of growth, a portion of the faculty for growth is given to the soul. When children go to school, they need to be able to learn. At puberty, children need to be able to form an opinion for themselves. Toward adulthood, they need to be able to step into the world on their own. These three events occur after the three phases of stretching. After the phases of filling out, previous developments are consolidated—they become more inward and richer. The first third of each of the initial three seven-year periods is accompanied by growth of the head. We should take "growth of the head" figuratively. We should see it as an individualization process, a shaping of the head and chiseling of the features. In the first third of the seven-year periods, the young person will show a preference for certain things and will make choices about the direction of his or her life.

97

The acceleration phase of growth in puberty does not rhythmically alternate between stretching and filling out. This growth pattern has a different character; it is discontinuous and unpredictable, with pauses and spurts. The astral body that is about to be born directs this phase of growth. Sex hormones play an important role during this time, much more so than before or after. In addition, growth during puberty calls itself to a halt by stimulating the closure of the growth plates in the bones. This would not occur in a rhythmic continuous growth, which would be able to continue (within biological bounds) forever.

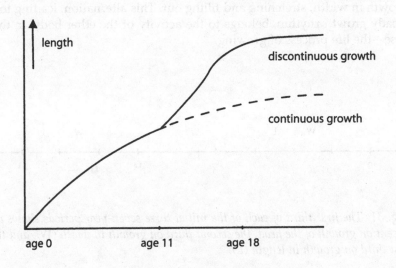

Fig. 32 The growth of the child has two aspects.

In the first seven years of childhood, we only meet growth processes that are regulated by the ether body. The child gradually leaves heredity behind and finds him- or herself. Growing can be understood as being on the way toward something and seeking the future.

Which organs are responsible for physiological growth? The work-place is obvious—the whole body of the child grows. Initially everything can and does grow. Growing lengthwise is made possible particularly by the growth plates of the bones, the epiphyses. Sense organs, nerves, and brain have essentially finished growing before the child is three. All other organs continue to grow until adulthood. Some organs are able to grow throughout life. Muscles grow when they are used. The liver restores itself when part of it is lost (the fifth, sixth, and seventh life processes cooperating). Often the earlobe of old people still grows. In pregnant women, the uterus and breasts will grow. For most people, fatty tissue can grow throughout life. The organs, therefore, are very different with regard to growth and regeneration. The phenomenon of growth also includes the opposite movement—becoming smaller (involution). After a certain age, we become smaller, mainly because the fluid content of the tissues decreases. We can see this as a decrease of the process of maintaining. Some organs have their maximum size during childhood (thymus and tonsils) and then become considerably smaller. Obviously these organs are mainly regulated by the growth processes of the first phase of life—the rhythmic continuous growth.

The body has many substances to regulate organ growth—factors that stimulate and factors that inhibit growth. These substances are hormones or hormone-like substances, the best known of which is the growth hormone. Insulin, thyroid hormone, and the hormones of the adrenal cortex also clearly affect growth.

There are limits to growth. When there are no substances provided (the fifth life process—maintaining), there is no growth. Without taking in substances, adapting, and digesting (the first, second, and third life processes), there will be no growth. Healthy growth remains between boundaries set by the building plan, the blueprint of the human body. Wound healing is a good example of this; growth will not go beyond remodeling the perfect skin. This principle applies also to other organisms. A kindergarten class must not grow beyond its purpose.

In the example of the physiological processes in the eye, we followed the light from its being taken in, to being adapted, and being broken down. The organism "behind the eye" re-creates the light through the fifth life process (maintaining). The process of growing gives the proper size to the image brought by the light, so that it can find its right relation to other images that come from memory or from direct perception. In this situation, growth means "making it fit the actual conditions."

99

Bringing into being: The seventh life process

The previous six life processes all have a goal, a purpose. All of them are directed toward forming the body. This form stands as a model for all life processes and is brought into reality by the seventh life process. In calling it *Reproduktion* (reproduction), Rudolf Steiner indicates that procreation belongs to this seventh life process. He also called it *Hervorbringung* (bringing forth). I have chosen the term "bringing into being."

In this seventh life process, we meet the capacity to call into being the specific form that belongs to the organism. This capacity causes— out of the identical forces of maintaining and growing—one plant to become a dandelion, another plant a poppy. Human embryological development results in the creation of an individualized human form. Some trees, plants, and lower animals have the capacity to repair damage done to their form. In an early phase of their embryological development, the same applies to all animals. Experiments with tadpoles have shown this. Even for the human being, an intact form will still come into being even when cells are taken away at a very early stage in the development of the human embryo. After birth, the process of body formation is less pronounced, even though the human form adapts to the circumstances and requirements of development throughout life. We have to assume that the seventh life process plays a role in this. It will also be active—along with the life process of maintaining—when a wound or broken bone needs to heal.

Creating the proper form has to do with heredity. The genetic material that is stored in the nucleus of the cell is not the only factor determining the human form, but it will set limits to the variability. The metabolism of the cell takes place in the cytoplasm, and through this, the influence of the environment can call for variations on the theme set by the genetic material. I have previously called this theme the *model*. The seventh life process regulates the interaction between the factors that bring limitations and the factors that bring opportunities. It works where the earthly and the non-earthly meet. It also sets boundaries—first of all the boundaries of the contours of the human form as a whole and, in addition, all internal boundaries of tissues and organs through which the overall contours become possible. When forms have to change—because of growth processes, for instance—the seventh life process needs to cooperate with the sixth (growing) and the fifth (maintaining). Through the central life process (sorting), the I has access to the choices that have to be made— does this belong to my human form or does it not? The first life process (taking in) is also responsible for a threshold—the boundary between the living inner world and the ether forces from the outer world. Without the activity of the first life process, the seventh could not succeed in forming the body. On the other hand, there would be no taking in, if there were no human being doing it. Thus both the first and seventh life processes work at a threshold—the first at the threshold between the ether world and the human being, the seventh at the threshold between the human being and the physical world. Between these two boundaries, they maintain human life in cooperation with the other five life processes.

In serving procreation, the processes of bringing into being attain yet another function—reproduction. There we touch on another boundary—the bridge across which human beings can enter the earthly world. After the physical body is impregnated, the ether body of the mother works along with the ether body of the child to create a new form. It is primarily the mother who takes on the task of substance formation and growth. However, the I of the child is right there when choices have to be made.

In connection with the seventh life process, we meet gender differentiation. The differentiation between male and female only plays a role on earth. The organs connected to this seventh life process are different for boys and girls. The genital organs play a key role in the protection and handing over of genetic material. Boys use a different part of the corresponding ether force for the forming of their genital organs than girls do. The complementary part of this ether force is then not used for physical processes. Therefore the seventh life process appears as a duality. The part of the ether body that is directed toward the physical body adapts itself to the physical constitution. The free part has the opposite gender and can be used for consciousness from the seventh year onward. The part of the ether body that is bound to the reproductive organs will not become free at the birth of the ether body and therefore cannot be used for consciousness, as it is in the other organs. In the reproductive organs the ether body has to remain available for reproduction.[5]

There is another organ, which was referred to before, that has to do with the form of the body. This organ includes the skin and membranes, the tendon sheaths and ligaments, the organ surfaces and cell walls, all of which are surface boundaries used to shape the proper body form.

I will take the skin as an example. The skin as a boundary is not firm and fixed. There are only a few other organs that have such a short cycle of regeneration. It takes only a few days for a germinal skin cell to develop into a fully differentiated cell and then into a dead cell (without a nucleus) that peels off. A stream of newly formed skin cells (human substance) is continuously working its way from within the organism to the outside. This unstable boundary is constantly creating itself anew. Nonetheless, it is the true boundary of the human form. The radiating body warmth, the exhaled breath, and the body odor are not to be understood as belonging to the human form. The seventh life process does not extend beyond the human skin.

Not only does the skin peel off; other organs do the same. For the intestinal mucous membranes, this process takes a few days; for the nails a few weeks; for the bones a few years. After seven years, all human substance has been replaced by new human substance. Nothing has remained the same; the entire human body is renewed every seven years. The seventh life process ensures that this cycle of renewal remains within the boundaries of the individual human form.

How does this seventh life process work in the eye? The picture from the outer world has gone through a process—it has been taken in, digested, assimilated, and it has grown. Now it can reappear in a form that is accessible to the human soul. In the ether body, a form arises—an image that can be perceived by the sentient soul. The higher levels of conscious activity, such as judgment, can work further with this.

Summary

I have described the four types of ether as the etheric substance with which the ether body can work. Since each of them constitutes a polarity, they produce eight instruments for body formation: warming up/cooling down (warmth ether), making appear/making disappear (light ether), creating bonds/disconnecting bonds (chemical ether), and bringing to life/leading to death (life ether).

Organisms have seven processes at their disposal, which work as a unity and can be put to work anywhere. These processes work together in pairs and are regulated "from the middle" by a central process. The cooperation between the first and the seventh process consists in the first process taking up from the outer world that which the seventh process needs for creating the proper form. The cooperation between the second process and the sixth process consists in the second process providing adaptation to the inner conditions of the body in order that the sixth process can provide growth adapted to the actual conditions. The third process breaks down the substances of the outer world so that they can be assimilated by the fifth process to maintain the body.

The four types of ether as substance of the ether body and the seven life processes as its operational tools are given to the child at birth. This is the working of heredity, which is more than chromosomes and DNA. Everything that nature has given to the child can be understood as heredity.

Reciprocal education of the upper and lower pole

In this part of the third chapter, I will describe the birth of the ether body in two ways. In each description, we will meet the duality of capacities given by heredity on the one hand, and of the work that one does to develop these capacities on the other hand.

First I will explain how capacities have an innate tendency to evolve and mature. Working to develop skills out of these evolving capacities makes children independent.

Then I will describe how the upper and lower poles have the opportunity to influence one another because of the reversed arrangement of the four types of ether. What is central in the one pole is peripheral in the other.

In the third section I will discuss the birth process, which works from above downward and occurs in three phases of two and one-third years each. The process of maturation follows the same time schedule, but it takes the opposite direction—from below upward.

Duality: endowed by heredity
—acquired through one's individual activity

During prenatal life and the first seven years, the child makes use of what in the description of the seventh life process (bringing into being) I have called heredity. Who is this child? He or she is an eternal being, who has not yet fully appeared on earth. When the child is born, almost all of this being is still in a germinal state, and not much of it is visible yet. Only the physical body has left this germinal state—it is born. The germs of the ether body, the astral body, and the I-organization still rest within the physical body. They still have to come under the child's control. Each child initiates and completes the births of these bodies. The example of the birth of the physical body, described on pages 28–30, has shown us that giving birth is not an easy task. The child starts mastering the ether processes described earlier in this chapter. The child learns to control them, and the ether body becomes individualized. Children accomplish the birth of the individualized ether body by occupying themselves with everything the ether body has to offer, and they do this with much interest and meddlesomeness. Children penetrate into the activity range of gnomes, undines, fairies, and fire beings, trying to bring the seven life processes under their own direction; of course, they will only partly succeed, and the meddling will have some adverse effects too.

Luckily the child does not need to do this alone. Children's diseases and other illnesses that come with a fever, as well as prudent education, will help. The actual helper is the child's angel. As the midwife has the wisdom to do what helps the child to be born, the child's angel knows what the child needs to accomplish the birth of his or her ether body.

The fact that the ether body after its birth is not simply a variation of the ether body before its birth, but is actually new, indicates that the child has worked with forces coming out of the future. We have seen in the second chapter that the ether body is open for such an influence. Examples of this newness are the four times three molars of the permanent teeth, which were not there in the baby teeth. Also new is the faculty to think and the free use of mental pictures and memory pictures.

What the child has received through heredity has its own dynamics of development, which we could refer to as "maturation." In the second chapter, we have seen this in the plant. Each plant has a more or less predetermined pattern of germination, rooting, growing, going through metamorphoses, and forming flowers, fruit, and seeds.

It depends on the individuality of the child how this process of maturation evolves, and to what extent the child develops his or her hereditary capacities. The effect of the child's own activity I call "emancipation." Plants are completely dependent on their circumstances. When the winter is long, a plant will germinate late. When the summer is hot and dry, a plant will form fruit early. Each child's independence is partially influenced by the environment, and partially by the child him- or herself.

I will give an example of maturation and of emancipation. When the baby is born, the kidneys have not yet reached their full potential for concentrating urine. The full potential has only been reached after a year or so—the function has matured. Children have taken a developmental step that works in the direction of independence (emancipation) when at the age of three they control their bladder to such an extent that they do not wet their pants during the day or at night.

Maturation is a process that is innate to hereditary capacities. Emancipation gives the child control over the bodily functions. These two processes, maturation and emancipation, are interrelated. Something that is not given as a potential by heredity cannot be emancipated and

104

become independent. The seven-year rhythm of the births of the four bodies is a potential that comes out of heredity. Yet it is a matter of the child's individuality how he or she gives form to this potential and works with it. Maturation can only happen when the human being has been born and is alive. The presence of the child, however small, is a prerequisite. Yet maturation processes evolve autonomously. In children with developmental disabilities, for instance, the kidneys will also reach their full potential for concentrating urine after about a year.

Mutual interaction between the upper and lower pole

The four elements of the physical body and the corresponding types of ether work together as a unity within the human body. We can nonetheless find a clear order in the organization of the elements and of the ethers. The skeleton gives a notable example of this. In the head, the bones are on the outside whereas in the limbs they make up the inner core. I have described the skeleton as a picture of the life ether and connected it to the earth element. The life ether and the earth element, therefore, are placed at the periphery in the upper pole and at the center in the lower pole. The other elements and ether types are also placed in opposite positions respectively at the upper pole and at the lower pole, as we can see in figure 33.

There is, however, a difference in how the types of ether express themselves at each of the poles.

In the head, we encounter the four ether types as they have turned toward the physical body. The processes of the life ether crystallize, and they produce the skull. The chemical ether works into substance and produces cerebrospinal fluid as well as the blood circulation on the outside of the brain. The light ether makes things visible and produces the grey and white matter. The warmth ether produces warmth and works in the service of life-functions such as the regulation of respiration, circulation, and temperature in the brain stem.

In the lower pole—most clearly in the limbs—the types of ether are placed in the service of the acting, willing human being. At the center, we find the bones with bone marrow inside; the bone marrow is the source of blood production (life ether). Around the bones, we find the muscles, which are the greatest consumers of energy in the human body (chemical ether). Around these muscles—in and under the skin—we find the zone in which a network of nerves facilitates perception (light ether). Outside of this, we find the warmth that radiates beyond the skin, and the skin's complexion that is influenced by good blood circulation (warmth ether). This is presented in figure 34.

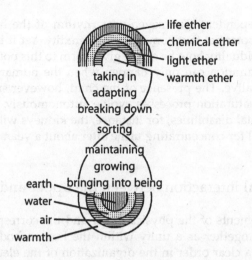

Fig. 33 *The arrangement of the elements and of the corresponding types of ether in the upper and in the lower pole. Above, the earth element and the life ether are on the periphery whereas the warmth element and the warmth ether are at the center. Below it is the reverse. Between the two poles, I have listed the seven life processes, since they are located in the middle region.*

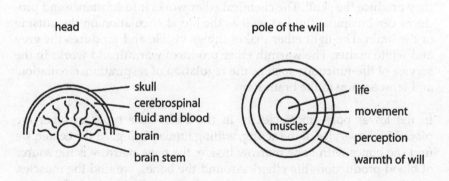

Fig. 34 *The arrangement of the types of ether in the upper and in the lower pole. For the head, I have indicated anatomical structures; for the limbs I have indicated functions that are in the service of the active human being.*

It is hard to describe the arrangement of the types of ether in the middle region. This is the region of the life processes. All the life processes are rhythmical and part of the rhythmic region, which is the middle region. There, the process aspect of the ethers comes to the fore rather than their substance aspect.

Since so far I have only mentioned the skull and its content, I will now proceed with describing the arrangement of the types of ether and of the four elements in the two poles.

With regard to the organs of the limbs (the muscles, nerves, arteries, and veins), the emphasis is not on their form but on their function in the service of the active human being. The head is unique in the sense that its organs are extremely physical. Because of this, we can attribute each type of ether to a specific organ. We cannot do this with the other visible organs of the human body. Those organs are penetrated by all types of ether and by all life processes.

The four types of ether in the head-pole are arranged in an order that is the reverse of the order in the will-pole, but this fact does not prevent the warmth ether of the head from being one with the warmth ether of the will. This is true for all types of ether. They work together and penetrate one another.

The head has a tendency to stillness and fossilization; the limbs have a tendency to activity and movement. When the child is born, the will-pole is active but without direction; the head-pole is sleeping but shaped to a high degree. These two start to interact. Through this interaction, the head is awakened by the will, and the will is directed by the head. Through this interaction—which the child activates by practicing and exercising—the child acquires the condition of controlled movement and an awakened head around the age of seven. The ether body has been born.

In the next section, I will describe for each type of ether its upper pole activity, its lower pole activity, and the interaction between these two.

Warmth ether

In the head
The functions of the warmth ether have almost matured at birth. The vital functions of respiration, blood circulation, and warmth regulation are normally well taken care of. How could it be otherwise? During the first months, the breathing rhythm might still be irregular, but after that—and generally earlier—it will stabilize. The infant has a rather fast pulse, but

the pulse regulation is functional at birth. The regulation of the body temperature, however, has not yet matured. It takes about a year before this will function normally so that, for instance, the child can have a fever in response to infections. This is often not quite possible at an earlier time. During the first year, some children even respond to infections with a decrease in body temperature.

In the will pole
The warmth ether in the lower pole does not manifest as body temperature. In the child, the warmth of the body is *warmth of the head*. In the lower pole, we have to look for warmth of will. That has to do with an intentional, directed will that brings the child into a true relationship with his or her environment. It is obvious that infants do not have this yet. Most of their movements are chaotic and undirected. During infancy, each directed movement is connected to reflexes, such as aiming for the nipple, sucking, or swallowing.

Interaction
The situations in the head pole and in the will pole interact, and they influence one another. The breathing, for instance, learns not only to attain a steady rhythm, but also to adapt to the activity of the will pole. When the child makes intensive movements (kicking, turning over, crawling, walking, or running), the breathing will quickly learn to adapt its rate. When the child is crying loudly, the breathing is completely devoted to an undirected will. When the child has learned to cry to get what he or she wants, the breathing is in the service of a directed will. When the child learns to speak, the breathing and the will must cooperate effectively. Exhaling puts itself in the service of speaking, and the undirected will allows itself to be formed by the speaking.

The following example is taken from warmth regulation. The regulation of the body temperature gradually becomes more flexible. When the child is very active or looks forward to something very much, the upper pole provides enough warmth to respond to this directed will and to support it.

In what way does the warmth of will allow itself to be educated by the warmth structures of the upper pole? It will accept rhythm, and through this it can be controlled. The child acquires a rhythm of alternating periods of rest (sleep) with periods of activity. The child acquires a rhythm by having regular meals; then the metabolic reflexes will be active in specific areas at regular times. The remaining time is then made free for directing the intention to the outer world. We can observe that infants are most able to direct their activity just after being fed, if they have not fallen asleep. In toddlers and preschoolers, rhythmic games are the means to educate undirected will.

Light ether

In the head

The brain and the fluid-filled ventricles are basically completed at birth, but are as yet in no way mature. New brain cells are added during the first year, and supportive cells during the first three years. The skull and brain grow tremendously during the first years, analogous to chest growth. The circumference of the head increases by almost five inches during the first year, in the second year by almost one inch, and after that a little more than one inch until the age of seven. Thus maturation takes one to three years. The functioning of the brain is not a matter of maturation but of its being used. I will not enter into the subject of brain functions as they are discussed in standard textbooks. It falls, however, within the scope of this book to depict the brain as a mirror—a mirror that has been made and polished by the light ether. Thanks to an incredibly intricate structure and by means of the fine-tuning of the interrelated different parts of the brain, the light ether has made a "device" that can register all experiences of the human body. All internal processes, all movements, and all sense perceptions can be registered by the brain and fixed. That is what the brain does. It is, of course, an incredible accomplishment to make a still-life picture of everything. The brain does this so that the human being can be conscious. Human consciousness cannot catch moving pictures and active forces; therefore it has to help itself with the "dead" still-life pictures provided by the brain. The brain itself does not "do" anything. The soul is active, and sometimes the I. In the mirror of the upper pole, the soul looks at the results of the fixation—at the pictures.

In the will pole

Throughout the body, the sense organs for touch and temperature perception are located just below the surface of the skin. In specific areas of the body (the nose and the mouth), the sense organs for smell and taste are also located just below the surface of the skin. The organs for the other senses are situated farther away from the periphery.

The human body is equipped with a network for the perception of the light ether, by which the soul receives messages from the twelve sectors of the sense world (see pages 125–128). These perceptions and sensations do not leave the human being untouched. They move us as adults. This is the opportunity for our will to know what is happening and what requires a response. How does this work in the young child? In the young child, the area of the light ether is still very undifferentiated, similar to what we observed with the warmth ether. The young child is stimulated by the inner world of his or her inner body and wakes up only slowly to the outer world.

Interaction
The partially formed mirror of the brain and the still undifferentiated chaotic perceptions of the will pole have a profound influence on one another. The mirror allows itself to be formed by everything the perceiving will experiences. The more perfect the mirror, the more differentiated the perceptions. Thus the exercising of the senses and nerves shapes the mirror. Because the brain transforms the chaotic sensations into pictures that can be perceived, the exercising becomes easier and easier, and the child will show this as skills. In the fourth chapter, I will discuss the senses.

Chemical ether

In the head
The brain and the spinal cord are surrounded by cerebrospinal fluid. This again is surrounded by an extensive network of blood vessels, among them broad blood vessels that are called sinusoids. The cerebrospinal fluid and the blood form a moving and living sphere around the static brain. Cerebrospinal fluid streams and pulsates more slowly than blood. Both respond to the respiratory rate. The cerebrospinal fluid makes the brain float. Because of this, the brain does not weigh 1500 grams but only 20. The function of this liquid cloak is to send the formative activities from the head throughout the whole body. The chemical ether is also known as the *tone ether*. This indicates that human substance needs to be penetrated by sound, structure, plasticity, and music.

The cloak of fluid inside the skull is the organ through which the tone ether can perform its function. Impulses are generated in the whole body, especially by the "perception organization" (i.e., the activity of the light ether in the will pole). The tone ether transmits these impulses—transformed into formative forces—to the growing body. The astral body does this by means of the cerebrospinal fluid, the ego-organization through the blood. The separation between the two—the barrier between the cerebrospinal fluid and the blood—is not yet completed at birth. In the newborn, substances from the blood easily pass into the cerebrospinal fluid. After a few weeks the barrier is completed.

In the will pole
In the lower pole, the sounding ether body has formed the "movement organization"—a preeminent musical composition of muscles, ligaments, tendons, joints, and bones.[6] The movement organization has the task to move with the surroundings and, through this, experience all that human beings are connected with, where they have a responsibility, or—to say it differently—where their destinies take them. Similar to other aspects

110

of the will pole, the movement organization is predominantly future oriented.

The movement organization still has another function—to lift up the physical body. The muscles—in the service of the ether body and especially of the tone ether—make the physical body weightless (see ppages 191–192). As long as we are not tired, we do not feel how many pounds we carry around. When we become tired, we start to feel our body weight. Newborns are not yet weightless, and they are not yet treading their path of destiny, at least not by themselves through their own deeds.

Interaction

Also at the level of the chemical ether, we encounter an intensive educating process between the upper and lower pole. The chaotic movements are formed and brought to rest by the quietly pulsing formative impulses from the head. Reflexes are made to disappear, covered by the impulses that the astral body and ego-organization imprint on the movement organization via the tone ether of the upper pole. Movements such as crawling, walking, or writing become habitual. The physical body is lifted out of gravity. Through this, voluntary movements can arise—the child is no longer moved by his or her muscles, but can now start to move from out of him- or herself. If enough incentives are provided, the child will start to move along with outer movements, imitating them. This is obvious in learning to speak. The movements that are necessary for speaking are specialized movements "lifted out" of the total movement opportunities. These speech movements attain their forms and become habitual by practicing them. The impulses from the tone ether of the upper pole bring the proper form to the speech movements. These impulses are generated by imitation. This way we can understand that there are children who practice certain movements inwardly and then suddenly show that they are able "to do it." Inwardly they have imitated and intensively moved with the outer impulses, and by doing this they have imprinted the new forms of movement into their movement organization. (See pages 186–193 for the development of the movement organization and pages 212–215 for imitation.)

Life ether

In the head

Through its crystallizing force, the life ether has been able to produce the skull. Bone has developed out of a stage of connective tissue, and calcium has been deposited into it. This bone must remain very alive because it has to adapt itself to the rapidly growing head. This is accomplished by breaking down bone substance on the inside of the skull and forming new bone substance at the outside of the skull. There we see how life ether works with substance. The skull can grow, in part because of the skull sutures. Where they meet is an open space—the fontanels. The time when these fontanels close is different for each child. The fontanel in the back of the head closes at about four months, while the large fontanel closes at about one to one and a half years. Then the process of maturation is complete. The skull growth, however, will continue for many more years, until puberty. The skull sutures—the movable connection between the bones of the skull—close only at about the age of forty. Of course we can say that the skull has the function of protecting the brain. The skull's essential function is, however, to bring the life ether process to a halt. This makes the head into a true skull. All processes of life and of movement that occur within the head come to a full stop in the skull. It is obvious that this is connected to the function of the upper pole. The other bones of the body serve different functions; the other parts of the skeleton belong to the movement organization; they are quite different in structure and development, as well as in their potential for being transformed and repaired.

In the will pole

At the lower pole, the life ether comes forward as the caretaker of the source of life. We can observe this in the bone marrow, but also in the pancreas, spleen, and liver. In all these organs, life is exuberant. The spleen and liver can also (under special circumstances) produce blood. For the yet unborn this is even normal. Around birth, the production of blood moves from these organs to the bones—a phenomenon of maturation.

It is significant that children are born with an abundance of hemoglobin, much more than is ever needed. During the first weeks after birth, this hemoglobin is broken down, and at about six months the baby might even be anemic. The tremendous exuberance of life forces is brought under control. Nevertheless, this life force is the foundation of the will. Every action requires energy. When the life force is too strong, as in the newborn, the human being cannot control it. Movement, perception, and intention will be flooded by it, as we can see in rage.

Interaction

I have described how the death processes of the upper pole and the life processes of the lower pole balance and educate one another. The upper pole has to learn to stay within its own territory—the upper pole. It must recede to allow for vitality and growth from birth till far into adolescence. After that, it must serve thinking in a matter-of-fact and unemotional way, and it will also govern the phenomena of aging. The vitality of the lower pole must learn to behave and must be willing to serve the movement impulses. It must provide sufficient metabolism to feed the will—neither too much (to prevent unruliness of the will), nor too little (to prevent apathy).

Having attained an overview of the organization of the four areas of interaction between the upper and lower pole, and seeing how these interactions work during the first seven years, we may have found the key to understanding Rudolf Steiner's saying that the limbs have to awaken the head and the head has to form the limbs.

Being born from above downward; maturing from below upward

In the previous section, I described the processes of the upper and lower poles as they influence and educate one another. The processes of the upper pole gain territory from above downward, whereas the processes of the lower pole do so from below upward. In the following section, I want to describe these two directions—from above downward and from below upward. The birth process of the ether body goes from above downward—first the head, then the rhythmic region, and then the lower pole. The process of maturation moves in the opposite direction. What finally comes to rest in the head started its journey in the dynamics of the lower pole. This second process is one of crystallization.

Being born

During the first seven years of childhood, the birth of the ether body takes place in three steps of two and one-third years each. First the ether body of the head is born, then the ether body of the middle region, and finally the ether body of the lower pole (see figure 35). We can again divide each step into three segments, so that different time-segments will overlap.

113

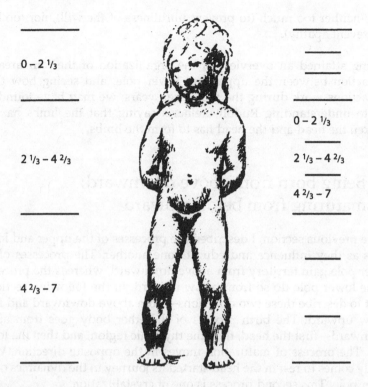

0 – 2 ⅓

0 – 2 ⅓

2 ⅓ – 4 ⅔

2 ⅓ – 4 ⅔

4 ⅔ – 7

4 ⅔ – 7

Fig. 35 The phases of the birth of the ether body. The primary segmentation of the time between birth and the age of seven is indicated on the left. The subsidiary segmentation is indicated on the right.

The body and its organs do not grow evenly in all their parts. Therefore the proportions of the human figure go through considerable change during the first seven years (see figures 36 and 37).

The lengthwise growth of the head stays behind compared to the growth in length of the torso and the legs; however, the volume of the head, especially the circumference, does increase significantly. At around the age of seven, the legs and torso have reached about identical length and this contributes to the impression of harmony that the body of that age evokes. Afterwards the legs grow more rapidly, and at the beginning of puberty they look disproportionately long.

During the embryonic stage and in the first year, the head of the child grows more rapidly. Afterwards the growth impulse shifts downward—first to the torso, then to the legs.

The ratio between the length of the arms on one hand and the length of the torso plus the legs on the other remains about the same until puberty. Children can place their fingertips against their upper legs halfway between the hip and the knee.

114

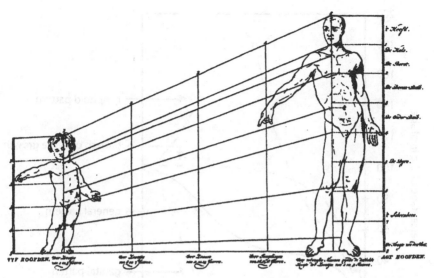

Fig. 36 The change in proportions of the human figure.

	birth	2 ½ years	7 years	adults
head	$3/12$	$1/5$	$2/12$	$1/8$
torso	$5/12$	$2/5$	$5/12$	$3/8$
legs	$4/12$	$2/5$	$5/12$	$4/8$

Fig. 37 The length of the head, torso, and legs as part of total body length, at various ages.

The ratio between the length of the arms and that of the head changes considerably. Babies can reach with their hands just to the top of their heads. Children who are ready for elementary school can reach with their arms and hands over their heads and touch the opposite ear.

The changes in the proportions of the human figure are so characteristic that they are a satisfactory basis for assessing the child's age more or less accurately.

Not only do the visible body parts have a varied pattern of growth, but the inner organs also grow at different rates. We can distinguish four growth patterns—the general type, the lymphoid type, the genital type, and the nerve type. The growth patterns are depicted in figure 38 with examples of the organs in each category.

115

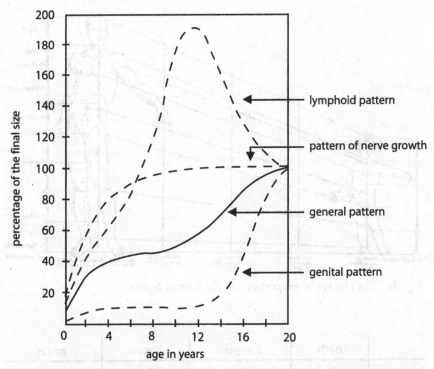

Fig. 38 The various growth patterns. The lymph nodes, thymus gland, and tonsils are among the organs that grow according to the lymphoid pattern. The brain, spinal cord, and nervous system grow according to the pattern of nerve growth. The human body as a totality as well as the muscles, heart, lung, and liver grow according to the general pattern. The sexual organs and adrenal glands grow according to the genital pattern.

In figure 38 we can observe that the general growth pattern of the muscles, heart, liver, lungs and the like, includes two periods of rapid growth—one in the first year and one during puberty. The fastest growing tissues are the nerves, especially the brain. This growth ends for the most part after the first few years and is completed after the seventh year. Genital tissue hardly grows until puberty and then reaches adult size within a few years. The sexual organs and adrenal glands show this pattern.

The lymphoid pattern deviates in a remarkable way. Organs such as the lymph nodes and thymus gland reach their greatest volume during the second seven-year period and decrease after puberty to adult size. As organs of the upper pole, the tonsils are something of an exception. They are the first lymphoid organs to grow and then already decrease during the second seven-year period.

If we ignore the exceptional pattern of the lymphoid system, we notice at once that the general growth pattern is composed of the patterns of the genital organs and the nerves.

Thus we can distinguish two growth impulses—one during childhood, extending into the second seven-year period, and the second during puberty, starting between the tenth and the twelfth year. Since this book focuses on the first seven years of childhood, I will not discuss the second growth impulse.

Head

The forehead grows during the first two years. The typical baby forehead attains its own specific form during this time. If we look at a photograph of a toddler, the forehead is already well recognizable. This is different for the middle part of the face—the nose, eyes, ears, and cheekbones. During preschool age, the middle part of the face starts to elongate. It opens up, one could say. We can observe this best in the gaze. Human eyes have the peculiar property that they can shed tears. The tear fluid is produced from the moment of birth and protects the outer layer of the eye from drying out. The newborn cannot yet shed tears when crying. This occurs around the third month. The tear gland is primarily an instrument of the ether body, and it especially serves secretion. The tear gland becomes activated when something irritates the eye, for instance dust, too much light, or onion fumes. When the soul is strongly touched, the eyes—as the soul's mirror—will show that. After three months, the small child might shed tears when crying because of physical sensations such as discomfort or pain. When can children cry because of sadness? When does sadness arise? Children must be well over three years old before they can shed tears out of sadness. In the middle of the second seven-year period, children learn to laugh with tears. What type of crying and shedding tears do youngsters learn in the middle of the third seven-year period?

Let us return to the middle part of the face. Around their third year, children learn to blow their nose and sniff. The air-filled cavities in the upper jaw—the sinuses—are formed in the middle of the first seven-year period. Simultaneously the middle part of the face elongates. The cavity in the forehead above the nose in the frontal bone develops only in the first part of the second seven-year period. The ears almost have their final shape at birth and they do not change much afterwards. They are not part of the face, but are halfway to the back of the head. The middle part of the face reaches its definitive form only during the second growth impulse at puberty.

Also the jaws and the mouth reach their definitive form only during the second growth impulse in puberty. During the first seven-year period they remain round and full. The baby teeth are completed at the age of two and a half, when the hereditary ether body of the head is born.

At the age of six to seven, the lower jaw will grow more. Because of this, the lower jaw will move forward in relation to the upper jaw by the length of half a molar. The teeth now have their defined occlusion, and in this position the permanent teeth can come in, as I have described in the second chapter.

Torso

The torso starts to grow when the neck elongates after the second year. Because of this, the child can move the head more easily and freely and can now turn it without simultaneously turning the shoulders with it.

The clavicle—part of the shoulder—is the first place in the skeleton where calcium is deposited for ossification, during the fifth month of pregnancy. The two clavicles are also the bones that are the last to fully ossify; this occurs at the age of eighteen.

The infant's chest is very short and is barrel shaped. The chest starts to elongate when the child is two; a second acceleration comes around the age of eight; and the third one occurs at puberty. The chest does not only elongate, but also the angle between the ribs right and left of the sternum changes gradually from a nearly horizontal line at birth to an acute angle when the child is ready to go to elementary school.

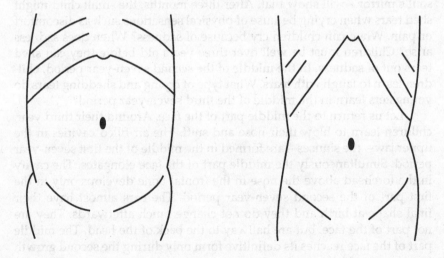

Fig. 39 The angle between the ribs right and left of the sternum is obtuse in the infant (left) and becomes more acute during the course of the first seven years (right).

118

The infant's abdomen is broad and weak. The toddler develops a hollow back and a protruding, firm, convex "toddler belly." This disappears in the fifth year. Around this time, the sexual organs could also have developed, but this does not happen. The growth of the genital organs is postponed for another seven years. Because of this, these years are like a gift to the child, so he or she may develop in a protected environment. We may look at the genital growth pattern as the result of an active inhibition of growth. Puberty is postponed for another seven years. We need this biological "retardation" to grow up harmoniously.

The birth process also goes from above downward within the torso.

Infants have little control over their breathing. The lungs are moved by muscles from the lower pole—the abdominal muscles. Around the age of three and a half, children can control their breathing, because the intercostal muscles, the diaphragm, and the abdominal muscles cooperate. When the physician asks these children to sigh, they can do so. The young toddler cannot do this. The control of breathing is exercised when children learn to speak. Children can already do this before they can sigh. There also, we see the birth process going from above downward.

The air passages and the alveoli in the lungs go through a development too. The trachea elongates and this expansion continues in the lungs toward the periphery and downward. Also the blood vessels develop, and in the three year old, the small arteries have reached the alveoli, whereas in the infant they did not extend this far down. The heart has the capacity to react "in an adult way" from shortly after birth onward. Its relative size decreases during the first years, and it situates itself in a more vertical way during the elongation of the chest.

The relation between the heart and the lungs can be expressed in a quotient. The ratio between respiratory rate and pulse rate is one to four in healthy adults at rest. Basically, this also holds true for youngsters.

	respiratory rate	pulse
newborn	30	120–140
seven years old	20	78–80

Fig. 40 Respiration and pulse rate per minute in the newborn and in the seven-year-old child.

The passage from the esophagus to the stomach will become more or less "safe" only after the first year. Before that, the content of the stomach can easily flow back into the esophagus. In figure 35 we do not find the phase of the closing of the entry to the stomach. If, however, we looked at the torso not as a unity but as divided into chest and abdomen, we could locate this phase of development. If we consider that the abdomen—below the diaphragm—also goes through a downward development in three phases, then development has reached the stomach after one year. This is confirmed by the fact that around this time the gastric juice reaches its adult level of acidity.

The kidneys are situated on a level with the stomach—right below the diaphragm. Around the age of one, they too should be able to function as they do in adults.

The intestines need more time to develop, and they adapt themselves to the food that is taken in. However, only when childhood is over can the child properly digest an adult diet.

Legs

Looking at the human figure as a whole, we may observe that the legs start to develop at the age of four and two-thirds. Until then, children do not seem to be walking with their legs, but rather it seems as if they were held by an invisible cord connected to their occiputs or shoulders. In the last third of the first seven years this impression fades away.

Another development begins right after birth. The upper third of the leg "is given to the child" during the first third of the first seven years, the middle part of the leg during the second third of the first seven years, and the lower third of the leg is "given" during the last third of the first seven years. The upper part of the leg includes the pelvis, the pelvic floor, the hips, and the thighs; the middle part of the leg includes the knees and the calves; and the lower part of the leg includes the ankles and the feet.

After they are two and one-third years old, children can keep their balance when they walk, because the pelvis has become firm and the sense of balance has started to function. Many children are potty trained at that age, because they can also control the muscles of the pelvic floor. The contour of the buttocks is determined by the gluteal muscles, rather than by the diapers.

When children are five, they can hop and skip. To hop and skip, they need to be able to use their knees freely.

At the age of seven, children can take off for a long jump. It means that the feet are then "born." Around this age, many children tend to have flat feet in spite of the fact that the foot had become arched around the age of four. This shows that the child has come down to earth around the age of seven. Usually the flat feet disappear again later.

Maturing

When children have gained some control over their movements, they can walk. This is a natural prerequisite for learning to speak, which, in its turn, is a prerequisite for learning to think. The developmental process of going from walking to speaking to thinking is a fine example of the direction from below upward. Learning to walk, speak, and think usually occurs during the first three years. I will discuss this in the fifth chapter.

The development of the breathing process presents another example of the upward direction. The infant breathes with the abdomen, then the diaphragm joins in, and at last the chest becomes involved. Chest respiration is dependent on the position of the ribs. The ribs of the infant have a rather horizontal orientation. In the child who is ready for elementary school, the ribs are directed diagonally downward. The intercostal muscles can make the ribs horizontal again, which leads to inhaling. Respiration matures in seven years.

During the first seven years, the relation between children and their environment changes in a process that also goes from below upward. During the first two or three years, children discover the world by touching, tasting, watching, crawling, walking, etc. In this first phase, they will experience the world mostly through physical sensations. Preschoolers start to experiment also on an emotional level. They start to experience the world through emotions such as joy, sadness, fear, and relief. These are all qualities of the middle region, which has a central position in the child's relation to the outer world in this phase. As they approach elementary school age, children will try to make mental pictures of things in the outer world: How would it be if I had a little brother? Could our house burn down also? What would it be like if I were the mother and you were the child? The three-year-old child cannot think in this way. This thinking is possible at age six, because in the upper pole the relation to the outer world is being consolidated.

The process from below upward starts in the metabolism where everything is in movement and prone to transformation. It ends in the head where rest and solidification rule. Maturing is a process in which differentiation, solidification, fixation, and crystallization play a role.

I will discuss this further in the fifth chapter.

Birth of the life processes

The life processes constitute the "toolkit" of the ether body. When the ether body is born, the life processes are also born. We cannot attribute a specific life process to a specific organ, because all of the seven life processes work in all organs.[7] In the following section, I want to describe

121

the direction of the birth of the life processes as an outcome of the two directions taken by *being born* on the one hand, and by *maturing* on the other hand, as I have described.

It is difficult to designate exactly what in a life process is *emancipation* and what is *maturation*. The life processes are given by nature. They are there as a fact, just as we take our own life and the life of others for granted. After the maturation process, they are perfect, in a sense. They are available to us with a degree of perfection to which nothing can be added.

I want to go deeper into two aspects of the birth of the ether body and of the life processes—one is how to take care of them, and the other is how to liberate oneself from them.

Life processes need to be cared for, otherwise they will wither away. When the child's digestive system has learned to cope with whole wheat bread, this capacity needs to be nurtured. The child needs to eat whole wheat bread regularly; otherwise, after some time the digestive system will not be able to cope with whole wheat bread anymore. An immune system that is regularly asked to be active in overcoming infections will be stronger than an immune system that has been idle for several years.

With the birth of the ether body, many of the capacities of the life processes become available to the soul, and the higher members of the human being can start using them. These capacities will, however, go through a thorough metamorphosis. This is necessary, because the human being would otherwise become ill. Growing has to come to a halt—otherwise the human being would become a giant. The forces that were used for growth until then can be used for thinking and memory. The life process of bringing into being does not have much to do anymore when the body formation is completed. Then these forces might be used, for example, for the forming of thoughts and the creation of poetry, painting, and sculpture. Even maintaining one's own body needs to be limited. If we were only maintaining, we would have no consciousness. The processes of destruction, aging, and crystallization are a necessity, because through them consciousness can arise.

When the three life processes that are directed inward take their forces away from the body, at least to a certain extent, and make them available to the soul, this will affect the life processes that are directed outward. The processes of taking-in, adapting, and breaking down will also become less active in the physical body, and they can become available partly for learning, memory, and intellectual thinking.

In what direction are the life processes born? It is away from the body and toward the soul. This occurs rhythmically. At night, the life processes are mainly directed toward the body, and in the daytime they are directed more toward the soul. Every day the soul-directed part increases, and each night the body-directed part decreases, until the metamorphosis is completed around the age of seven.

At a later age, the life processes can become directed again toward the body in situations such as sports or illness. This makes the birth of the life processes different from other births. For instance, we cannot temporarily undo the change of teeth. The life processes sustain the bridge between body and soul throughout life.

Summary

We can distinguish two directions taken by the child's developmental processes in the first seven years. As with other births, the direction of the birth process of the ether body goes from above downward. It is a process that gives children the opportunity to be emancipated, because they acquire capacities. These capacities can come forward because the ether body has worked intensively on the physical body and, in doing so, has gone through a learning process. The fruits of this learning process are then given to the soul. The other direction of the developmental process goes from below upward. This development consists of the unfolding of the potentials that organs and bodily organizations have by nature. The process of maturation begins in the lower pole, which is dynamic and prone to change, and ends in the tranquilizing and crystallizing activity of the head.

I have also described the developments during the first seven years by comparing the organization of ether substance in the upper pole with that in the lower pole. The arrangement of the four types of ether in the upper pole is the reverse of that in the lower pole. In the upper pole, the warmth ether is at the center, whereas in the lower pole it is at the periphery, and so on. In the upper pole, ether activity is directed toward organ formation; in the lower pole, it is directed toward the functioning of the active human being. The upper and lower poles can influence one another, because the warmth ether is a unity throughout the human body. The same holds true for the other types of ether, and so the upper and lower poles develop and educate one another. The formative forces of the ether types of the upper pole direct the dynamics of the lower pole. The life forces of the ether types of the lower pole awaken the faculties of the upper pole.

The life processes have a middle position. Over the first seven years, the life processes gradually become less directed toward the functioning of the body, and they dedicate their forces more toward the capacity to think and to remember. The direction of the development of the life processes is from an orientation toward the body to an orientation toward the soul. This development occurs in a rhythm of connecting and disconnecting.

4 Helpers with Perception:
The Twelve Senses and Their Development

In this chapter I will discuss the connection between the development of the senses and the development of the child. First I will make some introductory remarks about perception and the role the senses play in it. After that, I will focus on each of the senses separately. With each of the senses, I will ask the following questions: How does this sense perception develop? What can this sense perceive? and What does this sense contribute to the development of the child? Of course, I will stay within the scope of this book—the physiology of child development in the first seven years of childhood. You can find other aspects of this subject discussed in other literature.

Perception

Human beings learn about themselves, their fellow human beings, and other beings and things around them through their sensations. I will give some examples. When hungry babies are nursed on their mother's milk, their unpleasant sensations change abruptly into pleasant ones. When toddlers bump their heads against the leg of the table, they learn something about the world of furniture. Children who take their first steps experience joy and pride with this newly acquired capacity. By reading his or her mother's face, the preschooler senses that this is not the right moment to beg for candy. When children are teased at school, they learn in this way about fellow students as well as about themselves. Being in love for the first time opens up an unfamiliar area of experiences.

Not all sensations that children experience are based on sense perception. There is more than just sense perception involved when children experience pride, joy, being in love, their mother's mood, or humiliation. The same holds true for feelings such as sadness, depression, pain, or loneliness.

It is obvious that human beings do not have a specific sense organ for everything they can perceive. For instance, humans do not have sense organs to perceive the sensations that move in their soul, as in the examples just given. This is also true for perceptions in the supersensible world—many children are aware of gnomes, or have conversations with friends who are not physically present. There is also a world below the sense world, where we find the forces of electricity, magnetism, and all kinds of radiation. We cannot perceive those with our sense organs, but we can sometimes sense them.

What has been said so far makes it clear that the child encounters only a segment of reality when using the sense organs. This segment is commonly known as the *sense world*. Above the sense world is the super-sensible world, and below the threshold of sense perception is another world, which I have already mentioned. Soul experiences are not usually considered to be part of the sense world. Human beings live in the sense world, but what their souls experience does not belong to the sense world.

To come down to earth may be the most important task children have to fulfill in the first seven years, and the senses are indispensable helpers for this purpose. Without the senses, the child will not come down to earth. The senses make it possible for the child to become a "citizen of the earth."

I will present a description of twelve senses—more than are usually listed in textbooks on physiology. One could say that the healthy child has access to twelve gateways to the earth. Why are there twelve gates and not seven or twenty-one? I will not answer this question, but after reading the whole chapter, you may find that you know the answer.

The twelve senses

There are four prerequisites for sense perception.

1 A fully developed sense organ	— physical level
2 A healthy sense organ	— etheric level
3 A soul that is awake	— astral level
4 The will to perceive	— level of the I

Numbers 1 and 2 constitute the instrumental aspect of perception; numbers 3 and 4 constitute the functional aspect of perception. I will use the term *sense organ* to refer to the instrumental aspect of perception only. To indicate either aspect or the functional aspect only, I will use the word *sense*. I will now comment on each of the four prerequisites.

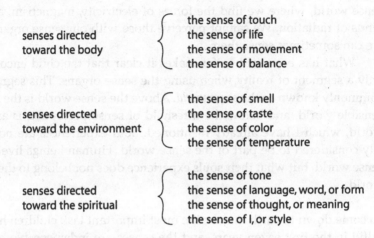

senses directed toward the body	{	the sense of touch the sense of life the sense of movement the sense of balance
senses directed toward the environment	{	the sense of smell the sense of taste the sense of color the sense of temperature
senses directed toward the spiritual	{	the sense of tone the sense of language, word, or form the sense of thought, or meaning the sense of I, or style

Fig. 41 The twelve senses.

Fully developed sense organs. Each sense has its own instrument—the sense organ. When the sense organ is perfectly developed, it may provide the soul with perfect sense-impressions. The sense organs are formed during embryonic development. After birth, the sense organs must be used; otherwise they will wither away. This holds true for all physical organs—they need to function to stay healthy.

The twelve sense organs can be related to the twelve signs of the zodiac. Anthroposophy teaches that cosmic forces are differentiated according to the directions they come from, and these directions are indicated by the twelve different constellations of the zodiac. These cosmic forces build the human physical body and, first of all, the sense organs. In studying the senses, we may learn about the activities of cosmic forces behind the zodiac as well as about the formation of the human physical body.

Healthy sense organs. A physical sense organ must be healthy to function properly. The seven life processes of the ether body must take good care of the sense organ. Therefore we should not use a sense organ without periodic rest. A period of activity must be followed by a phase of rest and recuperation. The eye presents a fine example for this. The light that enters the eye causes a biochemical reaction in the retina, in which rhodopsin—a substance which is sensitive to light—is converted and used up. This rhodopsin must be replenished by blinking before the same spot of the retina can be used again. This rhythmic process occurs throughout the day. We also need the day-night rhythm to keep our sense organs healthy.

The seven life processes are at work for the sense organs in yet another way. Nothing of the outer world is permitted to enter the inner world unchanged. This paradigm, which I described in the third chapter when writing about the life processes, also applies to sense impressions. The outer world—the sense impression—must be *taken in, adapted,* and *broken down* before it is allowed to enter the inner world to find its proper place. Each sense organ uses a specific modality of the life processes to receive and digest impressions such as temperature, touch, color, and tone. All processes have to function well to attain undistorted perception. When we are ill or exhausted, the life processes working in the sense organs are affected, and this, in turn, will affect perception. When we have a fever, for instance, we may experience our body as tiny or gigantic, and delicious fruit may lose its flavor. All life processes work rhythmically; rhythm is *the* prerequisite for life. We can observe the working of rhythmical processes in the structure of all organs. In particular, the sense organs show this in a surprising way. In the eye, we find the specific arrangement of rods and cones; in the inner ear—the cochlea—we find that the hair cells, which are sensitive to sound, are arranged in a special pattern; and we find the organs of touch rhythmically arranged in the skin.

A soul that is awake. During sleep, we do not perceive the sense world. The soul needs to be awake to be conscious of sense perceptions. As the ether body takes care of the sense organs and keeps them healthy, so the astral body takes care of the sense organs to keep them functional in the service of sense perception. The astral body's function is to enable the soul to leave the inner world behind and direct itself to the outer world. Each sense organ covers one-twelfth of the outer world. The soul can cross twelve bridges to learn about the outer world. Human perceptions are composed of the soul's experiences on these bridges. The soul's activities on the bridges are called the *sentient soul.* The impressions we receive through our sentient soul provide us with direct information about things in the outer world. We can rely on this information when the soul is awake and the sense organ is healthy and fully developed. The young child with a normally developed sense of touch can immediately perceive that a cup has a smooth surface. There is no need for reflection. The child may not yet know that we call this feature "smooth," but this is a matter of language, not perception.

The will to perceive. The difference between staring blankly and looking clarifies the effect of the I-activity in the sense organ. The I directs the gaze to the outer world. The I directs the soul to the outer world by means of a sense, with the intent to perceive. When the attention of the young child's soul *is drawn*—by color, sound, or speaking, for instance—the outer world has taken initiative. When children learn to open a book and read, they are asked to direct their gaze themselves from within and to activate the senses to "see" what is printed. Animals cannot do this. The hummingbird will not pay attention to the colored sugar water when it is not hungry. Its metabolism first needs to turn the bird's senses on to "search for food," and only then will the bird feeder arouse sensations in the bird, which are immediately translated into actions. Then there is no reflection, as there was no reflection in the example of the young child mentioned earlier.

In animals, the senses do not deceive them. Human beings can err when they connect an erroneous judgment to the sense perception. The senses only deceive us when our thinking occupies itself with the perceptions. Some graphic artists such as M. C. Escher in Holland have worked with this phenomenon in an artistic way. Human thinking may cause the senses to deceive, but human thinking can also correct the errors.

The effect of the way the human I works with the senses is twofold. It causes us to experience ourselves as the point of reference in perceiving; we relate our experiences to ourselves. It also makes us experience the difference between the outer world and ourselves, because we have to cross a bridge toward the world time and again. In other words, when using the senses, the I experiences both a center and a boundary. Animals do not know of this experience.

Educating the senses and being educated by them

Learning to use the senses can be compared to learning to use tools. When you have learned to use pliers, you have acquired two new skills. The first one is the capacity to use the pliers properly and for the proper aims. Because you have become acquainted with pliers, you will *notice* the occasions in life when pliers may be useful, and in addition you are *capable* of using the tool properly. The second skill arises because you will meet a force within yourself that can accomplish in a non-material sense what pliers can do in the outer world. The soul discovers its capacity to take hold of something.

Something similar occurs when children learn to play a musical instrument. They will be able to let music sound in a way they could not do before, and at the same time their souls will develop the specific quality that belongs to the musical instrument they have learned to play.

When exercising their senses, children also learn in a twofold way. They learn something new that enables them to perceive the outer world, and at the same time their soul acquires new capacities. The soul actually acquires twenty-four new faculties through the use of the senses. Twelve are related to the sense organs as instruments of perception (the content of the perceptions), and twelve are related to the inner world of the perceiving person (the newly acquired soul capacities). I will give examples when describing the specific senses.

Connections among the senses

If we arrange the twelve senses into groups of four, we may discover interesting connections. One of these is the relation of each group to the specific members of the human body (with the result that each of the four members of the human body is connected with three senses; see figure 42).

physical body	senses of touch, smell, and tone
ether body	senses of life, taste, and word
astral body	senses of movement, color, and thought
I-organization	senses of balance, temperature, and I

Fig. 42 The relation of the senses to the four members of the human body.

It is an important consideration in the physiology of child development that development of the four senses that are directed toward the spiritual (see figure 41) is closely related to the development of the four senses that are directed toward the body. The quality and differentiation of the senses that are directed toward the spiritual are to a large extent dependent on the degree of perfection to which the senses that are directed toward the body have been developed. We will come back to this in the section about the senses that are directed toward the spiritual.

sense of touch — sense of I, or style

sense of life — sense of thought, or meaning

sense of movement — sense of language, word, or form

sense of balance — sense of tone

The four senses directed toward the body

In the individual body the I can learn to perceive the outside world that is nearest to the soul. The I can make use of four senses to accomplish this—the senses of touch, life, movement, and balance. I will describe the following aspects of these four senses: (1) their development and education; (2) their fields of action; (3) some aspects of their physiology; (4) the soul capacities they activate; and (5) their sense organs.

Sense of touch

Development and education

Newborns already have the capacity to touch. The sense of touch is an important helper in the process of coming down to earth. When the baby is resting on the mother's belly after the delivery, the baby experiences touch for the first time. It can be said that, through the experience of touch, the child can experience the body as a dwelling enclosed by skin. A very special moment in the development of the sense of touch is when the child becomes sensitive to being tickled. While being tickled, the experience of touch becomes mingled with the experience of fear. The child responds to the increasing tension with muscle-contraction and laughing. Children show pleasure when they are tickled and like to instigate this kind of play because for them it is a pleasant way to exercise the sense of touch. However, the tickling game is not without danger, as we notice when laughing turns into crying.

Field of action

The sense of touch guides children from being connected to the cosmos to feeling at home in their own body. If this process is accomplished in the right manner, the child will also know that he or she can return to a connection with the spiritual world in a way that does not require leaving the body. This process will teach children to be within themselves with inner peace and confidence, knowing of their divine origin. For young children, the spiritual world is a matter of fact and not a mental picture. The sense of touch is the bridge over which the I can become a "citizen of the earth" while at the same time maintaining the full certainty of the presence of a spiritual world. The religious vocabulary that uses the expression "the fear of the Lord," refers to this inner peace. This fear needs to be distinguished from fear in the common sense of the word, which we will mention later in this section.

Some physiological aspects

The sense of touch is very earthly—through it the skin comes into contact with the physical world. It is the only way for children to learn that they are no longer part of cosmic interrelationships and that they are no longer enveloped by their physical periphery, as they were before birth when they were surrounded by amniotic fluid and the sheaths. On earth, children have to live with the limitations given by their physical bodies. This is the painful aspect of the sense of touch—it makes the child feel lonely and alone. This, however, can also lead to the conscious experience that "I live in my body."

The sense of touch has also pleasant aspects. When the child is carried by the mother and caressed, he or she can experience a sheltering that takes the loneliness away. It is very important that young children experience these two aspects of the sense of touch extensively—both the painful and the pleasant side—so that they may identify with their body in the right way. The type of fabric the infant's skin comes into contact with is very important. Later it is important that the child has a crib or a bed that has sideboards he or she can be aware of. Obviously it is also important that children are surrounded by objects that are made from substances created by nature, so that they may experience all the nuances that the sense of touch can convey to them—from smooth to rough, from round to pointy, from soft to firm. Adults around the child should know how important it is how they touch the child—the intention and certainty with which they lift, carry, or place the child. The primary function of the sense of touch is to let the human being experience the presence of a boundary.

When children approach adults to be cuddled, they are seeking these two aspects of the sense of touch—help me to experience that I have boundaries, and give me the feeling of security. When the cuddling becomes too intimate, the boundary experience as well as the security experience is derailed.

Soul capacities

The sense of touch provides the child with the secure feeling of "being home." The opposite feeling would be fear. Every child is also born with the ability to experience this fear. Behind fear stands the feeling of not being sheltered, not being carried, and being abandoned.

Every infant displays the "fear reflex" when he or she is startled by an unexpected sound, or for a short moment loses contact with the arm that is carrying him or her. Later on, this fear can metamorphose into the fear of something that is not pleasant to touch—such as a frog or a jellyfish; the fear of spanking, especially when unexpected; the fear of darkness that makes boundaries disappear; the fear of heights, when the touching gaze cannot span the space; or the fear of death, if the certainty of the presence of the spiritual world has been lost.

The sense of touch is accompanied by the soul capacities to experience fear and security. Learning to know fear and to overcome it provides the child with the experience of security and shelter. Not finding security and shelter causes the experience of fear in the child. Both aspects of the sense of touch need to have their place in education—fear should not be denied, and sheltering should not be exaggerated.

The sense organ

The organs of the sense of touch consist of simple free nerve endings around the hair follicles of hairy skin. In smooth skin the sense organs consist of encapsulated nerve endings (corpuscles) below the skin's surface. Especially in the fingers and the toes, the sense organs look like rhythmically arranged branches of nerve endings. The sense organ for touch is not localized in one spot, but is distributed over the entire surface of the body.

Initially one cannot differentiate the perceptions of the sense of touch. The young child cannot yet locate something that is bothersome. The process of differentiation occurs during the first years of life. At the age of seven, children have the ability to be very precise in indicating the exact spot on the skin that is touched. At the same time, the awareness of one's boundaries—a function of the sense of touch that hardly enters consciousness—is for children (and for adults) rather vague and nonspecific. When children start to use utensils such as crayons, pencils, spoons, and forks, they are practicing to extend their sense of touch through these utensils. When they stick the prongs of the fork in the bread, they are sensing with the fork. After a while they know that it feels different when they prick bread or when they prick an apple or applesauce. They also know that pencils touch the paper differently from the way crayons do.

Toward the end of preschool, children have developed a rather elastic, pliable touch-network, which coincides with the skin when it is not active, but can reach out far beyond the skin when activated. Also the gaze can touch, and it can be considered an instrument to use for touching. If the gaze cannot span the space it is looking at, fear may arise—fear of heights, for instance.

The sense of touch may be compared to the ropes with which the ship of the soul is moored in the harbor of the body.

Fig. 43 The touch corpuscles are rhythmically arranged protrusions of the nerves; this drawing shows the fingers of the left hand. (From Werner Spalteholz and Rudolf Spanner, Handatlas der Anatomie des Menschen, Amsterdam 1961.)

133

Sense of life

Development and education

The sense of touch teaches children where their physical boundaries are; the sense of life teaches them about the condition of their life processes. Similar to the sense of touch, the sense of life is functional from the child's birth onward. When infants are quiet and peaceful, open their eyes now and then, and make their characteristic movements or sleep in a relaxed position, they radiate contentment. The sense of life informs the child about this condition of contentment. The infant, of course, does not know consciously that he or she perceives contentment, but adults may observe it in the infant's behavior. When the child's sense of life does not perceive contentment, but experiences discomfort, nausea, cramps, or hunger, we may also see or hear this. From the way the child is crying, most mothers can distinguish whether the child is hungry or is experiencing some other discomfort. From the way the child is lying still, the mother knows whether the child is nauseous or comfortably relaxed. The sense of life is already functional at birth, but it needs to be educated and developed further.

The security of infancy, as well as breast milk, form the ideal soil and a favorable climate in which the sense of life can grow and develop. An important moment comes when the child is weaned and other food is introduced, because the sense of life starts to function then independently. The independently functioning of the sense of life will be postponed when the child is breast-fed for an unusually long time. If, for one reason or another, the child is not breast-fed at all or only briefly, the sense of life will have to be functional very early and will have less time to mature. This gives the caregivers of the child an additional responsibility to find other ways and means for providing the child's sense of life with the intimacy and security through which it may flourish. The climate in which the sense of life flourishes is that of a rhythmical succession of events. Plants grow in the rhythmical succession of day and night, humidity and dryness, higher and lower temperatures; so also will the sense of life grow well in a "climate" of a regular rhythm when there are smooth transitions between daily routines and variations on the standard procedures.

The education of the sense of life is furthered by playing with toys that are made from natural materials, and by eating natural food that is grown in an atmosphere of reverence for life. There should be a schedule of the day's activities, but it should be open to life and not restrictive. Customs and conventions should be clear, but followed with a degree of flexibility. The development of the sense of life has two sides to it. A favorable climate allows the sense of life to mature, but on the other hand there is a need for the child's consciousness to develop through pain, discomfort, and illness, which do cast shadows on the child's life.

Field of action

The sense of life gives information about the inner world of the body, not about inner soul life. When physiological processes run smoothly, the sense of life gives us a feeling of contentment, freshness, and of being rested. At the end of the day or after a long hike, the sense of life may inform us about the body's inner condition by presenting feelings of tiredness, weariness, and of having had enough. We may say that the sense of life functions as a mirror.

For a long time, adults who are close to the child can comfort the child and thereby repair the mirror of the sense of life when pain or any other discomfort displaces the feeling of contentment. Comforting is one of the most precious educators of the sense of life. In a certain sense, we may be grateful for pain and discomfort, because through the act of comforting, pain and discomfort remind the child and the parents to re-establish confidence that the child's body is functioning well. Yet we do not need to seek out pain and discomfort, because life always brings them to us.

As children grow a little older, parents will face questions related to giving in and spoiling the child. Sometimes this occurs already after the first weeks, but it will certainly come within a year. When is it appropriate to give in for the sake of harmony? In this book, I cannot go into the pedagogical aspects of this issue; however, giving in and spoiling also have physiological aspects. To give in means, in fact, to move the boundaries. This belongs to the field of activity of the sense of touch. To spoil is something quite different than to comfort. When we spoil a child, we might as well say, "Do not listen to your sense of life; have another candy even if it gives you nausea; stay up for another hour even if you can hardly stay awake." The spoiled child is taught not to take him- or herself seriously; and as a direct consequence, this child will face difficulties in developing the sense of thought or meaning later in life. He or she may end up in a world void of meaning.

Some physiological aspects

The sense of life works on the level of the ether body; it provides information about the functioning of the life processes. If all goes well, we are not aware of this functioning. When we are healthy, we do not feel our organs; they do not speak to us. Also the sense of life is silent when we are healthy.

We take the feeling of comfort, well known to us as the healthy vital base of our existence, for granted. The sense of touch enables the child to connect with the physical body; the sense of life enables the child to connect with the ether body. It forms the basis for the feeling later in life that it is self-evident that I live in my body as in my house, and that eating, drinking, and breathing are processes with which I gladly maintain my house. This culminates in the feeling: I am one with my body; *I am my body!*

Stomach aches, nausea, and similar experiences in which we are aware of our organs are not, strictly understood, perceptions of the sense of life. Organ sensations awaken consciousness in the soul without involving the sense of life. When we feel our organs, the mirroring surface that the sense of life spreads out over the organs is broken. With pain, it is somewhat different. Pain arises when a sensory stimulus is too strong, as in loud noise, bright light, or a strong taste. Pain also means that organ sensations are experienced directly by the soul; the sense of life is related to this condition in that it is suspended.

Soul capacities

We have seen that the sense of touch gives children security, and its opposite—fear. A well-developed sense of life gives children a *feeling of contentment*, which they may take for granted. But the sense of life also has another side. This other side manifests in the soul as *doubt and shame*, and it appears when the life functions do not carry the child's existence on earth as a matter of course. As the mirror of the sense of life is fashioned only gradually over time, so the ability to experience doubt and shame also needs time to develop, and it can appear when the child is a toddler. The capability to experience doubt and shame is a good gauge for the development of the sense of life. In doubt and shame, children confront themselves, as they do in another way with fear.

The sense organ

The organs of the sense of life are distributed throughout the body. We can consider the autonomic nervous system—which includes the sympathetic and the parasympathetic nervous systems—the sensitive instrument of the sense of life.

The autonomic or vegetative nervous system has the task to attune all movements and organ activities needed by the life processes.

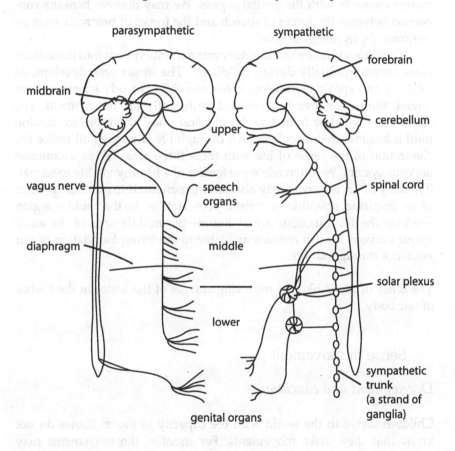

Fig. 44 *The autonomic nervous system. On the left is shown the parasympathetic system, on the right the sympathetic system; both are seen in their relation to the brain and the spinal cord. We can distinguish three areas: —an upper area that is related to speech and to the senses that are directed toward the environment; —a middle area that is related to the life processes such as respiration, digestion, and circulation; —and a lower area that is related to excretions and to the sexual organs.*

137

In young children, the functioning of the autonomic nervous system is hardly differentiated. In the course of the first fourteen years, a differentiation occurs. In its middle region, the autonomic nervous system is connected to the solar plexus, and this important part of it continues to function as the organ of the sense of life. Above and below this area, parasympathetic nerves branch off. Above, as the tenth cranial nerve (the vagus nerve), they connect directly with the heart and, interestingly, also with the speech organs. In the lower area, part of the autonomic nervous system connects with the genital organs. We may observe here the connection between the forces of speech and the forces of procreation on an anatomical-physiological level.

The differentiation of the autonomic nervous system into these three areas occurs gradually during childhood. The upper area develops, as thinking and speaking develop. When the child is ready for elementary school, the upper area has matured sufficiently for the moment. The lower area, which is bound to the physical body, continues to develop until it has matured at puberty. All through life, we may still notice the connection of the sense of life with these three areas of the autonomic nervous system. We often relate the feeling of a healthy vitality to sexuality; many of us, however, may also have experienced the vitalizing effect of an inspiring scientific or artistic presentation. In the middle region —where the life functions are at home—the middle area of the autonomic nervous system remains available to the living foundation of our existence throughout life.

The sense of life is like the mirroring surface of the water in the harbor of our body.

Sense of movement

Development and education

Children arrive in the world with the capacity to move. Babies do not know that they make movements. For months, the movements may seem accidental and uncoordinated. Some movements have the character of reflexes. Other movements seem to be inspired by inner feelings of comfort or discomfort. At the first breath, the baby has received his or her own air-organization as the carrier of the astral body; the other two instruments of the astral body—the nerves and the muscles—are still underdeveloped. This phenomenon manifests a striking difference between the newborn human being and the young gregarious animal that can keep up with the herd an hour after birth.

138

The sense of movement begins to develop when the chaotic movements of arms and legs come to a rest and the child begins to perceive movements. When children at first accidentally touch something or accidentally get something in their hands, only to let go of it again accidentally, then the impulse to grasp will gradually lead to gaining control over movements. A beautiful moment in the development of the sense of movement comes when the infant—at about three months old—observes one of his or her own hands come by and brings this movement to a halt with the other hand. Playing with one's own hands and later on with the feet, the stretching and the reaching, these all are joyful exercises in movement, which in turn support development of the sense of movement.

The development of the sense of movement does not demand much from the child's caregivers. Almost all children move, and they do so with pleasure. It may sound strange, but the best way caregivers can assist children in developing their sense of movement is to see to it that they have enough rest. Perception requires rest, coming to a standstill, and this holds true also in the children's task of perceiving their own movements. It can be of great help to young children when at certain moments of the day their leg movements are restrained from the outside, for instance by swaddling. Through this, the children will more easily be able to start controlling their arm movements. Too many movements and shapes around the child are not favorable for development of the sense of movement. A mood of joy and lightness around the child will stimulate it, as this mood indicates that those around the child have a well-developed sense of movement themselves. It is very important that children can develop their individual movement pattern, in their own way and at their own pace. It is not a good idea to try to teach children motor skills before they are ready for them. There are many good reasons for this; one is that it impedes the development of the sense of movement.

Movements often have a social aspect; we can express something with our movements. It is a significant occurrence when this happens for the first time. The first smile of the baby, when a few weeks old, indicates that his or her chaotic movements have come to a rest, at least to some degree. This condition of rest enables the child to perceive, and the child responds to this perception with the gesture of the smile. Usually the child perceives the mother on this occasion. When a movement is the expression of a feeling—such as aversion or affection—the movement becomes a gesture.

Gestures will become more and more important when the child grows older. This can justify why parents put so much emphasis on how children sit at the table. The *posture* of the human being is significant; it is the accomplishment of the sense of movement.

Field of action

The nature of movement is future oriented. A meaningful movement can therefore be made when there is a will to move and a mental image of the movement's purpose. For children, movements are meaningful when they fit their possibilities and life situations. Therefore it is not desirable to have children walk holding your hand when they would rather crawl; nor is it helpful to teach them to hop or skip when they are not yet eager to learn this. It goes against the nature of movement development to teach children certain movement patterns, because the child should be ready for them—as is advocated by certain types of movement therapy. Eurythmy can be an excellent help when there are problems with movement development, because its principle is only to practice movements that already exist in the child's ether body.

Some physiological aspects

The development of the sense of movement is closely related to the development of the child's movements, and to the child's movement possibilities. We cannot separate the sense of movement from the actual movement, because the sense of movement does not perceive anything when there is no movement. For the sense of movement, perception and the perceived object overlap to a large extent. What does the sense of movement perceive? Directed toward the inner world, the sense of movement enables the human being to determine the position of the limbs in relation to the body and to one another. Secondly, also directed toward the inner world, it provides information about the nature of the movement. The two-year-old knows exactly how far he or she has to open a hand to be able to hold a cup. It is as if the hand already holds the picture of the cup beforehand; the sense of movement tells the child—of course beyond the child's consciousness—how he or she has to hold the hand and the fingers so that the real cup will fit. We can be impressed by the capacity of the sense of movement to perceive complicated movement patterns. Look, for instance, with how much ease and skill the four-year-old goes down the steps; remember then how much practice has preceded this seemingly supple, effortless going down the steps. It might even be better to say that the sense of movement does not just perceive the movement, but "knows" it already beforehand, and the muscles can then adapt to the planned movement. Thirdly, the sense of movement teaches the child to perceive movement and form in the outer world. The shape of the bed,

140

of the pictures on the wall, of the furniture in the room—the sense of movement scans them with the child's eyes or feels them with the child's hands. The sense of movement constitutes the inner sounding board that also perceives moving objects, animals, or humans.

We can exercise the sense of movement throughout life; this sense might be the one that can be educated the most. Time and again, adults may learn new movements, such as those that belong to a new musical instrument, a new outfit, or a new style of handwriting.

Soul capacities

As children develop their sense of movement, more and more movements come under their control. In principle, movement is a part of the human body that is independent of inner pressure or outer necessity. Seen from this aspect, the sense of movement is an element of human freedom. When movements and the sense of movement are well developed, the *sense of freedom* will arise as a capacity of soul. The levity of the hopping, skipping, dancing child gives us a beautiful example of this.

We may observe the opposite of this sense of freedom in children who are handicapped in their ability to move freely. When the muscles cramp or do not cooperate, the sense of freedom does not arise; instead there is a feeling of being bound to the physical body. This may easily be accompanied by a chilling or cramping of the soul. The opposite occurs when the body has too little muscle tone, is hypotonic. The balance tips to the other side—the sense of freedom becomes too loose. In such a situation, it is very hard for the soul to connect with its physical instrument. In either situation, the feeling of *powerlessness* arises, and with it a soul quality of despondency or resignation. The will is not free but is *tied up*.

The sense organ

The organs of the sense of movement are located in the muscles. They include the muscle spindles, motor endplates, and all stretch-sensitive organs that are distributed over the entire movement organization, including the tendons and ligaments. Because of this, the body can perceive stretching, tension, relaxation, and position in relation to other parts of the body.

When we move, the entire body is involved even when we seem to move only one part of the body, such as a finger or an arm. The same

141

holds true when the sense of movement sends its feelers toward movements and forms in the outer world.

The entire movement organization of the human being serves as the sounding board for perception of movement. The perceiving consciousness of the upper pole needs nerves to become conscious of movement perceptions. For this purpose, it makes use of nerves called motor nerves. I present this picture to substitute the model chosen by science where motor nerves serve movement and sensory nerves serve perception. In the picture presented here, all nerves serve perception. The so-called motor nerves serve perception in the region of the will—in the lower pole (see also page 189 ff).

The sense of life creates a mirroring surface around the organs and thus *above* the life processes; the sense of movement penetrates *into* movements and, in so doing, serves the perception of these movements.

The sense of movement is like the wind in the sails of the ship and like the navigator who knows that he or she can sail into and out of any harbor.

Sense of balance

Development and education

The young infant does not yet perceive by means of the sense of balance. It is hard work for him or her to learn to be free and independent of gravity. The spatial position of the young infant is horizontal; he or she is given over to the forces to which the physical body is subjected from the moment of birth onward. At birth, the baby's body weight is about seven pounds. At the end of the first year, when the child can stand freely, weight is overcome. The scale will assess the one-year-old child at more than twenty pounds, but in another realm of reality—the reality of perception—the freestanding child's weight is zero. The child does not feel the pounds; he or she has just overcome them. The child is able to arrive at this great accomplishment by exercising endlessly. First infants are able to hold their head up more or less (balancing of the head); then they straighten the spine and can catch themselves when they lose their balance (sitting freely); after that children can pull themselves up (standing with support); and finally they can get on their feet from a crawling or sitting position without external support (standing freely). This development is closely connected to movement development, just as the development of the sense of balance is closely connected to the development of the sense of movement.

Field of action

We can describe what happens in the domain of the sense of balance in the first year as: The I eliminates the effect of gravity by commanding the muscles to lift up the physical body.

Penetrating the physical body, the I connects with the earthly law of gravity. The field of the I-forces neutralizes the field of the gravity forces.

I need to mention one prerequisite: The child must have role models. In an environment where there are no human beings around, the child will not attain uprightness. Children raised by wolves imitate the way wolves deal with gravity—going on all fours.[8] During the process of attaining upright posture, the child puts the sense of balance to work. Before that, the young child cannot lose his or her balance, because there is no balance yet. Young children will not suffer from seasickness or other nausea-producing phenomena that are based on a functioning sense of balance.

By attaining the capacity to stand freely in space, gravity is conquered—which is an important step in the development of the sense of balance. Now the child can take the next step—conquering space. Animals cannot take this step. Nature has allotted animals "their space," the boundaries of which are set by their instincts. The human being, however, can freely dispose of three-dimensional space. By watching children, we can observe how space is conquered. Each child has his or her own style for doing this. Some children practice endlessly, standing up and sitting down again at one spot in the room, before they venture their first steps. Other children practice walking for a long time, finding external support in furniture and the like. Then, much later than the caregiver had expected or hoped, they at last go through the room without external support. There are also children who never practice; they only watch. Suddenly and unexpectedly, they start to walk as if they had never done otherwise. The way the child discovers space speaks a clear language; the sense of balance is a developmental instrument that is very individual.

Initially children can only walk straight forward, and when they have to change direction, they turn their whole body. Children will fall over at each turn until they have learned the trick. After this, children start to master walking sideways. This is preceded by practicing walking alongside an object (such as a couch), moving one foot to the side and then bringing the other foot over next to the first one. Walking backward comes much later. Three-year-old children can move their legs in a direction that does not follow their nose, but they still look a bit scared. Only at about the age of ten, can children walk backward freely with a feeling of security and without turning their head. To do this, the child needs to feel secure about the space which he or she does not see.

After conquering the vertical axis (over and against gravity), the space to the left and to the right, and the space in front and behind, children also have to scout the space above and below.

It takes some time before the child, when sitting underneath the table, will stand up without bumping his or her head against the table top. The awareness that something might be there above the head comes slowly and painfully. We can observe how children deal with "below" by the way they pick things up from the floor. Initially the child will reach out to the object and fall over. The child has to lie down, sit, or—later— kneel to pick something up in a stable position. At a certain moment, the toddler has learned the technique of folding over double, reaching the floor, and straightening up again without losing balance. The preschooler is able to squat—with the head upright—and rise again from this position.

Some physiological aspects

Through the sense of balance, the I of the child makes contact with the forces of gravity and with the spatial directions—above and below, front and back, left and right. Also the spatial directions constitute a field of forces in which, during the initial years, a child has to learn to move freely.

The cube has its surfaces coinciding with the three spatial directions. When children play with a piece of wood that has the shape of a cube, it does not matter which side is up, left, or front; two sides of the cube take a different position when the cube is turned a quarter turn, and that does not matter. For the sense of balance, it is different; the three dimensions are not interchangeable; the forces from each of the three directions are different. Each of them has a specific function when the human organs are formed; each of them is the carrier of a specific soul force—thinking, feeling, or willing. Left-right is related to the faculty of mirroring and comparing; up-down is related to the faculty of empathy; and forward-backward is related to the faculty of choosing. This way we may understand that the earthly task of the sense of balance can be considered a tall order. The sense of balance helps the child to come down to the earth with its laws of gravity and three-dimensional space. At the same time, the child learns to know the creative forces of the three directions and to find a balance among those. Of course, all of this happens unconsciously.

Soul capacities

Exercising the sense of balance cultivates a very special capability. It provides the child with the certainty that in this three-dimensional world he or she continues to be the same person. "Whether I lie down or stand, move or rest—in my bedroom or in the living room—*it is always I myself*. I do not yield to gravity or to the forces from the spatial directions. I am I." Because of this experience, the child can start to say I (referring to him- or herself) at around the age of two-and-a-half to three years old. This indicates that the child starts to separate from the surroundings. It dawns on the child's consciousness that something is essentially different from all other things—that is I. This experience is a direct consequence of starting to use the sense of balance. Thinking does not mediate this, neither is it a perception by the sense of I (which I will discuss later).

The sense of balance does not only have this "asocial" aspect; it also has a social aspect. When human beings feel secure and stable in three-dimensional surroundings, they can start to share this space with fellow human beings. From their own standpoint—where all coordinates intersect—they can perceive that every other human being also stands at the point of intersection of all coordinates. The human being can then decide to share his or her space—at least partially—with others.

The opposite of this ability also belongs to the sense of balance. How is it when a person does not succeed in attaining a harmonious coexistence with gravity and space? The experience of seasickness gives us an example. I have asked many people how they felt when they were seasick. They say that one desire prevails: not to be there—"I wish I were dead."

This impulse to destroy oneself can also metamorphose into an outwardly directed destructive impulse. Is it possible that acts of terror—with no respect for fellow human beings—are committed by people who have not succeeded in attaining a harmonious relationship with the creative forces of the spatial directions?

The sense organ

The sense of balance makes use of specific organs. In the petrous portion of the temporal bones on either side of the head, near the ears, we find tiny organs. One part has the function to perceive our position in relation to gravity. Floating in fluid, small calcium carbonate crystals rest on sensitive hairs, which are under a certain pressure from these crystals when we are in a vertical position. When we are not in an exact vertical

145

position, the crystals are pulled to the side. When we move up or down in a vertical line, for instance in an elevator, the pressure on the hairs increases or decreases correspondingly. This organ could be called the levity-gravity organ.

The function of the other part of the sense organ of balance—the three semicircular canals—is to perceive our movements in three-dimensional space. The three curved canals, perpendicularly positioned like the surfaces of a cube, contain fluid. This fluid is never at rest; it streams in rhythmic movements correlated to the breathing. Every movement of the body affects the streaming of this fluid, which then can give us exact information about the direction of the movement of our body.

Rhythmically streaming fluid is the point of reference for spatial orientation. Through breathing, this streaming is related to our feeling and to our capacity of judgment.

The three semicircular canals are not static. They do not constitute an organ of gravity, but are a picture of our active relation to the three spatial directions of the world. We could call them our sense organ of orientation. When they function well, we can move freely and as if weightless. If there is a disturbance, we become dizzy and fall over.

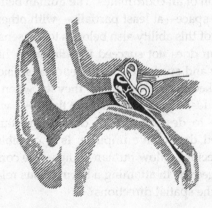

Fig. 45 The ear, the sense organ of hearing, and the sense organ of balance. (From Lothar Vogel, Der dreigliedrige Mensch, Dornach 1992[3].)

The organs in the petrous portion of the temporal bones are not the only organs of the sense of balance. The sense of balance makes use of the whole muscular system. When we close our eyes, we feel that it is much harder to maintain our balance than with our eyes open. Visual orientation is important for the function of the sense of balance. A specific eye muscle, the superior oblique muscle—or pulley muscle—of the eyeball, perceives balance in the field of vision. It might be better to say: the sense of balance uses the pulley muscles to inform the soul about the balance in the field of vision. The pulley muscles of the eyeballs have their own nerve supply, which is different from the optic nerve and the nerves connected to the other eyeball muscles.

To perceive three-dimensional space outside of us, it is essential that the axes of the eyes intersect. When acrobats stretch their arms or hold a long pole, they extend their sense of balance to their fingertips or to the ends of the pole.

The sense of balance is like the albatross that keeps its course as if effortlessly, freely gliding, even during a storm.

Summary

The human soul receives information about its own body through the senses of touch, life, movement, and balance. For the soul, its own body is that part of the outside world that has come nearest to itself. The sense of touch is related to the boundaries of the physical body. The sense of life is related to the activities of the ether body. The sense of movement is related to the movements of the astral body. The sense of balance is related to the standpoint of the I-organization. After their development within the body, these organs can also be used for the perception of related qualities in the outer world.

Exercising the senses provides the child with skills and with new capacities. The skills are the well-developed functions of the sense organs; the capacities arise in the soul and are prerequisites for the healthy functioning of the sense organs. The capacities include four sets of opposites, which are:

for the sense of touch	security (I own my body) and fear
for the sense of life	contentment (I am my body) and shame, doubt
for the sense of movement	sense of freedom (my body is no hindrance) and powerlessness
for the sense of balance	uniqueness (I am I) and impulse toward (self-)destruction

147

The organs of these four senses are not localized in one specific area, but each of them is distributed over the entire body.

The four senses directed toward the environment

We have four senses that convey information about the quality of the environment to us. The sense of smell conveys physical properties. The sense of taste conveys etheric properties. The sense of color conveys astral properties. The sense of temperature conveys spiritual properties. These four senses have their field of action outside the human being, in the environment. The four senses directed toward the individual body develop and are trained in connection with the body. Later they can also be directed toward the outer world. The four senses that are directed toward the environment develop and are trained in connection with the outer world; this direction does not change throughout life.

I will approach these senses also from the viewpoints of education and development, field of action, some physiological aspects, related soul capacities, and the sense organ.

Sense of smell

Development and education

When do children start to use the sense of smell? Odors enter the nose of the baby from the outset. Yet nothing indicates that babies perceive odors. Infants and young toddlers cannot smell yet. The two-year-old is neither attracted nor repelled by odors. As soon as children have learned to sniff, they can learn to smell. We do not sniff in for something that is icy cold, ugly in color, or has a bitter taste, but we do sniff for something that stinks.

Children cannot blow their nose before they are three years old. From then on, they can also become conscious of what they smell. Before that, odors are not perceived. Infants calm down as soon as they "smell" their mother, but this is not a perception they are aware of. The sense of smell develops between the ages of three and nine, although mostly unconsciously. After that, children can relate to the world of odors. They might smell their dirty socks; they may no longer want to cuddle with their parents in bed on Sunday morning, because they do not like the way the parents smell.

148

The sense of smell does not need to be educated to function. People are different in what they are able to smell; this, however, is not a result of educating the sense of smell, but a matter of a person's inherent abilities.

Field of action

Things give away their hidden property through their odor. We smell food to discover whether it is fresh or spoiled. The scent of a fruit is an indication of its ripeness. The human body odor when a person is just getting up is different from the odor when one has been up for an hour or so. We can smell it when a person is fearful. A child who is sick has a different odor from the way he or she usually smells. The young child still has a neutral smell; when puberty starts, the body odor becomes acid and penetrating.

When something that is or has been alive starts to give off an odor, this indicates that processes of ripening or breaking down are occurring, or—to say it in another way—it indicates that the astral body has started to push back etheric processes. The ripening of the fruit is the stage before it starts to rot; when a flower starts to give forth a scent, this is the stage before it fades. Fear causes chemical breakdown reactions; the hormonal changes during puberty do the same, although in another way.

The variety of odors is unlimited. It is hard to code them. Often we try to define a specific odor by way of comparison—something smells like lavender. From the fresh scents of spring to the moldy odors of the fall and from the inviting smell of cooking to the appalling odor of tainted meat, they all are expressing a degree of breakdown caused by the astral body entering the etheric domain. Breakdown processes are dying processes. The sense of smell informs the soul about the relation of the created world to death.

Some physiological aspects

The sense of smell is relentless. We must breathe, and when we breathe we smell. Yet nature has also been gracious—the perception of a smell disappears after a few minutes, even though the odor is still there. The other senses also demonstrate this phenomenon—that the perception can disappear for a while, but as soon as we direct our conscious attention to the sense perception again, it will come back. We feel again that the wristband is too tight, for instance, or we see that the flower has an orange color indeed. This is not so with the sense of smell. Smells do not naturally come back when we focus on them again. The nose first needs to perceive a different odor; then it can smell the previous one again.

This phenomenon can be better understood when we look at the function of the sense of smell in animals. The sense of smell is very important in animals, since it rules their instincts to a large extent. In particular, dogs are known for their sense of smell. We could consider the dog an extended nose. Sniffing makes dogs active, enthusiastic, and excited. Male dogs mark their trail with an odor of urine and so inform the other dogs. Typical dog behavior can also be seen in other animals, where their instincts and behavior are ruled by what they smell. In many animals, the sense of smell has a distinct relation to propagation. In propagation, butterflies are completely dependent on fragrances. The fragrance of their companions guides butterflies over distances of many miles. Their instinct, as well as their physical form, confine and determine the behavior of animal species. These are two sides of the same coin. Instinct and physical appearance are both properties of the animal's physical body, and they confine and determine its behavior.

For the human being, this is also true, although only partly. The fragrance industry has developed refined techniques to appeal to human instincts, while excluding human consciousness. Compared to animals, however, we are not good at smelling, and also our instincts are degenerated compared to those of animals. This enables us as human beings to act out of other impulses than just out of instinct.

The phenomenon that the sense of smell is relentless is related to the instinctual aspect of animals and humans. The phenomenon that human beings cannot perceive a smell for longer than a couple of minutes is related to the fact that they are given the possibility to choose freely.

The sense of smell is peculiarly and closely related to memory. Odors can open the door to experiences we had long thought forgotten. When I smell a type of furniture wax, I see my grandmother's room with its polished furniture, wood floor, and fireplace. Remembering a smell makes a specific corner of one's memories accessible again. We may understand the relation between memory and the sense of smell somewhat better when we look again at the difference between humans and animals. Instinctive behavior and behavior based on the sense of smell coincides in animals to a large extent. Instinct may be seen as memory fixed to the body. The limitations and possibilities given by its external form determine the behavior of the animal, and they "remind" the animal continuously of what is to be done. This is triggered by the sense of smell; animals smell something and they know what to do without having to reflect on it.

Animals do not remember previous experiences; their instinct *is* the memory for their behavior. This compelling knot is loosened in human beings, in order that they may act out of freedom, but remnants of it are still present. It would be interesting to research how much our childhood memories of smell influence our actions and whether adults who had a refined sense of smell during childhood are more inclined to be influenced in their actions by memories of smell than do adults who, as a child, could not smell as well or whether it is the other way round.

Soul capacities

The sense of smell is less developed in humans than it is in animals. Yet it is important that children exercise their sense of smell. They have to learn to trust their nose, and to distinguish all kinds of odors. Later on in life this helps the child to "have a nose for things." This expression refers to the capacity to know about inner qualities of people or situations with "instinctive" certainty. Human beings go through a transformation, which is made possible by the sense of smell, when they metamorphose their dependence on instincts into an active surrendering of themselves to the moral quality of their environment.

The sense organ

The nose is the sense organ of smell. A small portion of the nasal mucosa contains free nerve endings that have a direct and short connection to a small part of the brain that is situated right above the nose. This is an ancient part of the brain from the point of view of the history of human development. In order to smell, we have to inhale through our nose; the directing of the inhaled air through the nostrils may also be seen as belonging to the sense organ of smell.

The sense of smell is the compass with which the skipper determines his or her course.

Sense of taste

Development and education

Infants can already taste. At least we may assume this from watching their facial expressions when they are given something sweet or some-

151

thing bitter to eat. They will start making faces when they taste the bitter, and they will show contentment and relaxation when they taste the sweet. The infant's ability to taste, however, might be different from that of the older child or the adult. Adults may find the taste of soymilk, for instance, appalling whereas infants drink it without further ado. Infants may also be very selective in their choice of nourishment when it does not taste exactly like mother's milk. This is an issue especially in the second half of the first year, when the mother tries to feed the child fruits and vegetables. We cannot be certain, however, whether it is the sense of taste that is decisive here or the sense of touch and/or the sense of smell, because besides taste, fruits and vegetables also have different consistency and aroma. The somewhat older child, two or three years old, might notice that there are onions in a baked vegetable pie. However, the question remains whether children would also notice the presence of substances they dislike if they were blindfolded and had a clothespin on their nose. We can ask the same question in regard to ourselves as adults: what would our sense of taste perceive if we were blindfolded and had our noses pinched?

The variety of odors our noses can smell is broad and hard to classify. The variety of flavors our mouths can taste is narrow and can be basically categorized. We could distinguish six elementary taste qualities—tart, salt, and sweet (which are usually pleasant to the taste, if not too strong), soap-like (or earthy), sour, and bitter (which are usually unpleasant to the taste). We might say that tart contracts, salt gives support, and sweet provides space. We might experience that bitter evokes resistance, soap-like is appalling, and sour conserves. Tastes that are too strong are unpleasant, and they can make us sick to our stomach. Unlike fragrances, flavors do not come toward us. If we want to taste something, we have to put it into our mouth. We can only taste a substance that is dissolved in water. We cannot taste a pebble, for instance. When we taste a mineral it needs to be dissolved by the saliva. Think of kitchen salt. Substances derived from plants or animals usually have already been partly dissolved when we taste them. Usually the roots of plants offer salty, bitter, and soap-like (or earthy) flavors, whereas fruits offer tart, sweet, and sour flavors.

Flavors belong to plants. The taste of the plant's leaves, roots, and fruit is significant for the plant. It determines the plant's healing properties to a large extent. The taste indicates, in a way, the value of the plant for the animal or human who consumes it. Through its taste, the plant shows the characteristics of its specific place between the earth and the cosmos.

How does the sense of taste develop? After an undifferentiated phase, the healthy child develops a healthy instinct for what to eat and what not to eat. It is remarkable to see how precise children can be in deciding what is good for them in a certain phase of development and what is not. This pertains not only to the taste of food, but also to the quantity. This instinct is no longer reliable for many children today. For instance, when children eat too much candy or have certain food allergies, they lose this healthy instinct. The development of the sense of taste needs the mouth free of any tasting in between meals or snack times. When the mouth is continuously filled with something, it lacks the experience of the pause that is needed to taste food properly when digestion starts. The mixing together of several types of vegetables or the use of seasoning or flavors to make the food tasty, does not contribute to the differentiation of the sense of taste.

Field of action

The field of activity of the sense of taste is the nutrients. The taste of a nutrient tells something about the quality of the food. The way food tastes in the mouth often predicts how it will be digested. Tasting prepares the process of digestion. Food that is swallowed without having been tasted encounters an unprepared digestive system. To be tasted properly, the food needs to come into extensive contact with the mucous membranes of the mouth, especially with the tongue. Flavors are set free when the food is chewed well, and thus the perception of taste coincides with the beginning of the digestive process. The tasting process continues also after the food is swallowed. Then, however, we are no longer conscious of taste perception, but all along the digestive process we continue unconsciously tasting the food intensively. Throughout the digestive process, from mouth to intestines, we gauge the quality of the food, its nutritional value, and its "inner" properties.

Some physiological aspects

The sense of taste opens the door to the etheric world, to the "inner world" of substances. I already mentioned that we do not taste a substance unless it is dissolved, opened up, digested. In the third chapter, in describing the life processes, I stated that nothing from the outer world is allowed to enter the inner world unchanged. Everything must be taken in, assessed, and digested before the human body can make use of it. The sense of taste plays an important role in this process as it relates to our food.

153

It is important that children learn to taste well. When they taste well, children educate their digestive processes. The digestive process responds in detail and appropriately to the perceptions of the sense of taste. Children who have learned to taste nutrients well may also in other situations have a sense for the quality of a situation, because they have learned to perceive the "inner side" of things.

Civilization has occupied itself extensively with the culture of tasting and eating (think of gourmets). Having a meal together is an important social event. This fits the fact that tasting is perceiving the etheric. The ether body is an excellent cultivator of relationships. A good meal in pleasant surroundings where the food can be digested well and the participants can nurture their social relationships, is an artwork from the sense of taste studio.

Soul capacities

"To have good taste" is a metaphor that describes a human capability that can be applied to all areas of life—artistic, philosophical, and practical.

What does it mean to perceive the "inside" of substances, as the sense of taste makes us do unconsciously? If we were to do it consciously, we would perceive the elemental world. We would perceive pictures of the formative forces of the substances. The substance that is responsible for a specific taste would determine the picture to a large extent. The sweet carrot would give quite a different picture from the sharp horseradish. There are not many people who consciously perceive pictures when they taste something. The sense of taste, however, has the power to evoke this capacity.

The sense organ

The taste buds on the tongue are the sense organs of taste. The buds are arranged in a specific order—we taste sweetness at the tip of the tongue; at the base of the tongue we taste bitterness; in between we taste saltiness. Along the sides of the tongue we taste tartness more toward the front, sourness more toward the back, and the flat taste in between. Saliva may be considered a part of the sense organ of taste; if the tongue were completely dry, we could not taste anything.

Whether the tasting that extends farther along the digestive tract belongs to the sense organ of taste can be debated. If we consider it to be so, then the sense of taste closely cooperates with the sense of life to assess how the food is received by the body.

Tasting is connected to the mouth as smelling is to the nose. When we do not like the taste of the food, we can spit it out until it passes the very end of the oral cavity where the food must be swallowed.

In earlier times, seafarers could determine their position by tasting the seawater. The sextant took the place of this ancient art of navigating, and today we have very advanced equipment to guide ships safely across the oceans.

Sense of color

Development and education

It is difficult to assess exactly when children start to perceive colors consciously. I work with the assumption that it is when they, out of themselves, begin to ask questions about the names of colors. Since the optical instrument—the eye—is functional at birth, we can assume that children are not conscious of the colors that penetrate their eyes, before they indicate that they are aware of them. Yet these colors work upon and affect the organism from the outset.

At the age of about one and a half, children start to draw. If they have colors available they will use them to make colorful compositions of scribbles. Initially the child does not consciously select the colors or use them in a specific sequence. Yet it is remarkable that children seem to use the lighter colors first and only later add the darker colors in their drawings. Then comes the moment when children do not just make drawings, but also start looking at them. From this moment on, children may select in advance the color they will use next. When they are about three years old, children will inquire about the names of the colors. This may be the moment that they first perceive colors consciously. Some children have a special relationship to colors; they are outspoken in how they use them and they may have a favorite color. Other children seem to be less particular about them. When children start to make figures representing the outer world, most of them will soon make a yellow sun, a blue sky, and green grass. This is natural. For houses and human figures, children usually use a variety of colors.

It is important for the education of the child's sense of color that the colors in the child's environment are true. That is to say—the color of a person or an object should express something about the essential properties of the person or object.

Colors appeal directly to the soul. It is important for the education of the child's soul that the colors are in harmony with the mood of the situation. The mood of spring asks for different colors than the mood of fall.

Field of action

What does the ability to perceive colors bring to us? What would happen to us if we could not see colors? It would affect our life of soul most certainly if we were only able to see degrees of grey. Colors give brightness, differentiation, and variation to life. Colors speak directly to the soul. When people are depressed, they will usually not want to wear yellow clothes, while during a carefree summer vacation, a person may actually like to wear yellow and red. This also applies to our environment. Minerals, plants, and animals express themselves in colors and show this on the surface of their external appearance. The dandelion must be yellow and the pomegranate must be red. Nature is naturally green, the sky blue, and not the other way round. We can perform the mental exercise of picturing the reverse. But we know that it *cannot* be true. It cannot be true, because in nature colors are objective and true. Colors tell something about the essence of things; they present the picture of this essence. This is different with taste; people can attribute different tastes to the same thing. This is even more so with smells; the odor of things is perceived in a very subjective way. Color appears at the surface of an object and does not separate from it. To perceive color, we only need to open our eyes; we do not have to go to the object, we do not have to smell it, we do not have to taste it, we do not have to touch it. Even when we close our eyes to it, we can recall the color with our mind's eye.

The field of action of the sense of color is the world of qualities, of moods, and of other properties that appeal to the soul. It is the astral world that gives objects their color, gives birds their colorful array of feathers, zebras their stripes, and gives the sunset its enchanting orange-red. In the colors, the subjective world of qualities appears in quite an objective way. Through the sense of color, we gain access to this astral world.

Some physiological aspects

Colors are born where light and darkness meet. From this point of view, colors are beings that are born and exist. When we watch the rainbow, we become aware how fleeting the existence of colors can be. The rainbow has factual existence but it does not last and does not leave a trace. Something similar occurs with the complementary colors, which always are born the moment the physical eye perceives a color. The mind's eye perceives this complementary color—an objective reality, but fleeting. Seen from this point of view, colors connected to the surface of objects have died. The light-beings are not free—as in the rainbow—but are bound to the earth by the color pigment.

There are artists who, to some extent, are able to loosen this bind. You may know some examples of this. The ether forces working in the organ of the sense of color do something similar. The direction of the color is reversed in the eye—the color appears as the complementary color as it is freed from its bonding with the earth.[9]

Soul capacities

The creative world in nature mirrors itself in colors, which work objectively. The eye provides the soul with a perception and a counter image. The eye can train itself to listen to the message of a color. Then the capacity can arise that belongs to the sense of color—to learn to perceive the creative world. When the soul has learned to perceive the ether world, it receives pictures of the forces that are active in this ether world. These pictures are known as imaginations. Through the sense of color, we might be able to exercise this capacity to come to imaginations. A person can have "a good eye" for situations. This is different from having "a good nose" or "good taste." Having "a good eye" indicates that a person has learned to perceive the outside of things as an image of what is inside.

The sense organ

The eye is a perfect instrument for the perception of color. The activity of the pupil reduces the light that enters the eye to the proper intensity. The cones in the retina are the color sensitive elements. Through them, the retina becomes an ingenious optic apparatus that the sense of color can use.

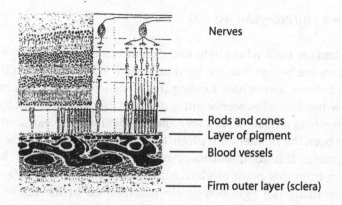

Nerves

Rods and cones
Layer of pigment
Blood vessels

Firm outer layer (sclera)

Fig. 46 Diagram of the back of the eyeball. Above is the inner core of the eyeball which receives the light. Below is the outer layer of the back of the eyeball with the blood vessels. (From Lothar Vogel, Der dreigliedrige Mensch, Dornach 1992[3].)

However, the eye does much more than perceive color. The clarity of perception is determined by the rods, the light sensitive elements in the retina. We can perceive the outline of a form because the eye follows its contours; this is an activity of the sense of movement. Through the sense of balance, the eye perceives whether or not the painting on the wall is hanging level. Three other senses, which I still have to describe—the senses of form, meaning, and I—also make use of the eye. All these perceptions are brought together in the field of vision.

The sense of color is the star-strewn heaven by which the skipper can determine his or her course.

Sense of temperature

Development and education

We can observe how the sense of temperature, also known as the sense of warmth, functions when we observe children's reactions to heat or cold. Babies who are dressed too warmly or too lightly will either whine or be too silent. This reaction indicates that their sense of temperature is functioning. It will still take some years, though, before children can regulate their own body temperature with the help of their own sense of warmth. Adults are responsible for how warmly children are dressed until they can do it themselves. Even rather independent preschoolers may not think of taking off their jacket when they sweat or—even more so—putting on a jacket when their teeth are chattering because they are too cold.

Even when they are still young, children react adequately when they sense that an object is cold or warm, extremely cold or hot. Obviously, they can use their sense of temperature from early on. To develop this sense further, children need to be surrounded by a physically pleasant degree of warmth to move freely within the boundaries of their body, without being cramped from the cold or dissolving in the heat. To develop the sense of temperature properly, children also need a degree of psychological warmth in their environment, in which they can flourish and even can become angry now and then. When the child's environment is too tolerant psychologically (I could also say, when the range of psychological warmth is too broad), or when (figuratively speaking) too often heat waves or cold fronts are passing by unexpectedly, the free development of the child's sense of temperature will be affected. The I will then have to deal with an instrument that is not properly adjusted, or too rigid; it will not be able to make the right judgments with respect to warmth that is coming toward it or that is expected from it. This can lead to physical or mental illness—physical illness, because heat or cold can surprise and overcome the body; mental illness, because a person can become confused when he or she is not able to assess properly, for instance, tokens of sympathy or antipathy.

Field of action

With our sense of temperature, we perceive whether something in the outer world is warmer or colder than we are. In essence, this sense reveals just two facts—something is warmer than I am, or something is colder than I am. The "warmer" or the "colder" may consist of a broad range of degrees, but this does not change the simple duality of the perception. Compared to, for instance, the sense of color and the sense of smell, the sense of temperature is a very simple sense.

Temperature is closely related to movement. Change in temperature gives an impulse to movement. Warmth works centrifugally—it radiates out and connects with everything it meets. Cold works centripetally—it sucks everything toward a center. Variations in temperature are responsible for the movements of ocean currents and of air currents in the atmosphere. Warmth and cold determine climates and seasons.

It is interesting to reflect for a moment on the differences between warmth and, for instance, color and odor. A color remains physically with the object it belongs to—the gemstone, the flower, the butterfly, the rainbow. When we say that a color comes toward us, we are using a metaphor. Odors can come toward us literally. Odor disperses physically from a source. I have already mentioned that butterflies can smell their companions over a distance of many miles. Warmth also leaves its source. Warmth is a property that can go from one object to another, Warmth fully penetrates objects. Using a metaphor, I could say: warmth is contagious. In this quality, it is different from the objects of perception of the other senses.

The working of the sense of temperature is as strong as it is simple. Its field of activity is the home of the I. The I also moves in two directions—radiating and connecting with the environment; or sucking in and relating everything to itself. The I-organization is structured according to these two principles: in the upper pole the quality of sucking in prevails; in the lower pole the radiating quality prevails. When I described the types of ether (beginning on page 105), I approached this phenomenon from another side.

Some physiological aspects

The sense of warmth functions normally within a rather narrow range of body temperatures. For most people this lies between 97.5 and 99.5 degrees Fahrenheit [36.5°–37.5°C]. When our body temperature is a few degrees lower, we may still be able to perceive the temperature of objects accurately. However when we have really cold hands, we cannot trust our sense of temperature any longer. This sense has narrow operating margins, and at the same time it affects the organism strongly.

Perceptions of the sense of temperature make us move. When we become too cold, our teeth start to chatter, and we want to move and put on more clothes. When we become too hot, we start to perspire and take off clothing. In fever, the life processes become very active; with an extremely low body temperature, the life processes slow down to a near standstill. In either situation it is difficult to maintain normal consciousness and awareness. In the cold, our thinking slows down; in the heat, our thinking evaporates.

The body temperature is lower in the morning than it is in the evening. This indicates that human beings will be more focused on processes of the upper pole in the morning, whereas in the evening they will be more focused on processes of the lower pole. The structure of the I-organization moves in the polarity between warm and cold, between lower pole and upper pole.

The I-organization and the sense of temperature, as well as warmth itself, are closely related. This reveals itself also in the temperature changes in the human body during a 24-hour period. During the night, the outside of the body is relatively warm, which allows the loosened I to leave the body. During the day, the skin is relatively cool and the core temperature is highest. This condition fits the incarnated I, which works from the center. The sense of temperature follows the changes of the day and night rhythm. Instead of feeling that we become warmer, we become sleepy at bedtime. If we need to get out of bed at night, we are easily chilled. During the first year of life, this pattern of alternation in the warmth-organization stabilizes as the child develops a distinct day and night rhythm.

Soul capacities

When children learn to use their sense of temperature well, they not only gain the capacity to perceive physical warmth and cold but also the capacity to perceive and deal with warmth and cold in a metaphorical sense. They will be able to distinguish between words spoken with warmth and sincere enthusiasm, and words spoken out of political considerations or greed. This ability leads to perceptions expressed in phrases such as "it warmed my soul" and "it leaves me cold." People who have gained these capabilities know not only what they want but also what the next step is in any situation.

The sense organ

The sense organ of temperature is composed of free nerve endings in the skin that respond directly to changes in temperature. They are distributed over the skin as are the nerve endings of the sense organ of touch. For a long time, scientists did not distinguish between perceptions of touch and of temperature. The perception of temperature as well as the perception of touch does not have the same degree of exactness in all areas of the skin. The palms of the hands and the inside of the arms, for instance, are more sensitive to temperature perception than the back of the hand and the outside of the arm. The skin on the back is relatively insensitive to warmth and cold perception. It takes us a moment to realize whether the water from the shower on our back is icy cold or hot.

161

Through the sense of temperature, the seafarer can become "a skipper second in command to God."

Summary

Perceptions of the senses of smell, taste, color, and temperature provide us with direct information about physical, etheric, astral, and spiritual qualities of the environment. By using these senses, the human soul not only develops sensory skills, it also develops capacities. The sense of smell enables the soul to have a nose for the moral quality of something, a person, or a situation. The sense of taste enables the soul to be aware of the inner quality of something. The sense of color enables the soul to have an eye for the image character of objects or phenomena. The sense of temperature enables the soul to have a feeling for what may become of something.

Exercising the four senses that are directed toward one's own body teaches the children to deal with the foundation of their earthly existence and with their existential doubts about it. Exercising the four senses that are directed toward the environment teaches them to know their own soul, because they recognize soul qualities in the environment. For the children to develop and educate these four senses, the inner aspects of their environment must correspond to its outer aspects in the areas of smell, taste, color, and temperature. Three of the four senses that are directed toward the environment have a distinct, small part of the body as their organs—the nose, the tongue, and the eyes; the sense of temperature, however, has the entire skin as its organ.

The four senses directed toward the spiritual

The soul directs itself toward its own body when it perceives with the four senses that are directed toward the body. The individual body is the first part of the outer world that children should become acquainted with. Thereafter, the four senses that are directed toward the environment help children meet the surrounding world. The child must share this world with other people. The spiritual world, perceived with the four senses that are directed toward the spiritual, is familiar to children. They were there before birth. However, children do not yet know how the spiritual world manifests itself here on earth. They will be taught about this by the four senses which are directed toward the spiritual. Children will learn to recognize sounds, words, thoughts, and human beings as earthly manifestations of the spiritual world. These earthly manifestations of the spiritual can be perceived directly; they do not appear as images. This is different from the perceptions of the other senses. The four senses directed toward the environment perceive how the spiritual world presents itself in picture form (images) in the world around us, which it created. The four senses directed toward one's own body teach the human being how the spiritual reveals itself in the body. Through the four senses directed toward the spiritual, the spiritual reveals itself directly in the sense perceptions themselves. This does not imply that the human being can perceive the spiritual world. For that purpose, the soul needs to develop specific sense organs; the physical sense organs are inadequate for that.

Before I discuss the last four senses separately, I want to present them as a group. The sense of tone is related to the physical level; the sense of language, word, or form is related to the etheric level; the sense of thought, or meaning is related to the astral level; and the sense of I, or style is related to the spiritual level.

The capacity to perceive sound—the sense of tone—is present at birth. Together with the eight senses previously mentioned, these nine senses are given by nature. The remaining three senses are given as potential, but their development is entirely dependent on education. Through education, the sounds that children perceive will begin to reveal meaning; for instance, the children will perceive thoughts that are expressed in language. Not only sounds, but also letters, gestures, and colors (to name a few) will reveal meaning when we use the three highest senses. Through education, children will learn to understand what they read; they will understand non-verbal communication, and art objects will speak to them. The three highest senses integrate the perceptions of the other nine senses.

I will give three examples to clarify the place of the three highest senses. When we hear a violin sonata by Bach played by a professional musician on a well-tuned instrument, we use all four senses that are directed toward the spiritual. With our sense of tone, we hear the notes being played. With our sense of form, we hear the type and quality of the instrument. With our sense of thought, we hear the melody and the structure of the sonata. With our sense of I, we hear that Bach was the composer.

When we listen to a lecturer, we consciously need to activate our sense of tone to hear the pitch of the voice. While we are doing that, it is very hard to listen to the content of the lecture. A peculiarity in the way

163

the lecturer is speaking—for instance, a lisp—activates our sense of language, probably with the effect that it takes a while before we can focus on the content of the talk with our sense of thought. Normally we do not listen to the vowels and consonants. We may abruptly hear the lisp again when the speaker makes a statement we do not agree with. Then our sense of thought retracts, and our sense of word or language makes us hear the pronunciation of the consonants again. When we are again focusing on the content of the talk with our activated sense of thought, we might perceive that the speaker makes a statement, quoting somebody else with whom the speaker is not in agreement. It is our sense of I that perceives that the lecturer does not connect him- or herself fully with the spoken thoughts for a moment.

At an exhibition of sculptures by Henry Moore, we have the opportunity to observe a number of his works. We perceive the materials they are made of—granite or bronze—with the help of our sense of color. With our sense of form, we perceive concave surfaces, convex surfaces, corners, and edges. Our sense of thought discerns the meaning of each sculpture, even when we do not read the titles. With our sense of I, we might be able to recognize a Moore sculpture later on when we encounter a collection of sculptures by various artists.

These three examples show us that the perception of a higher sense overrules the perception of a lower sense. We may formulate this also in the following way: the sense of tone serves the sense of word or form, which serves the sense of thought or meaning, which serves the sense to perceive what is characteristic about the other person. Common language uses the word "hearing" for much more than the perception of tone. Similar to the way we perceive just colors with our sense of color, we actually perceive just tones and their properties with our sense of tone. We need the sense of meaning to perceive the meaning of a color, a sound, or a word.

Again, I will approach these senses from the same viewpoints that I used when describing the previous eight senses.

Sense of tone

Development and education

There is no doubt that the healthy infant can hear sounds. Babies may even discern subtleties, because they will react to their mother's singing differently from the way they do to someone else's singing. In such a

164

situation, the sense of tone is not the only sense that plays a role for the baby—the three highest senses will also be involved. We may assume that the sense of tone is active in young children in all its nuances. In music therapy, it is generally known how even very young children react explicitly to specific sounds they are offered. At a later age, other perceptions are added to the tone perception that do not have to do with the sense of tone, but with the other three spiritual senses. For instance, the capacity to recognize the difference between the sound of an oboe and the sound of a violin has to do with the sense of language, word, or form.

The capacity to perceive tone, and all that belongs to this, is given to the child by nature at birth. It does not evolve with age. People are very different in this respect. One person is much more aurally alert than another. When we have gone through childhood without damage to our hearing—which is becoming more of an exception these days—the capacity to hear the higher tones decreases steadily after the age of twenty-one. The phenomenon of a decreasing capacity of the sense organ with increasing age is also found in the other eight senses given by nature. We will later see that the sense of tone reveals the inner quality of the created world. Children enjoy tremendously hearing the different sounds when people in the kitchen are using pots, pans, glassware, and china, or when they themselves are allowed to play with some of the kitchenware. This experience teaches children to connect sounds to the objects that are sounding, so they become aware that sounds are related to the essence of things. Sounds that are reproduced mechanically do not have this true relationship between sound and the sounding object. Sounds coming through an amplifier have no connection to the materials the device is made of. For the education of the sense of tone, it is more helpful for children to hear the breaking of glass, or the sound of silverware hitting a pot, than to listen to a CD player or a Walkman.

Field of action

To discover a tone, we have to be active. If we want to know whether a beam is rotten or not, we have to knock on the wood. To know more about the differences between lead and silver, we might strike a triangle made of lead and one made of silver. Tone reveals the inner quality of a substance, but only when movement has come into play. The tone needs to be liberated; it needs to be loosened by vibrations.

Tone is not material; it is spiritual. Why can we hear it, even if we have no psychic powers? It is special indeed that we can hear tones. To accomplish this, both the ear and tone itself have gone through a special

165

development. Ear and tone abstain from something very important; they sacrifice for the sake of sense perception.

On earth, tone incorporates itself in air vibrations. Each tone has a specific wavelength. The world of the tones is structured according to mathematical laws. Intervals (such as the octave or the fifth) can be expressed in quotients of whole numbers. A tone is not identical with its wavelength, as the archetype (for instance, the archetypal birch tree) is not identical with its physical manifestation (a specific birch tree). Sounds have been incorporated in the created physical world; they are freed from the objects when these are brought to vibration. The silver triangle and the wooden xylophone are examples of these magical occurrences. When we bring these instruments into movement, the spiritual tones appear in the physical air vibrations. This is the sacrifice made by tone.

The other sacrifice is made by the ear. In its structure, the middle ear is an organ of movement. It is a tiny limb with bones and muscles. This limb, however, is not meant to move actively by itself; it has to be moved. Air vibrations make it move. The ear presents a physical picture of sacrifice, because it is a sacrificial deed when a person who is very capable deliberately does not use this capacity but makes it available to others without reward. We will also meet the principles of renunciation and service in the three highest senses. Through the occurrences in the middle ear and subsequently in the inner ear, the air vibrations disappear. Then physical sound has disappeared. The soul can now perceive the tone reborn in its true form, no longer the captive of its physical carrier—the wavelength.

The field of activity of the sense of tone is "the inside" of the created world, of that which through movement can be made to sound. The more pure the material and the harder it is, the easier it is to make it sound.

The perceptions of the sense of tone are as limited as they are varied. A tone can be soft or loud, low or high, short or long. Only these three aspects of a tone, in almost unlimited variation, can be perceived by the sense of tone. All other auditory perceptions are not connected to the sense of tone.

Some physiological aspects

To know what a tone is, we will have to answer the question of why the sense of tone is included in the category of senses that are directed toward the spiritual. Why does tone not belong to the same category as color or smell? It would belong to the category of senses directed toward the environment, if the environment did not only have smell, taste, color,

166

and temperature, but also had sound. That, however, is not so. Minerals and plants do not sound by themselves. The animal world is also rather silent. Only human beings create sounds—music, speech, and mechanically created noise. What about the murmur of a creek, the dashing of the waves, or the rustling of leaves? These sounds are not inherent to the water or the leaves, but are caused by movement. The prevailing silence in the animal world finds its exceptions, such as in birds or in mammals in the rutting season. A strong astral influence can make animals give up their silence. Yet, whereas the created world exposes itself in smell, taste, color, and temperature, it conceals the tone.

Comparative anatomy discloses that parts of the jaws and the mastication muscles of the lower animals are transformed into the middle ear of higher mammals and humans. What initially has been part of the lower pole has been taken away and given to the upper pole. Some of the capacity to chew is sacrificed in the service of perception directed toward the spiritual.

The cochlea in the inner ear, which is the organ of the sense of tone (as we will see later), is built like a snail shell. It is a perfect spiral. There are more structures in the human body which have the form of a spiral, for instance the heart muscles, the uterus muscles, and the turns of the small intestines. Wherever we encounter a spiral, we face the border between two worlds—the one appearing, the other disappearing. The spiral is a picture of the transition from the spiritual world to the physical world, or vice versa. The cochlea is such a picture of the sense of tone.

Soul capacities

The soul acquires an ability when it exercises the sense of tone. It is the ability to hear what a specific situation has to say. The senses directed toward the environment prepare the soul to perceive imaginations. The sense of tone prepares the human being to receive inspirations, to hear the spirit speak. John the Evangelist wrote the Apocalypse—the last book of the New Testament of the Bible—on the basis of inspirations. Great composers note down their inspirations. True reality sounds in inspirations.

The sense organ

The cochlea is the sophisticated instrument of the sense of tone. The fluid-filled spiraling tube is equipped with hairs that are extremely sensitive to vibrations. One end of the hair moves freely in the liquid, whereas the other end of the hair is connected to nerve fibers of the auditory (vestibular/cochlear) nerve. Movements in the fluid caused by sound waves are transmitted to the hairs and are perceived with the help of the auditory nerve. You may find a picture of the cochlea in books on anatomy and physiology (see also figure 45, page 147). The complexity of this organ distinguishes itself, for instance, from the simplicity of the organ of touch. The cochlea of the inner ear is located inside the petrous portion of the temporal bones, next to the organ of the sense of balance. The sense of tone and the sense of balance make use of the same cranial nerve.

The functioning of the inner ear is prepared by the functions of the middle ear and the external ear. The middle ear and the auricle are built to move. They have many small muscles that, however, do not serve movement, but serve perception. The middle ear is equipped with an ingenious setup to prevent strong air vibrations from damaging the inner ear. The sense organs of the left and right ears provide the listening soul with perfectly identical perception. That is quite different for the eyes; the perception of the left eye is never completely identical with the perception of the right eye. The organs of the sense of tone are so mathematically perfect that they can function perfectly when they are healthy.

There is still another organ for the perception of sound. Tones, sounds, and music do something with us. A sudden noise may make us contract, merry music will make us dance. Sound affects our movements in a magical way. This is not so with color or other sensations. Odors can also do it, but they do it indirectly by affecting our desires. Sounds affect us directly; for instance, we wake up with the trumpet and go to sleep with the cello. This indicates that sound has access to our movement organization. It is not that we hear the music with our ears and then decide to dance; music makes us dance and, when we hold still for a moment, our ears hear the music.

The two organs of the sense of tone serve two different aspects of the perception of tone. Firstly, the tone, the sound, and the music affect our will directly. The will is put into movement by the power of the sound. When we resist this magic and do not move outwardly, we will notice how the sound affects us, how we become, for instance, melancholy or joyful. Secondly, the cochlea is designed to perceive the wavelength of the air vibrations. This organ provides us with exact perceptions of pitch, intensity, and duration of the sound.

Since the same sounds are simultaneously perceived by our movement organization (our will) and by our inner ears, the two perceptions meet in the soul of the listener. The perception by the will bears the risk of infringing upon human freedom of choice, as can happen with war music or pop concerts, which are meant to arouse people. The perception by the cochlea is the physical picture of a sacrifice out of free will (as I have described). In the sense of tone, the two polarities of the human will come to expression, and they then have to be integrated by one and the same human being.

Sense of language, speech, or form

Development and education

The young child notices neither forms nor language. The capacity to perceive forms and spoken words needs to be developed through exercise. We can have an idea how the perception of language or form begins to develop when we pay attention to the infant who begins to "speak." At the age of about eight months, children start to babble. They practice contentedly, moving their lips and cheeks and making all kinds of sounds, which shape the currents of the exhaled air. When they practice this sufficiently, they will later on be able to move along with these sounds when they hear them. If they then do not move outwardly with the sounds but only move along inwardly, they will be able to "hear" the forms of the sounds.

This is similar to starting to "see" the forms of objects—the table, the chairs, the plants, the animals, and so on. Initially children literally have to move those forms. Children must have them in their hands; they must bump against, endlessly walk around, crawl under, and creep over the table; they must follow all forms and shapes around themselves with their eye-movements. When they have practiced this sufficiently, and if they place their experience of movement in the service of the sense of form and do not physically move along with those forms, then they will be able to perceive spatial forms.

The sense of language makes spoken tones into a language. It is even better to say: with the help of the sense of language we hear how specific tones form a language. We experience this clearly when we are in a country where we do not understand the language of the people. Concepts are not the building stones of a language. The same concept expresses itself in different languages through different words. It is the genius of the language that makes tones into a language. We could compare this to the sculptor who expresses the form-language of the sculpture in granite. As the lifeless granite comes to life in the sculpture, so the dead tones become alive in the language. This is the field of activity of the creative formative forces that work in the ether.

169

The sense of language is only given as potential. Depending on the place on earth where the child is born, on the forms the child experiences (at home and in the environment), depending on the language(s) the child learns—depending on all such factors—the sense of form will develop into an instrument. This instrument belongs to that particular place on earth. When children go to kindergarten and have to establish their position among others, it is essential that they can speak their mother tongue more or less fluently. The sense of language anchors people in their social environment. Even if the child does not understand the teacher or the other children but is familiar with the sounds of what they say, the anchoring will occur.

Throughout life, we can learn new forms and gestures. We do this, for instance, when we learn to speak a new language and enjoy familiarizing ourselves with the unusual intonations and tongue twisters.

The basis for the development of the sense of language or form is laid when the child has the opportunity to develop the sense of movement freely. Proper development of the sense of movement requires that children develop their motor skills at their own pace and in their own way. In addition, children should learn to control their movements. This requires sufficient rest and restriction, and, especially, repetition and rhythmic games. For the development of the sense of language itself, it is important that the adults around the children articulate their mother tongue well and do not use abbreviations. Whether a bilingual situation works favorably or unfavorably on the child depends on his or her constitution and on the consistency with which the two languages are used at home.

The sense of form develops by itself as long as there are forms and structures to be touched and to be seen. *How* the sense of form develops depends on the nature and variety of the forms around the child. It is obvious that living in an old farmhouse will affect children differently from living in a tall apartment building.

Field of action

The sense of form perceives the process of shapes being formed out of substance, in space or in time. In language, this process would consist of vowels and consonants connecting to form words. In music, the form arises out of the characteristic sounds of each instrument, including the human voice. In sculpture, forms are concave or convex, pointed toward the outside or toward the inside, edged or dented. In written language, there are the shapes of the characters; the reader translates these sym-

170

bols back into vowels and consonants. The gestures of sign language or eurythmy also are perceived by the sense of language or form.

Some physiological aspects

Perceiving forms and structures in space and in time is an activity that makes a connection with the formative forces of nature, of the human being, and of other formative beings such as the geniuses of language (see also page 199, where I describe the role of the genius of language in learning to speak). The formative forces make use of the ether world to cause a form to be seen, heard, or felt. The sense of tone gives an indication of the hidden physical qualities of a substance; the sense of form tells us about the ether forces that have worked on this substance.

We need to suppress the perception of the substance when we want to perceive the form. As long as I read the characters, I cannot perceive the word, and when I focus on the pitch of the tone I do not perceive that it is an oboe playing. The sculpture is just a block of granite when I focus on the material, and I will only see paint and brush strokes when I look at a painting from a few inches away.

The perception of the sense of form supersedes the perception of substance. Form is frozen movement. To perceive form, we must first move along with the movements that composed the form, and then we have to suppress the movement. The prerequisites of a proper development of the sense of form are inner and outer flexibility and a well-educated sense of movement.

Soul capacities

When we exercise the sense of language, word, or form, we develop the capacity to listen in such a way that we know: this has to do with me, it affects me. The sense of tone makes it possible to receive inspirations. The sense of form enables us, in addition, to perceive our specific place in life, in a spiritual sense. Then we will also know what we have to do to worthily take this place.

The sense organ

The way the sense of form functions is closely related to the way the sense of movement functions. Accordingly, the sense organ of form is to be found in the human being who moves with purpose. A characteristic for the development of movement is that a variety of chaotic movement patterns must be suppressed, that reflexes are suppressed, and that the human being controls unnecessary movements in order to accomplish a single movement willfully. The essence of movement development is mainly to bring movement to rest (see also page 191 ff.). For that purpose, the human body is equipped with an extensive network of nerves. This complex system of nerves extends from the brain to the lower end of the spine and is known as the pyramidal tract. When the pyramidal tract is well trained, it becomes the well-tuned instrument for perceiving tones and forms.

Sense of thought or meaning

Development and education

The first awakening of the sense of thought or meaning may be at the time that the child first does not look at your hand when you are pointing your finger at something, but looks in the direction you are pointing. In doing this, the child indicates that he or she perceives the meaning of the gesture and does not stop short by looking at the gesture itself. The sense of thought develops gradually at the age of about eighteen months. Children start to think for themselves in their third year.

The sense of thought, therefore, has already been functional for some time when the child starts to think, and it continues to develop throughout life. Every new concept we take in broadens our sense of thought.

We *perceive* the meaning of a gesture, a word (written, spoken, or in eurythmy), or of an art object; we do not *think* it. If, in the twilight, you take a juniper tree for a robber, or if, in a conversation, you hear "comic" when somebody says "cosmic," the sense of meaning is at work; however, it does so on the basis of an incorrect perception of the underlying sense of form. When we do not perceive correctly, we cannot understand correctly. When the sense of meaning is at a loss, fantasy becomes active. We have then left the field of sense perception.

Children grow up with a multitude of thoughts incorporated in pictures, gestures, and tones. This is the material with which they exercise their sense of thought. This way, they train their capacity to perceive the meaning of a new situation.

When adults learn a new language, they have no problem learning a different word for a familiar concept; they do face difficulties, though, when

172

the new language presents them with unfamiliar concepts. We encounter similar situations when children raised in a religious milieu sleep over with friends raised in an atheistic environment, and vice versa.

The sense of thought or meaning is a rather decisive factor in the development of the child. This sense forms the framework for the concepts with which we meet the world; in addition, the concepts that we have available (in the sense of "stand by to be used for perceptions") determine and restrict *what* we will see, hear, and touch. If we have never learned to distinguish between firs and pines, we might see conifers but not firs and pines, because we lack those concepts.

When we speak a rich and differentiated language, we do the greatest service to the education of the children's sense of thought, since children will then have access to a rich and differentiated source of concepts later on. The use of proverbs and sayings is also important from this point of view.

Field of action

The sense of thought enables a person to perceive the thoughts of other people. The sense of thought has access to an area that is superior to the areas of tone and language. Language gives expression to thoughts. Language is the material through which thoughts and concepts can be expressed. Thoughts are not abstractions; they are formative, creative forces. These are not the formative forces of the etheric, but the formative, creative forces of the astral world. In the regions of the spiritual world where things come into being when they are spoken, concepts are living realities. This region of the creative word is also known as the Logos whom John the Evangelist writes about at the beginning of his gospel.

The creative power of concepts does not only work through spoken language. We can also read a train of thought in a written publication, and we can understand the meaning of a gesture with the help of the sense of thought.

When looking at a painting by Van Gogh—one of his dark paintings with a weaving loom—I perceive brush strokes of dark paint when I look at it from a few inches away; I notice a bent figure and a dark framework when I look from a somewhat greater distance; from still farther away I see a small, poorly lit room, an antique weaving loom, and a weaver, probably a male figure. After a while, I also observe the poverty and the desolation of the situation; I do this with the help of the sense of thought. It can also happen that I realize somewhere during this process that this is a very early painting by Van Gogh. This, then, is an activity of the sense of style.

Some physiological aspects

Where in the human body can we locate the homeland of the sense of thought or meaning? Where in the human being can we find the formative, creative wisdom of the world of concepts?

We would not find it in the astral body. Through its connection with the I-organization, the astral body is too personal, not universal enough. We can find it in the ether body. The picture given in the Old Testament—that God created the human being with His breath—conveys this reality. All human beings have an area in their ether body, in their constitution, where all concepts are at home. The sense of meaning relates to this area. The Logos has spoken the ether body. In the human organism this process is repeated when the part of the ether body that is available for thinking is born. This part of the ether body is formed by the language that the child speaks. Through this formative process children learn to think in a way that corresponds to their mother tongue.

The sense of life enables us to perceive our constitution. Knowing the individual constitution through the development of the sense of life is a prerequisite for the functioning sense of thought. Different from the sense of life, the sense of thought does not *perceive* the individual constitution, but uses it as a point of reference. When we hear another person speak, this field of reference needs to be silent and not try to speak itself; it must be a sounding board for the thoughts that the other person is expressing. When we listen, we renounce tone and language in order to hear what the other person is saying. We thus renounce the activity of our own constitution. When this is quiet and silent, the other person expresses him- or herself in it.

Soul capacities

Exercising the sense of thought will lead to an ability that has to do with encounters. If I sincerely want to meet a person, I am obliged to listen. I need to create space in order that the other person can become manifest in me. Something similar occurs when we meet a concept. The sense of thought is active when I perceive the concept. When I play with the concept in my own thinking, I am dealing with a *picture* of the concept. If I then suddenly realize that I am not only dealing with a thought, but with a reality, then I myself change through the meeting with the concept. This happens when children suddenly understand what multiplication is, or when adults make a new concept their own.

The sense organ

When children learn to speak, they imprint the thoughts they express into their ether body. This happens with the help of the upper part of the autonomic nervous system, which is connected with the larynx. (See page 137—the organ of the sense of life.) Speaking develops this part of the nervous system to such an extent that it can become the sounding board for the sense of thought or meaning. When we hear others speak, we inwardly speak the words along with them. Small children, as well as some adults, cannot hold this back—they start to speak aloud themselves, because the speaking impulse has been activated. Then they can no longer hear what the other person is saying. When people are angry, they force themselves not to speak inwardly what the other person is saying. Then their inner being speaks its own language and the other person might as well stop speaking to them. Yet when people are able to listen and understand, they have learned to hold back what they have learned with so much effort—speaking.

Sense of I or sense of style

Development and education

It is characteristic for the sense of I that it perceives something invisible. How do we notice whether someone is "right there" or "not home"? By the person's gaze. How do we meet what manifests the person's essence? By looking the person in the eye. Why do caregivers demand that children look at them when they have something important to say? Because then the children are right there. When I look in the other person's eyes, I see myself reflected. I "see" the other person when I look in the dark of the pupil of his or her eye.

When babies start to look at their mother and smile, the sense of I dawns upon them. The sense of I develops between people who love one another and trust one another unconditionally. The child's field of perception expands only slowly beyond the first few familiar faces. The child may not recognize people when they are in an unusual place. For children, the perception of another human being is not separated from the perception of the environment. This changes around the age of ten.

The sense of I can only be developed in an atmosphere of trust. Children can practice the discerning capacity of the sense of I when they are

175

around adults who set the example of differentiating. Generalized judgments, about professions or nationalities and the like, do not educate the sense of I. Those types of judgment reduce the human being, perceived by the sense of I, to the manifestation of a species.

Field of action

The sense of I perceives what is personal. Therefore we could also name it the sense of style. When the child hears a distinct creaking of wood and then knows his or her mother is coming up the stairs, the child makes use of the sense of I. We can also recognize people by the way they move, speak, or think. The sense of I is directed to the perception of one single object—the I. Still it can perceive as many egos as there are human beings. The sense of style also recognizes civilizations, periods of art history, and the like. The use of this sense must be practiced; it can be exercised throughout life. Children practice this sense only in relation to the people they know. Adults tend to limit the practice of this sense to their field of interest.

The sense of I or style does not work with general concepts. When I am able to perceive Bach with my sense of style, this does not mean that I can also perceive Beethoven.

Some physiological aspects

An atmosphere of complete trust is necessary to practice the sense of I, because the technique that the soul uses in applying it is very dangerous. What happens? When I perceive another human being with my sense of I, my soul leaves my body and submerges itself into the soul of the other person. When my soul leaves my body, I fall asleep. When part of my soul leaves my body to perceive the I of another person, I partially fall asleep. Since other persons cannot bear my soul invading their soul, they put up their defenses, and my soul returns to my body. This process repeats itself several times, probably reciprocally, until we have attained security: I encounter the I of the person I am meeting.

Before birth, the soul of the child is completely submerged in the spiritual world. In that world, we do not need the sense of I to meet other beings; we meet other beings directly, unhindered by the veils of the sense world. After birth, the soul is dependent on the physical body. Children need to learn to trust their physical body, and the sense of touch helps them to achieve that. With increasing trust, a faculty grows for coping with the defense system that belongs to the sense of I.

The first defense of the child becomes visible in the contact with his or her mother, when the child—still an infant—smiles. The infant's smile is a token of trust *and* of distance. The degree to which the child, gradually and unconsciously, has learned to know its own physical body determines how much this child is ready for encounters that require the activity of the sense of I. This means that the other soul must be allowed to be within the child for a moment and that the child as a physical human being must pull back for that moment. This cannot last very long. No one can endure this for more than a few very short moments, without the risk of losing him- or herself. The perception of the I is a very quick perception—it happens in an instant.

Soul capacities

It is obvious that the sense of I has to do with meeting others. The capacity connected with this sense remains close to the sense itself. The ability to meet others indicates that the sense of I is functioning well. It is not relevant how the other being appears to us at the time of the meeting; the point is that we meet the essence of the other being. We can take the example of a near-death experience. Some people have described how they have encountered a light-filled figure. They cannot say much more about it, but it changes their lives to the very core.

The sense organ

How does the sense of I perceive its object? Let me describe it in the following way. The short moment that I fall asleep in the soul of the other person is an experience that I subsequently take back with me into my own soul. There I compare the soul of the other person to my bodily organization. The unconscious picture of my body, which the sense of touch has given me, is the sense organ for perceiving the individuality of the other. This happens when I meet the other being in person; it can also happen when I meet a piece of art created by him or her.

From what has been said, we may understand that the sense of I is closely connected with the sense of touch. The sense of touch provides me with a picture of the boundaries of my bodily organization. This process occurs within the safety and security of the first years of childhood. Without this, I cannot arrive at a proper picture of myself, and, consequently, my sense of I cannot reach an optimal functioning.

177

Summary

The four senses that are directed toward the spiritual enable us to perceive the way spiritual qualities manifest themselves directly on earth. On a physical level, this manifestation occurs with tone, on the etheric level with language, on the astral level with thoughts, and on the level of the I-organization, it occurs with other human beings. From this point of view, we can name these four senses: the senses of tone, language, thought, and I. The last three senses perceive more than the sense of tone does. From this wider perspective, we can also name these three: the senses of form, meaning, and style. It is a characteristic of all the four senses directed toward the spirit that they are designed to serve; I have used the word sacrifice to indicate this. The soul capacities that they help to develop are inspiration and the capacity for true encounter.

The interaction of the senses

So far we have looked at the senses separately. I have already paid some attention to their interaction, but I would like to focus more on their interrelations. When we take a walk, listen to a concert, or work in our profession, there is never a moment when one sense functions alone. In normal circumstances, the senses work together whenever we have sense perceptions. Therefore, to understand what happens in reality when we have a sense perception, we need to picture in our thoughts how the senses work together. Let me present an example of such a mental exercise.

What can we experience when we taste a cranberry? We experience the characteristic fruity, slightly sour flavor of the cranberry. Then we ask ourselves what the other eleven senses experience when they perceive this specific taste. What does the sense of touch experience when it perceives the taste of a cranberry? I would say: rather smooth and firm. The sense of life tells me that the taste of a cranberry is fresh and brisk. The sense of movement informs me that the cranberry taste makes a fast movement away from me. The sense of balance might say that this taste is vertical and perpendicular. The sense of smell: the smell of a morning in the spring. The sense of color: the color of the cranberry taste is not crimson—as is the berry—but rather yellow-green, as is the color of young leaves of spring flowers on a bright cold morning. The sense of temperature: rather cool. The sense of tone: a short and rather high-pitched tone. The sense of form: the timbre of a violin. The sense of thought: a modern composition, or polyphony of the early Middle Ages. The sense of style: not Brahms or Mahler; possibly Mozart or even Schönberg.

We could do the same experiment, for instance, with the smell of frankincense, the color of an emerald, and the sound of a choir of croaking frogs. We would then ask ourselves: what do the other eleven senses experience when they perceive this smell, this color, and this sound? When we do this in a group of people who are well acquainted with the twelve senses, we will notice that people have compatible experiences. We are not dealing here with fantasies, but we are experiencing the actual interrelationship among the senses. When we are conscious about this, it helps us to be exact when we perceive an object interactively in participatory observation. For artists, this is a must.

The sense-world manifests itself in three areas of activity: the field of touch, the field of vision, and the auditory field.

The sense of touch—one of the senses directed toward the body—gives the foundation for experiences in the field of touch. The sense of color—one of the senses directed toward the environment—gives the foundation for experiences in the field of vision. The sense of tone—one of the senses directed toward the spiritual—gives the foundation for experiences in the auditory field.

The field of vision. We can experience its existence when we press a finger against our eyeball from the side and notice that our vision becomes blurred. Our field of vision is determined by the sense of color, working together with the senses of movement and balance. Objects that appear in our field of vision are perceived as shape, form, concept, or style. The three highest senses (of form, meaning, and style) enable us to move beyond the perception of patches of color and see a table, a candleholder, a drawing, an original Rembrandt. The three highest senses integrate what we perceive in the field of vision.

The auditory field. If we are not deaf, our auditory field is always around us. We cannot close our ears as we close our eyes to extinguish our field of vision. The auditory field is determined by cooperation between the sense of tone and the four senses that are directed toward the body. Because of this, we can spatially orient ourselves by listening. The three highest senses help us to recognize what we hear, to understand the meaning of the sounds, and to integrate the auditory perceptions.

The field of touch. We are less conscious of this field than we are of the other two. Yet its existence is obvious when the sense perception is obstructed. When our arm, hand, or leg is "asleep," for instance, we cannot have experiences in the field of touch with this limb. In fever,

179

the experience of touch has changed, and we may experience ourselves bigger than we are. In the field of touch, the sense of touch cooperates with the other three senses directed toward the body and with the sense of temperature. The three highest senses have the task of integrating the experiences in this field.

In the field of vision, the created world manifests itself around us. In the auditory field, the created world unveils its spiritual qualities. In the field of touch, the created world becomes a physical reality that we can experience directly.

When children have problems with perceiving in one of the three regions of perception, it may sometimes be possible to let them have experiences in the areas where they have no problems. For instance, when a child has a problem with taste, the taste quality may be presented in the area of touch. The child may then experience that silk is different from wool and wool from cotton and may so develop a "taste" for such differences. Caregivers can influence what the three areas of perception have to offer the children and should try to find good material on which to have the children exercise their senses. Doing this, they will develop, train, and guide the cooperation among the senses as well.

Three of the twelve senses are connected with the physical level. The sense of touch acquaints us with the outside of our body; the sense of tone teaches us about the inside of physical substance; the sense of smell informs us about the degree to which death has entered into physical substance.

Three senses are connected with the etheric level. The sense of life informs us about the health of one's own body; the sense of form teaches us about the formative forces that have been active in matter; and the sense of taste lets us know whether or not we can digest our food properly.

Three senses are connected with the astral level. The sense of movement informs us about our inner and outer flexibility; the sense of meaning tells us about what moved the spiritual world in shaping things; and the sense of color teaches us about the innate qualities of the creative world.

The remaining three senses are connected with the level of the I-organization. The sense of balance gives the I-organization access to the physical world; the sense of I gives the other person access to me; and the sense of temperature creates a bridge between my own will and the world.

5 Helpers with Becoming Human

In this chapter, I will discuss some familiar and common capacities with which children are endowed. In the first part of the chapter, I will discuss walking, speaking, and thinking. In the second part, I will discuss in pairs the qualities of imitation and habits, imagination and reverence. All of these are general human capacities that make the child human; we may call them all-human capacities. They help the child become a citizen of the earth, a fellow human being, as well as a personality; they nurture the child's relationship to day-to-day reality, as well as the child's creative and religious potential. Once again, I will take up the two developmental directions described in the last part of the third chapter—the downward direction of the birth process, and the upward direction of the maturation process (chapter 3). These two aspects, which represent the past and the future respectively, will enable us to place the capacities we will discuss in a wider perspective.

Walking—speaking—thinking

How children conquer the ability to walk upright, how they take up speaking their mother tongue, and how their thinking lights up in them, is very individual. Those who have the opportunity to closely watch these processes unfold can learn much about the uniqueness of the individual child. Yet the development of these processes occurs in accordance with certain natural laws. The acquisition of motor skills, for instance, is dependent on a strict sequence in which each step must be taken, one after the other.

The aim of this chapter is to draw attention to the physiological and developmental processes that are available to all children so that they can find their own place on earth in this incarnation. For that purpose, I will first make some remarks on the two developmental directions. Then I will describe the actual steps in development that children have to take. There is an abundance of literature on early childhood development. I hope that this chapter can help you, the reader of this book, to orient yourself in the maze of facts, data, variations, and hypotheses you might encounter.

Direction of development

Children take hold of their physical instruments from above downward, following the direction of the birth process. In the third chapter I discussed how the birth of the ether body takes this direction. Children activate the faculties that are hidden in the instrument of their bodies by practicing and exercising.

However, the developmental steps of walking—speaking—thinking take the opposite direction, from below upward: first the limbs, then the respiration, and finally the head. As a matter of fact, it could not be otherwise.

Starting with the early chaotic movements, the young infant must continue to work on an intensive process of exercising the motor skills to arrive at upright posture and walking. Only when the child has succeeded in this to some extent can some movements—those in the region of the larynx—be refined to serve the development of speech. And only after the child has sufficiently practiced and exercised speaking a language—both understanding the thoughts as well as naming the objects—can speaking be held back and refined to allow thinking in the upper pole.

The process of motor development brings order in the uncontrolled sounds of the infant. When the sounds can be controlled, the child can practice the mother tongue by imitating. The development of speech into a means of communication structures the brain's vital forces and transforms the brain into an organ of thinking.

Nature does not give us ready-made capacities of walking, speaking, and thinking, as it gives us teeth, for instance. Teeth will erupt whether we want them to or not and whether we are active in the process or not. To be able to walk, to speak, or to think, we need the will to do it, and then we need to actually do it; otherwise thinking, for instance, would lie dormant. At birth, nature has given us the movement system, the speech organs, and the brain. When these organs are correctly formed, it depends on the child whether he or she elicits walking, speaking, and thinking from them. Along with the movement system, nature has given us a multitude of reflexes and involuntary movements; these have to be conquered and subdued. Along with the speech organs, nature has given us tones, volume, and sound patterns; these have to be put in the service of speaking. Along with the brain, nature has given us imprints of cosmic wisdom; these need to be read.[10]

Origin

By learning to walk, speak, and think, children not only start to make use of the three regions of their body, but they also prepare these regions for the soul functions of willing, feeling, and thinking later. To be more precise—children cultivate the three regions of their body in such a way that their I can find its way in them later. *Its* way means: finding the I's specific destiny, meeting the people with whom this person is karmically connected, finding access to those themes in contemporary civilization with which, before birth, the I decided to occupy itself with.

What kind of primordial human capacities are these? Why are walking, speaking, and thinking all-human as well as individual capacities?

First I will discuss the all-human aspect. Doing this, I need to mention the angels. We can only attain a true picture of the developmental steps during the first three years of childhood—walking, speaking, and thinking—when we take the role of angels into account. Angels are spiritual beings who are further developed than human beings. They are the lowest rank of the spiritual hierarchies, and they are closest to the human being. Every human being has his or her angel as a companion, who keeps an eye on his or her personal destiny. Groups of human beings, such as nations, are connected with higher spiritual beings known as archangels. The Bible mentions the names of Michael, Gabriel, and Raphael; there are many more. Humanity as a whole is connected with still higher spiritual beings, the spirits of personality or archai.

Taking the direction opposite to the actual developmental sequence, I will start with thinking. Our thoughts are the most personal thing we have. We are alone, even lonely, in our thoughts. Yet in our thoughts, our angel is with us. Our angels communicate with us especially through thoughts, and so we can turn to our angels through thinking.

Speaking a language makes us members of a human community. There is not much sense in speaking with oneself; one might as well just think the thoughts. We feel related to and connected with the human beings with whom we share a language. I may even feel ashamed when people who speak my language misbehave in a foreign country, or I may be proud when they accomplish something of value abroad. The genius of the language determines the national character. This genius is an archangel, who is connected not only to me but to the group into which I was born.

The upright posture and walk is the most general characteristic trait of all humans. The body of the human being is especially designed for it. Whatever the differences are among people in build, color, language, customs, or patterns of thought, we can recognize fellow human beings by their upright gait, and we may speak to their feelings of respect, compassion, and generosity. We would not expect these qualities from a cat or a chimpanzee. Human beings have received these all-human moral qualities as a gift from the archai. Humanity has not always used the gift of morality in the same way, but has specialized in one or another aspect of it through the ages. This time aspect belongs also to the domain of the archai.

In moving from thinking to speaking to walking, we have followed a path from the personal to the universal, from our angels to the archai. However, we can also describe the same direction, moving from thinking to speaking to walking, as a path from the universal to the personal. We will do this not for a thought-game, but in order to observe a different reality.

As there is only one mathematical reality all over the world, so there is also only one world of ideas, which is accessible to all people. On the level of thinking, an Italian Roman Catholic can communicate with a Tibetan Buddhist. However, what from the general world of ideas we take up and how we take it up restricts the thinking, so that the thinking becomes culturally and personally determined. The world of thoughts itself is most universal; my own world of thoughts is most personal.

Although speaking is an all-human capacity, speaking a certain language restricts the universality of the world of thoughts. In any language, it is hardly possible to find the exact words for all possible thoughts. Translating thoughts from one language into another is difficult, and translations will most likely have different nuances from the original.

My standpoint is most personal. Where I am standing, no one else can stand. I choose my own path. The human capacity to stand and walk leads to the situation where each human being has his or her specific place on earth, which cannot be shared with anyone else.

From this point of view, the moving from thinking to speaking to walking is a path from the all-human to the personal. Just before taking this last point of view, we described the same direction—going from thinking to speaking to walking—as a path from the personal to the all-human. How do these two opposites relate?

The direction from the personal to the all-human applies to humanity, to all human beings. The direction from the all-human to the personal applies to the single human being, to a person. In their first developmental step, children take control of the all-human capacity of standing upright and walking. The archai watch this with interest, I would think. In taking their second developmental step, children learn to speak. The all-human narrows down to being part of a group. Yet this also makes children more social as they relate to the group of people who are connected to the same archangel. In taking their third developmental step, children become individuals by taking on first the thinking patterns of their family, and then developing their own thinking. Guided by their angels, they can still gain access to the universal world of ideas.

This development, moving from walking to speaking to thinking, makes children citizens of the earth and puts them on their own feet, keeping them connected to the universal at the same time. Archai, archangels, and angels guide this development. These beings act on behalf of the central Being of the earth and of humanity—the Christ. It is important to recognize that, in their first three years, children learn to walk, to speak, and to think under the guidance of the Christ. The development of these capacities in the child is the working of the Christ. The caregivers of the child cooperate in this process in His name, albeit largely unconsciously. When all goes well, this development will provide the children with the foundation for morality in walking their path, for truth in their speaking, and for life in their thinking (see figure 47).

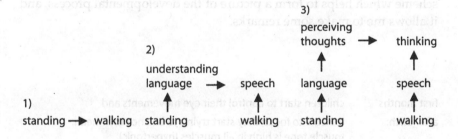

Fig. 47 Firstly, children learn to stand still, in order that they can start to walk. Secondly, children learn to listen, and by doing this, their sense of language develops; through this, they can start to speak, which is a refined movement. Thirdly, thoughts start to arise; the individual thinking develops from an inner speaking.

The development from learning to walk to learning to speak to learning to think is a process of maturation. When children have examples to imitate, this process occurs spontaneously. Then, children take control of these capacities and make them their own. Practicing this, they go to find their unique place on the earth and in the cosmos. This is a process of emancipation.

I will now discuss the development of each of the three capacities—walking, speaking, and thinking.

Learning to walk — lifting oneself up, standing upright, and moving forward

Once children have learned to walk, it is hard to imagine that just a year earlier they were lying on their back and moving their legs helplessly. They have gone through an extensive learning process during that time and have taken steps in a rather strict sequence.

Steps in motor development

I will start with presenting an overview of the development of children's movements between birth and seven years of age. It is a generalized scheme which helps to form a picture of the developmental process, and it allows me to make some remarks.

first months after birth:	children start to control their eye movements and are able to focus; they start trying to balance their head; muscle tone is high in all muscles (hypertonic)
10 weeks:	children discover their own hands
16 weeks:	children can direct their grabbing; their eyes follow their hands
20 weeks:	children can keep their head in balance by controlling their neck muscles
26 weeks:	children discover their own feet, are able to roll over, and can sit straight up in a chair
28 weeks:	children can transfer objects from one hand to the other
32 weeks:	children can sit with their legs supported and try to grab objects out of their reach

36 weeks:	children move forward like a creeping tiger and can pull themselves up with the help of the edge of the bed or playpen
40 weeks:	children can sit without leg support, start to crawl on hands and knees, follow their movements with their eyes when grabbing at something, and stand up from a sitting or crawling position
52 weeks:	children can bring thumb and index finger together and walk like a bear
after one year:	children take their first steps, walk with legs far apart and with a fixed pelvis; the legs seem to dangle; they breathe in when walking and breathe out when standing still; they walk from their hips
15 months:	walking is initiated from the upper legs; movements are not articulated at the joints and muscles are relatively hypotonic
18 months:	walking is from the knees; legs are still rather far apart
2 years:	walking is from the ankles; the feet do not yet curve from heel to toes when touching the floor, which makes for a sauntering gait; the children can walk fast with relaxed continuous breathing while walking; when they climb stairs, the free foot is placed next to the foot that has taken a step
3 years:	the posture is upright; legs and feet are facing forward; when children stand still, their feet are flat and the ball of the foot is wide; however, the feet have an arch when children are walking; children can stand on one leg and pull the other leg up from the hip; they can jump down from a step; the movements are no longer unarticulated and look more graceful; the muscle tone moves from one group of muscles to another; when children learn a new movement this movement becomes unarticulated again; children can climb stairs using the free foot to take the next step
4 years:	the feet are also arched when the child is standing still; when walking, the children make light, loose, and graceful movements "of a smooth and ingenuous fluency, naive and uninhibited, that cannot be imitated by adults" (Buytendijk); children can jump like frogs
5 years:	children can hop on one leg, which, however, still gives the impression of heaviness
6 years:	children can hop in a light and supple way using both legs; can walk normally without a dancing quality; can jump rope and twist without falling over; they can quickly change direction when running; they no longer move limbs that are not involved in the intended activity to the degree they did before; they can perceive objects while walking or running

Fig. 48 Steps in motor development.

Children go through the developmental direction from above downward a few times. In the first year, the movement control descends from the head to the feet—then the child can walk. Till about the age of four, the movements increase in fluidity. The child makes the movements with pleasure and with ease. After that, until the age of seven, children learn to maintain this fluidity also when they consciously give direction to the movements. The movements of the seven-year-old child do not become clumsy when the child consciously pays attention to the movements.

Figure 48 did not list everything the child has to unlearn. All kinds of innate reflexes and movement patterns, such as the sucking reflex, search reflex, postural reactions, walk-, stand-, and crawl-movements, and the grab reflex are covered over by the acquired coordinated movements. In abnormal situations, the innate reflexes may appear again. Postural reactions may come to the fore again in specific normal situations, as when children fall over and catch themselves with their hands.

Muscle tone also goes through a development. The infant, when awake, is hypertonic. The toddler is rather hypotonic. The preschooler alternates flexing and relaxing of the muscles. This third phase is the proper time for practicing rhythmical movements. These are preceded by crawling, which is typically a movement that exercises alternating muscle tone. Scratching also exercises alternating muscle tone; it is an innate movement and has the character of a reflex.

Two developmental processes occur simultaneously—the process of coming to the upright position, and the process of moving forward. The process of *coming to the upright position* is composed of the phases of lying on the abdomen, sitting, and standing. The direction of development is from below upward. The process of *moving forward* starts with looking, pointing, grabbing; next comes creeping like a tiger, rolling, and crawling; it culminates in taking steps. The direction of development is from above downward. Learning to move forward, the child has to practice rhythmically alternating movements with perseverance. This even happens while the child is still lying on the back and making cycling movements with the legs, and also when the child is just able to stand and holds on to the chair, and then makes those well-known up and down movements.

The small child is either perceiving, when at rest, or moving actively. Breathing follows this alternation. Children who have just learned to walk take steps on a fixed inhalation; when they exhale they take a pause from moving forward. During this pause, they can look around to see where they want to go next. Only at about the age of three does walking become so familiar that the child can look around and talk while moving.

Each child has his or her specific way of coming to the upright position. Some children lie quietly on their back for a long time before they pull themselves up and stand. Other children cannot wait to pull themselves up and try this even before they can keep their balance. There are children who are active when they are still lying on their belly, they creep forward like a tiger, do not crawl, and stand up early. There are children who move forward on their knees for a long time. There are also children who crawl for a long time, become very adept in doing it, and postpone the wearisome walking.

The graceful dancing gait of the three- or four-year-old child is not the result of consciously controlled movements. To the contrary, when children of this age are asked to do something consciously, we might notice that the movements become clumsy and awkward. The Dutch scholar Buytendijk (in *Algemene theorie der menselijke houding en beweging*) has described the spontaneous movements of these children in the following lyrical way:

It is simultaneously a spontaneous moving and a being moved;
the child is dependent on the moving force of the situation.
Youthful dynamics are like a piece of music that is improvised
and that is filled with feelings, yet also dissonant and without
a continuity that connects the past to the future.[11]

Until they are ready for elementary school, children unconsciously move muscles that do not need to be activated for the specific activity they are engaged in—parallel movements. Muscles that are not in use and not fixed imitate the voluntary muscle movements. Especially the facial muscles are used this way, and we may notice this parallelism even in adults. The process of maturation causes the gradual disappearance of movement parallelism; it is accompanied by a decrease in the distribution of stimuli in the nervous system. This is a process of active inhibition, which does not work as well when we are tired or when we have expended a lot of energy. An insufficient decrease of movement parallelism is a type of developmental retardation. Some types of hyperactivity show this phenomenon.

Physiology of movement

In this section I will focus on the role that the four members of the human body play in movement. I will ask some questions and then try to answer them.

The first question is—who is moving? The commonly given answer is—the muscles move. The next question is—what roles do the muscles and the nerves play in movement? The usual answer is—the muscles move and the nerves send the movement impulse to the correct place. The third question is—who or what makes us move; why do we move? The standard answer is—because we want to. We will look at these questions more in depth and will have to modify the above answers considerably.

The first question: Who is moving?

In the previous section of this chapter, we discussed the process by which children attain direction in their movements. The result of this process is a hopping preschooler who does not have to put much effort into hopping and moves freely. Of the four members of the human body, it can only be the I that moves the child. The physical body is being moved; by itself it is heavy. The physical body is lifted up to levity. This is done by the activities of the ether body and the astral body, as we will see later. Children enjoy moving, therefore their souls and also their astral bodies are actively involved in the process.

It is the child him- or herself who is moving. The entire movement organization is in service of the I which activates and directs the I-organization. In young children, the I is to a large extent outside the body, and thus children start to gain control of their movements from outside. To bring the child's body into movement, the I of the child finds many objects that are attractive, desirable, and lovely to the child's soul—parents; other children; the dog and the cat; things to eat, to touch, to carry around, or to make noise with. When children become older, the I offers stimuli from within in addition to those from without. Now the desire for pancakes or ice cream comes not only when the objects are perceived, but the child can create a picture of these goodies. Memory and the capacity to make mental images are required for this. In a still later phase, the outer world can present impulses to move by appealing to the child's soul, such as a piteous animal that needs to be taken care of. Throughout life, new motives can arise that call us to movement and action. It is always the I that takes the initiative to move. It can do this more or less consciously and more or less independently of external events.

The second question: What roles do muscles and nerves play in movement?

What is the role of the muscles?

The I moves the body, but the I can only move a physical body that has no weight. The I wants to be connected to its physical body, and it calls in the help of the muscles to lift the body out of gravity. A good movement is weightless; we do not carry our pounds with us throughout the day. The main task of the muscles is to keep the body in balance and under all circumstances away from gravity, so that we do not fall over. The developmental process of the young child indicates the moment when the child's muscles can do this; at about the age of four, children have attained a graceful, free, and dancing gait. The muscles are now in the service of the ether body. It is the task of the ether body to conquer gravity and support levity. The physical body is subject to gravity—the ether body lifts the physical body out of it. Movements can be supple and fluid when the ether body is working in the muscles, which is when the muscles are organs of the ether body. We notice the importance of this phenomenon when we are tired; then the muscles can no longer keep our body out of the reach of gravity, and we start to feel the pounds we are carrying with us.

The muscles have another important function—to inhibit movement. In the young infant we can still observe that the fountain of the movement-will pole is full of dynamic vitality and unrestricted movement. Before birth and conception, this is even stronger—the spiritual world does not know rest, and is always in movement. These dynamics have to come to rest within the physical world. At least almost all of them. Only a few movements may remain—the movements that fit the moment. From this point of view, the muscles help the I to attain the stillness and quietness that is necessary for thoughtful perception.

The muscles have yet a third function—they imitate the movements in the outer world. When we see a four-year-old child dance, we move with this child inwardly, but we do not act it out. When our eyes follow the contours of an object, our muscles make those movements, but we do not act correspondingly. We imitate all movements inwardly; by inhibiting the corresponding outward activity of the muscles, we are able to perceive the nature and the form of these movements. A well-trained muscular system is the sounding board for the perception of movement in the world around us. I mentioned this already when describing the sense of movement in the fourth chapter.

What is the role of the nerves?

The I moves the physical body with the help of the muscles. In order to do this, the I needs all possible information about the facts and situations inside and outside the body. The information about the outer world is provided by the senses. The senses directed toward one's own body provide information about that body—the nearest part of the outer world. The sense of movement informs the soul about the position of the limbs and about the form of the movements the limbs are making. We are still missing information from the inner world about the essence of the deed: do the movements of our action correspond to our intentions, and how do the effects of our action relate to our ideals? The soul receives the information needed to answer these types of questions, related to the inner world of the human body, by way of the so-called motor nerves. Nerve tissue is never an acting agent; it is always only a throughway. Nerves do nothing; they serve perception. In this case, they serve the perception of our own movements with respect to their form (the sense of movement) and their content (nerves connected to the muscles). The astral body, as an instrument of the soul, uses the senses and the nerves to provide the I with the information the I needs in relation to the movement situation.

If not the nerves, is the brain then the initiator of movement? Literature on biology and physiology might present that picture. Previously we came to the conclusion that it is the I that is the initiator of human actions. If this is so, what role does the brain have? It is obvious that the brain is very important for making proper movements. Movement patterns are disturbed when the brain does not work properly because of a trauma or, for instance, use of alcohol or drugs. In the third chapter, I gave the picture of the brain as an organ of mirroring. This holds true also for the mirroring of movements. All pictures delivered by the outer world and by the inner world via the nervous system are received by the brain and fixed into pictures that can be perceived by the soul. Only if one's mirror is perfect can one's movement be perfect.

So far we have looked at the role of the four members of the human body with regard to movement. We came to the conclusion that the physical body is brought to movement, that the ether body makes the physical body weightless with the help of the muscles, that the astral body serves the perception of movement with the help of the muscles and the nerves, and that the I is the initiator of the movements with the help of the I-organization.

The third question: Why do we move?

What makes the I want to move the body? Let us see where we come to by comparing human movements with the movements of minerals, plants, and animals.

When a rock falls down, or dust moves up into the air, there is always a cause in the immediate past. Water has loosened the rock from its base, or the wind came around the corner and took the dust along.

With plants, it is different. Growth movements of plants are related to air, warmth, light, and humid soil. The plant itself in momentary cooperation with its environment "causes" the growth movements.

Movement of animals comes more from within, but is always related to their environment. The squirrel jumps from branch to branch high up in the tree; the mole creeps under the ground in search of food. Why? What makes animals move? Animals are not aware of past or future; they follow their instincts here and now. There is no choice, no doubt, no regret, no intent.

Movements of human beings occur on a different level. When I fall out of a tree, my physical body is like the rock. When the child has grown five inches, the body is like the plant. When the toddler crawls very fast toward what his or her eyes have noticed, this is like the instinctive behavior of an animal. However, all activities that are truly human are not predetermined. They are not only a response to a situation in the outer world. Human activity starts in the future. The human being can have an intent, a plan to move. The physical body follows this intent as well as it is able to. In answering the two previous questions we have seen how the body does this. In this respect, human movements are different from all other movements. That is why animals can move much better than humans. They also have a movement plan; this, however, is placed in their bodies at an early age and is no longer subject to change. The human being is rather clumsy compared to animals. Yet the human being has the capacity and the responsibility to move in such a way that he or she shows and develops morality and respect.

It is obvious that not all human activities are coming out of the future. We have plenty of habits and automatism that become movements. It might even be true that most of our movements belong to this category. Nevertheless, each human being on a day-to-day basis has the choice to opt for the familiar routine or for doing things differently, for nonchalance or for precision, for automatism or for conscious presence of mind. It is up to the human being whether and where to find a source of inspiration for his or her movements.

Learning to speak — understanding language, and the capacity to speak

The development of the capacity to speak is closely connected with the development of the understanding of language. The capacity to speak requires control of the muscles that are used when we speak. The progress children make in controlling the muscles of their speech organs goes parallel with the possibility to use the exhaled air as a vehicle for speech. Sign language works similarly; in sign language too the controlled muscle movements serve the expression of meaning.[12] The gestures with which some people accompany their speaking have the same origin as the language itself.[13] In the history of humanity, meaningful expressive movements preceded spoken language. The same still holds true for the young child. By learning to control the unrestrained movement of screaming, children learn to form sounds in the exhaled air. At the same time, the other movements are also calming down, so that the child can experience the stillness and quiet that is necessary for listening. The next step is a further refinement of specific movements so that tongue and lips become available for articulation.

I will discuss the steps in speech development, the physiology of speech, and the threefold nature of the speech organism. I will conclude with some remarks about the origin of language.

Steps in speech development

As with the steps in motor development, I will start by presenting a diagram that gives a brief overview of the steps in speech development.

from birth:	screaming and crying
1 month:	evolving social process; the child responds to being spoken to, for example, with a cooing sound
2 months:	differentiating sounds; babbling is independent of what the child is hearing
3 or 4 months:	imitating sounds and practicing them
5 months:	more or less conscious cooperation between hearing and uttering sounds
6 or 7 months:	imitating in a whisper what is heard (sounds) and seen (lip reading)
11 months:	understanding a few words and making corresponding gestures
from 1 year:	practicing imitation and speaking
from 1 1/2 years:	naming objects and pictures; the first phase of asking questions
from 2 years:	beginning to make sentences; understanding simple instructions
from 3 years:	answering simple questions; the second phase of asking questions

Fig. 49 Steps in speech development.

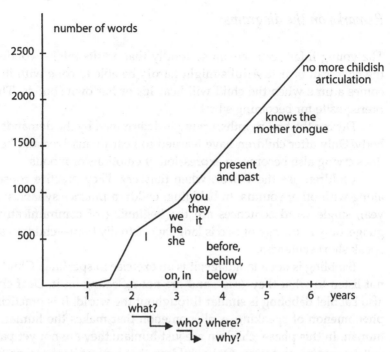

Fig. 50 This diagram indicates the number of words children know during the first six years; it is an average, of course. It also indicates some accomplishments in learning grammar.

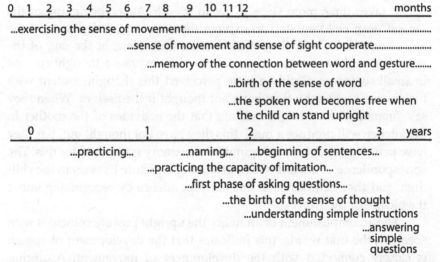

Fig. 51 Phases of speech development out of the thinking, and of the sense of thought out of speaking.

Remarks on the diagrams:

The young infant can scream so loudly that adults might wonder how the child can bear it. Adults might hardly be able to cope with it. There comes a time when the child will hear his or her own sounds. This is a prerequisite for becoming silent.

During the first months, crying is determined by the demands of the body. Only after children have learned to hear themselves and be silent does crying also become an expression of emotions or moods.

Children use the vowels when they cry. They practice consonants along with other sounds. In babbling, children practice syllables; at one year, single word sentences are the beginning of communicative language; only at the age of two is language actually born—children start to speak short sentences.

Babbling is not a language; it is an exercise in speaking. Children do not listen to what they "say" and are not reflecting on it. Deaf children also babble! Babbling is similar throughout the world. It is practicing the phenomenon of speaking, a phenomenon that makes the human being human. In this phase, children are just human; they are not yet part of a culture, group, or nation. Only children that are not deaf can go further and take the next step.[14] They become part of a community because some sounds from the world of sounds around them start to have a meaning for them. In this phase, a word carries for them an extended and encompassing meaning.

It takes three more steps to get to speech. At the beginning of the second year, children start to express themselves verbally; around the age of one and a half, they start to point and name; at the end of the second year, they start to communicate—they express a thought content in small sentences. Children have perceived this thought content with their sense of thought; they have not thought it themselves. When they say "mamma," they might indicate that the activities of the mother in the kitchen will produce a meal; this they have not thought out, but they have perceived it. Yet some beginning of memory is required for this. The correspondence of a word with a gesture or a picture lives on in the children, and they can call back this correspondence by recognizing either the picture or the word.

The accomplishment of attaining the upright posture coincides with speaking the first words; this indicates that the development of speech is closely connected with the development of movement. Acquiring an individual standpoint and expressing oneself in language belong together in time.

Between the ages of one and one-and-a-half, children practice only a few words; they exercise speaking, rather than language. After the age of one-and-a-half, new words come in large quantities. The acquisition of new words might continue throughout life, but this exuberance is never repeated.

The ages I have indicated are approximate and average. Each child has his or her own pace in taking the required steps.

Prerequisites for speaking

There are two kinds of prerequisites for speech to develop and function; one has to do with the child, the other with the environment.

Prerequisites that have to do with the child. There is no speaking when there is no *speech organism* within the child. This has a threefold nature—the speech movements, the breathing, and the meaning of the language.

Speech movements are part of the entire human movement organization. In young children, the development of the entire movement system goes parallel with the development of the speech movements. Children who suffer from a disturbance in their motor development will also face a speech problem.[15] To speak without hindrances, the human body—except for the speech organs—needs to be still and silent; the body needs at least to have the potential to be at rest. The one-and-a-half-year-old child cannot walk and speak at the same time. This capacity comes later. Since it is closely connected to speech, the entire movement organization is the sounding board for the speech movements.

Children must be able to direct their breath. We speak on our exhaling. All air processes in the body lead to exhaling. In normal breathing, the exhaling exclusively serves the physiological processes of the exchange of gasses, the life processes. The "living air" that the human body has collected is exhaled and given to the outer world, to nature. When we speak, something new occurs. The exhaling receives an additional function—the exhaled air becomes a substance to which the speaking gives movement, sound, and meaning. Exhaling now serves a creative process—the human being expresses him- or herself.

The meaning of the spoken words is the third aspect of the speech organism. When we have nothing to say, we keep our mouth shut. For speaking, we need perception, interest, and purpose. When I am too tired, my head feels empty. When there has been too much talking in a meeting, the words do not want to come anymore. Children can arrive at the meaning of the spoken word when they are perceptive and stand in the world with interest and with an active memory. It may seem as if this happens without effort. Caregivers should pay attention to the quality of the child's perceptions, the direction of the child's interests, and (as we will see later) the degree to which memories are restrictive for the child.

Prerequisites in the environment of the child. Speech cannot develop without an active *language organism* around the child. This also has a threefold nature—the spoken language of the caregivers, language as a connecting agent between people, and the genius of the language.

Children need to be surrounded by human language. They need an example to imitate. On this first level, children are shown which of the wide range of sounds are important for them. Some consonants, as we all know, are pronounced differently in different languages and dialects. The language as an instrument is offered to the child to imitate.

Language only makes sense when there are people who speak it. Then language can be a connecting agent between people with different degrees of education or development and with different views on various issues. When someone does not understand your language, coaxing words or insults miss their mark. The more the children become at home in the language, the more they experience the way the gap can be bridged between them and the world, and between other human beings. The social element of the language becomes part of children's security framework within which they can feel at home. It gives a familiar feeling that I do not experience when, for example, a bus driver in Indonesia announces something and everyone rushes to get off the bus.

From the world of art, we know that there is an artist behind every piece of art, a creator behind every creation. It is the same with language. Behind a living language is the presence of the genius of that language (archangel). The young child meets this genius. Children meet the genius of the language indirectly through other people speaking; they meet the genius directly before birth and every night when they are asleep and are given the ability to work with the language. Meeting the genius of the language as the inspirer and guardian of a distinct social group of people is as important to the children as meeting the archai. Before birth and during sleep, the archai teach children to develop morality in their actions; the archangels teach them to connect with people through the language.

Physiology of speaking

Learning to speak is an artistic process. An artist depicts something from another world; children make a picture of reality in their speaking. Language gives each child an instrument with which to make his or her appearance in the reality of the human world. This is similar to the artist's situation. It might seem that language comes to children without any effort on their part; this is not the case—children have to work hard for it, but they do it with pleasure.

Most adults cannot learn a new language with the ease and creativity with which toddlers learn to speak. Adults struggle with the instrumental aspect of language—grammar, meaning, and exceptions. Usually it takes years before adults are as much at ease with a foreign language as they are with their mother tongue. If they succeed in this, they have become part of another language community. Language is an instrument that the genius of the language can make use of.

I will describe the physiology of the instrument of speech. I choose a threefold approach for this rather than the fourfold approach I used in discussing movement development. In each verbal expression we can distinguish *force, sound,* and *meaning.*

Some people talk in such a soft voice that you can hardly hear them when it is noisy; others speak so loudly that you can hear their opinion through closed doors. This has to do with the strength of the voice that is determined by the force of the exhaling, in which the diaphragm plays an important role.

The second aspect—the sound or the melody—indicates the feeling that accompanies the words. For instance, when the child calls "maaam" in a particular way, the pitch somewhat higher than usual, and with somewhat more modulation than usual, the mother will know that the child is coming to ask a favor. This aspect has to do with pitch, modulation, and rhythm. In particular, the vowels can be used for this aspect.

The third aspect—the meaning—is expressed through articulation. To form the consonants, throat, tongue, teeth, and lips have to work together. We can emphasize this aspect when we speak emphatically. When we whisper, we abstain from using force and sound, and concentrate on meaning. It is really difficult to convey an emotional message through whispering!

When young children learn to speak, they take the steps—force, sound, and meaning—in sequence. This development is directed from below upward, which is the direction of maturation. This is a small-scale version of the big steps of walking, speaking, and thinking.

Understanding language is also a three-step process. I discussed this in the chapter on the senses. We perceive the voice elements—the sounds, which are the basis for speech—with our sense of hearing. The sound is short or long, high or low, and loud or soft. We perceive the building stones of the language—vowels, consonants, syllables, words, and sentences—with our sense of word. We perceive the meaning of what is spoken with our sense of thought. For the sense of thought, it is irrelevant which language is used.

Summary

Newborn babies produce sound without restriction. After they have learned to hear themselves, they will be able to coo contently. Then they can become inwardly so quiet that there is space to perceive the language. This leads to babbling—the spontaneous practice of all kinds of sounds. After that, children will begin to imitate the sounds of their mother tongue. Around the first birthday, the first words with a meaning are "born." After about half a year of practice in expressing themselves, the children begin to name objects. The young child conquers the world very quickly by naming the things, as Adam did. Real language is born only at about the age of two—then the speaking also attains a social function. Numerous personal inventions and trials help children to become at home in the world of concepts. This creative phase ends when the child is five years old or thereabout. At that age children make it a point to speak the same way as the older children and adults around them. They still speak with a characteristic childish tone of voice and this then disappears when they are seven years old. Only at the age of seven will children develop their own language, say what they want to say, and keep to themselves what they do not want to say. Word games carefully make their appearance, which is a playing with language that would be blasphemy to the very young child. During the first seven years, language helps the child greatly to incarnate and therefore it should be taken seriously.

Speech development assists children to work through their entire threefold bodily organization in seven years and to shape it. By learning to control exhalation, the children exercise the force and the dynamics of the lower pole. By learning to manipulate the sound or melody of their voice, they learn to express a broad range of feelings from the middle region. This confronts them with the social effects of their words. By learning to carefully articulate and by trying to make clear what exactly they want to say, they learn to create clarity in the upper pole.

Closing remark

Is it correct for us to take the child's physical birth as the starting point for discussing the development of speech and language? In a way it is not. Creation started with "the word," the Logos; this is also true for the creation of each new human being. During the embryonic stage, and also before, the human being is spoken. Creative powers are speaking the human form. In this situation, language does not have the function of sounding, but of condensing. The human being is created as God's image, because divine spiritual powers expressed themselves to condense some of their own spirituality into the form that is the human being. For some time after birth, spiritual powers continue to speak, working directly on the human being. This decreases as the child's capacity to speak develops. Then the children themselves start to practice the process of creation through language, on a human level. Shaping the exhaled air, they speak, and with it they express themselves, their environment, and their thoughts. To the degree that speaking can put itself at the service of thinking, children become independent creators themselves rather than imitators in the process of creation.

Learning to think — imitating, making mental pictures, and thinking

The development of thinking is an obscure process; there is literature on child development that does not even mention it. This is understandable. The steps in movement development are obvious for anybody; the development of speech is more elusive. We all can hear the sounds children make, but it needs expertise to assess what is occurring. Parents very often remember the occasion when their child took the first steps; they often do not remember when their child first used verbs. The beginning of thinking is even more obscure. Thinking mostly dresses itself in the cloak of language. This, however, can be a source of error. When children speak a sentence with meaning, this does not necessarily indicate that they have thought it out of themselves; it might be just imitation. When children give the impression of intelligence, it does not mean that we are meeting the intelligence of these children. In addition, we sometimes can conclude that children indeed have taken a step in thinking, not only by listening to what they say, but also by observing what they do, and sometimes by what they don't do. Let me give an example. Two-and-a-half-year-old Johnny always starts to scream when his older brother takes one of his toys. The parents are always dismayed and often threaten him with punishment. One day the parents announce that the family will go to the zoo and then eat ice cream in the afternoon. Before midday the older brother "borrows" one of Johnny's toys without asking—Johnny does not scream!

This example demonstrates that there are various conditions that have to be fulfilled before Johnny could accomplish the step in thinking he has taken. Johnny needs to have acquired the capacity to remember previous situations and also to be aware of the time-concept "this afternoon." With these abilities, he could understand the possible consequences of his throwing a tantrum, and he could choose to keep quiet.

I will now discuss the steps in cognitive development, the prerequisites of cognitive development, and the physiology of thinking.

Steps in cognitive development

The age from two to four. At this age, children spontaneously begin to think of naming things, animals, and people. The child might ask where the papa of the kittens is. When children have only seen milk in a carton or beans on the shelves of the grocery store, they might conclude that milk is made in cartons and that beans grow in the store. This then indicates that these children have been thinking, because they are not imitating what adults were thinking or saying, nor are they expressing what they had been taught. The first step in the development of thinking is the naming phase.

The age from three to five. This is the phase of comparing, weighing, and reflecting. "If the weather is nice tonight, we might barbecue." "When I have my birthday, I will go to school." "Which locomotive do you like? I like this one, because the headlights turn on when it goes." The child might pour forth judgments; these judgments are based on actual situations surrounding the child. Direct life experiences provide material to compare, and children try to relate these experiences to themselves in thought. They discover that, indeed, thoughts can build a bridge between themselves and the world; this experience makes children sigh with relief. The exercise of building this bridge is the real fun; the actual content of the spoken words is less significant. This is an important phase, which precedes the later one in which it becomes essential to have a correct judgment about situations. For young children their only point of reference is themselves. We should be grateful when in this phase children seriously consider themselves the center of the world. Children gain self-confidence through this attitude; the content of the thoughts they express is not important.

The age of four to six. In the previous phase the thoughts were there to play with; in this phase, the child starts to take them seriously. Children begin to experience reality in their own thoughts. The thoughts become as real as their feet, abdomen, bellyache, joy, and sadness. "I told you so," the little girl tells her mother indignantly after a pile of books fell over. Her mother had not heeded her when she had said that the pile did not look stable. In this phase, children can experience severe pain of soul if something happens to someone they had wished dead. They think that their thoughts have caused the accident or illness. They experience the magical power of thoughts—if I like you, you *are* a nice person; if I expect to get an apple, I *am* entitled to it. This magical power may easily exceed what we consider normal. The child thinks of Aunt Penny, and that afternoon Aunt Penny unexpectedly stops by. The girl thinks that she is not allowed to play with her little brother, and thus she has to pinch him. "Why did you do that?"—"I don't know; I had to do it." In this phase, the magical power of thoughts is far ahead of the accomplishments of the children to express themselves verbally. The children think much more than they can say; the thinking does run the risk of going its own way and leaving the children behind. There is not yet enough reality-testing to handle this runaway thinking. Allow me to express it this way—in this phase of childhood, reality is much less factual and bare than later on. The yet unborn ether body does not allow the separation of the inner and the outer world. Thinking is experiencing. "Something is thinking in the child"; the child receives it and thinks it as his or her reality. In the section on the physiology of thinking, I will pay attention to what this "something" is that is thinking in the child.

The three phases in the development of thinking, which I discussed just now, precede the more mature thinking that becomes possible at the age of six or seven. This, then, becomes a thinking that maintains its character of reality independent of the child's experiences. The thinking that is needed for math or grammar has, at that time, nothing to do with the reality that the child is experiencing. These thought movements are needed to bring flexibility and suppleness to the newborn thinking. When caregivers call in the help of this more mature thinking before the children have reached the age of six or seven years, they are not heeding the natural steps of the development of thinking.

Prerequisites for cognitive development

In the beginning of this chapter, I indicated that thinking develops from speaking and speaking from movement. Because children learn to know their mother tongue, they also learn to perceive thoughts. Children learn to perceive language because they have learned to stand upright and be quiet inwardly. Children practice their thinking by speaking the thoughts of others, over and over again.

As the child practices and exercises speaking, the mother tongue becomes the language of the child and an obedient instrument for the thinking. Language has to develop within the child, and soon after that, it has to make itself available for something new—the perception of thoughts and thinking.

The development of thinking requires stillness. Speaking develops from the control of movements. Moving has to be brought to a complete rest for thinking to be there. Movement and activity, as well as the dynamic vitality of the body, hinder thinking. Thinking expands *itself*. Other body functions hinder this expansion. A well-known example of this is the headache, in which metabolic activity within the head obstructs the thinking. In the brain, rest and minimal vitality is the normal condition. The brain must have matured to a certain extent before it can serve as an organ that supports thinking.

If each moment were new, if nothing from previous impressions and mental pictures remained, if there were no background of experiences—in short, without memory—no thought of our own could arise. The development of thinking is closely connected with the development of memory. As long as the memory of children is dependent on the place where they are, the children can only have thoughts about the situations they are in. Only when children have free access to their memory content can they also use their thinking power freely. This is the situation when children are ready for elementary school.[16]

It is a decisive step when children go from "re-thinking" to "pre-thinking." Children start with re-thinking the thoughts of others. Adults do the same; if we ask ourselves how many times a day we don't think new original thoughts, we will be able to recognize this re-thinking. Children come to creative thinking by calling on their imagination to meet a situation. True thinking comes when we reflect on "it can be done this way, but it must be possible to do it another way also." Childhood usually is blessed by the presence of an active imagination. As the midwife carefully helps the child come to earth, so does imagination help with the birth of thinking.

It is very difficult to think about something that we cannot make a mental picture of. When we want to develop thoughts about a subject, we usually first try to collect experiences. For example: when parents want to form a judgment about their child's being left-handed, they very likely start reading about left-handedness and ask other parents about their experiences. They might have the child go through various tests to find out about the dominance of the eye, the ear, the arm, the hand, the leg, and the foot. They will try to assess how the presence of cross dominance could affect the future of their child.

It is the same with toddlers. They need mental pictures of time and space before they can take the first steps in thinking. They must be able to orient themselves in the three spatial dimensions, and, especially, they must be able to make mental pictures of what is in front or in back, to the left or the right, and on top or below. Without this capacity, thinking lacks the structure through which it can become orderly thinking. Children who cannot "see" that the table is higher than the chair will never come to the idea to make a slide from the tabletop down to the chair.

It is similar with the concepts of time—yesterday, tomorrow, and so on. To think that tomorrow, today will be yesterday requires a power of thinking that the three-year-old child will not have; the six-year-old child might have it. As long as the time concept does not yet have an inner structure in children's minds, they cannot move with their thoughts in this area.

There are no thoughts when we cannot perceive thoughts; there is no thinking when we do not have the sense of thought. This statement helps to understand the difference between one's own thinking, on the one hand, and the perception of the thoughts of other people, on the other hand. Young children discover with their senses that there is something like "thoughts." The discovery that "our dog" indicates an existing object and that "please come and sit at the table" are not just words but have a meaning, is an experience that is based on the perception of thoughts. Children have to think themselves to discover that not only "our dog" exists but that there is "the dog" as a species. When children hide just before the mother calls "please come and sit at the table," they indicate that they have been thinking actively. Thus the development of the sense of thought is a prerequisite for the development of thinking. I have discussed this also in the fourth chapter (beginning on page 172).

Physiology of thinking

What processes occur within the body when we think? Before answering this question, I need to give some attention to the structure of thinking. It is evident that there are the two aspects—form and content. When someone asks me what the weather will be this afternoon, I might answer—thunderstorms. I also might give an elaborate answer explaining that, because of the barometer reading, the humidity, the temperature, and the like, thunderstorms are likely to occur. In both answers, the content is more or less the same; the form, however, is different. The form is the cloak in which the thought is dressed. When I do not want to think about the question, there will be no form, no content, and no mentioning of thunderstorms. The existence of a thought process underlies the aspects of content and form. Thus we can distinguish the thought process, the thought content, and the form in which the thoughts are expressed.

The thought activity is composed of the following elements: first the *will* to think is mobilized; then the thought *process* begins—thought *substance* is worked on, and the thought *content* is created; finally the thought receives a *form*.

The will to think

Thinking is an activity. We all know from experience that tiredness slows the thinking down. Thinking requires a force that is akin to the force of regeneration and building up. When we are ill, we usually do not want to study difficult literature, and mothers who breastfeed their babies often do not have the utmost clarity of thought when nursing. After a good night's sleep, thinking can find creative solutions it could not find the night before.[17]

Directing the will to think—what is this? How does it relate to the fact that rest is a prerequisite of thinking? Don't we consider will to be an activity?

We need to distinguish some aspects of the will. On the one hand, there is vital dynamism as a will activity that rules the infant and the toddler. Throughout life, it may even determine a larger or smaller portion of adults' actions. On the other hand, there is the directed will as a will activity, directed by the human I, which rides the horse of the vital dynamism. It guides, makes choices, knows restrictions, and aims at a goal. The I is at work in it. The vital dynamism in the thinking needs to be controlled to such an extent that the directed will has free access to the thinking. The directed will tries to find its way in the multitude of pictures and phenomena.

The thought process

Can we find the seven life processes—which we discussed in the third chapter—in the thinking? We have met them as processes that, working below the threshold of our consciousness, allow the ether body to transform the outer world into an inner world and to free energy.

For children who want to think, the thought substance that the elemental beings provide is outer world. It is somewhat alien to them; they do not "own" it yet, but they recognize it nevertheless. We could compare this with food that children like—they are eager to eat it, but then they still have to digest it. Also for adults, an unfamiliar thought content is outer world and somewhat alien. Figure 52 shows the stages of the thought process.

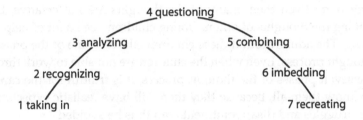

Fig. 52 The seven life processes of thinking.

The first phase of the thought process is taking in—learning to know and observing over and over again. Something alien is allowed to enter one's own thought organization. The second phase is trying to recognize it by comparing: "Is it similar to a thought I have had before? What does it make me think of? When I modify it somewhat, can I recognize it?" The "alien" is taken in somewhat further and adapted to existing thought patterns. The third phase is analyzing. Young children cannot do this yet, but adults can. The effect of taking our train of thought apart is that we are left with only fragments, and the overall structure is lost. The fourth, the *central life process*, has witnessed the three previous phases with a critical eye and ear. Now it can decide whether and how the thought process might continue. Part of the alien thought is useful and can be accepted; another part is not yet useful and must be excreted. This fourth phase is the phase of sorting in and sorting out; it requires that we interrogate the outer world that is entering our thought organization, that we ask questions. What has been accepted and sorted-in will now become a part of our own thought world in three steps. The fifth phase of the thought process is to do the opposite of analyzing; we have to put the pieces we decide to use together again. We are making a new composition of the thought

207

fragments. This might be similar to the original "alien" thought, or not. But this is not sufficient; we need to take two more steps. The sixth phase is to place this thought composition in the world of our experiences. We give it a place among previous thoughts, memories, mental pictures, and experiences. Here it becomes part of our ether body and can grow further. The seventh and last step is that the new thought becomes so much part of our own ether body that we are able to speak it or bring it into action. In doing so, we show the result of the thought process to the outer world and to our own soul.

In the young child, some of these seven steps are not functioning yet. At the age of three children begin with the first, the fourth, and the seventh step. The digestive process is not there yet. Only at puberty can children go through all the seven phases and experience a thought as their own. Even then, many of the thoughts are not creative, but a rethinking the thoughts of others. Young children need a lot of help with thinking. The adults around these children take on some of the phases of the thought process. Even when the children are not able to work through all the seven phases of the thought process, it is fruitful for the caregivers to know them all, because they then will have realistic expectations. Many struggles and disappointments can thus be avoided.

Thought substance

I have already shown that thinking has to do with the ether body. We have seen that the seven etheric life processes have gone through a metamorphosis when they appear in the thinking. Now we may ask the question: how do the four types of ether manifest in thinking? In the third chapter, I mentioned that there are four categories of elemental beings that form the life ether, the tone ether, the light ether, and the warmth ether (see page 82ff). The life ether spans the polarity of life processes and death processes; the tone ether connects and separates substances; the light ether makes things appear and disappear; and the warmth ether causes the warming up and cooling down.

During childhood, the elemental beings have the task of making the human form visible. They let the complex blueprint of the human body appear in physical substance, with the help of the four pairs of polar activities just mentioned. They implement the divine creative thoughts. When they have accomplished their task, initially at birth and then further during the first seven years of childhood, their work and their experience become available to the child. Of course, some repair and maintenance will always be necessary; this does occur at least every night.

The work and the expertise of the elemental beings become available to the child, but there is a potential risk when there is no master and no field of activity. Think of adolescents who are bored—not much good comes from that. The elemental beings, however, do have a new master and a new field of activity—the child and his or her thinking.

The life ether manifests in thinking as life force and death force. They manifest in fruitful thoughts that present an overview, but these thoughts will die in time and provide space for new life. The tone ether manifests in the analytic and the synthetic qualities of thinking. They appear in hair-splitting arguments and endless differentiating, but also in clear compositions that show coherence among all the thought elements. The light ether plays a main role in the thinking. Thinking sheds light on things. However, where there is light, there is also shadow. So the thinking can also leave things in the dark and let them disappear. The warmth ether brings a purpose to the thinking. We owe to the warmth ether in the thinking that we can hold a thought, give it reality, and translate it into action, and also that we can moderate and modify a thought.

This etheric thought substance is the factual living reality of each child. The elemental beings, who provide children with this thought substance, know each child, and they are willing to share this knowledge with the child.

Thought content
The thought content is dependent on the sources the thinking human being has access to. Memories, stories, pictures, observations, previous thoughts, facts, and fantasies—all of these constitute sources for thoughts. This source material is not kept in chaos; it is kept orderly in structures. The context of a specific happening, or the situation in which a story was heard gives a specific place to the corresponding memories. The name of a friend from elementary school evokes a wide range of memory pictures that the thinking can make use of. Thus not only facts are available for thought content, but also their context. One has access to everything—chaotic mazes, paved ways of thinking, or alternative thinking patterns.

We do not retrieve the thought content from a type of reservoir or from complicated archives. There is a source, or there are sources, the water of which has a special quality. It can give all that is humanly possible. It nurtures, renews, replenishes, shows familiar routes, and also shows new trails where no one has gone before.

It is our memory that constitutes this source. Our memories provide the content of our thinking. Please do not understand this in too narrow a sense. Memories that we are not conscious of, from this life, from past lives, or from the times in between incarnations; memories from the history of the development of humanity—all these are also, in principle, accessible to our thinking. In day-to-day life we can draw only from a small part of this source consciously, because the superficiality of our day-to-day memory leaves large segments of this source in the dark. Young children are not yet burdened by this; therefore they can think sometimes with remarkable wisdom.

Thought form

At last the thought is "born" in a specific form. This can be an unspoken idea, a statement, a question, a remark, a letter, or a brochure. It can be a declaration of love, or a token of compassion. It also can appear as an action; the thought that someone is immoral, for instance, can make one turn away from that person. The way the thought makes its appearance is dependent on personality factors such as age, experience, character, habits, and the like. The thought has value when it can be meaningful not only to the person who created the thought but also to others; or, said differently, it has value when the thought manifests an aspect—no matter how small—of what is universal, of that which each human being has the potential to recognize.

Can we recognize properties of the ether body in the form in which thoughts become manifest? Usually we use properties of the physical world to describe the form in which a thought is written or spoken, such as sharp or round, closed or open, simple or complex, clear or murky, complete or fragmented. This nomenclature we can also use for plant parts such as the leaves, flowers, fruits, or seeds. As the plant is an etheric formation, the organs of the plant have become the way they are because ether forces have made them so. We can compare the form in which a thought appears with plant formation. The four types of ether create, in the given situation and from the available substance, the final form in which either plant or thought appears. We can see the form of plants with our eyes; we can "see" the form of thoughts with our sense of language, word, or form.

Summary

I have described three physiological aspects of thinking.
    1. The will to think. This is the most individual decision to use one's

210

will and imagination to start thinking in a controlled, goal-directed, and unbiased manner. The will to think makes use of the seven life processes.

2. Thought substance. Partially it is composed of the four types of ether as the all-human ether substance. Partially it is the thought content that has been derived from the source of memory.

3. Thought manifestation. This is the result of the thought process at a given moment. It is very individual, but one might hope that other people can also make use of it.

In respect to time, we can find future, past, and present in the thought process. I would like to place this in an even larger framework. Divine beings have first thought everything that is in the world. Divine thinking is a creative force. A great deal was needed before the human being could be created.[18] This phase of creation is repeated in child development. This we can observe especially in embryonic development; each coming into being of a child manifests a repetition of the original creation by the divinity. This is the first occasion where the child comes into connection with thinking—each individual child is the manifestation of divine thinking.

The second occasion where the child comes into connection with thinking is when the child learns to perceive the thoughts of other human beings. Meeting human thoughts enkindles in the child the will to acquire the capacity to think human thoughts.

The third occasion where the child comes in connection with thinking is when the child learns to think. The capacity to do so is conceived in the time between three and seven, is born around the age of seven, and is subject to development throughout life.

Four helpers in educating the will

Parents often lament their child's strong will. When asked, they specify that the main issue is that the child does *not* want to do certain things. The lament narrows down to the issue that it is so difficult to influence the child's will. Most, if not all, children will now and then bring their parents and educators to despair. How can adults manage that their children are willing to do what the adults think is beneficial, such as eating vegetables or practicing the violin? Is it correct to influence the child's will, or is this an abuse of power? This type of question plays an important role in education. This book will not provide answers, but it will shed light on four human qualities that are important in education.

211

Nature helps children in their development in four ways. All children can by nature imitate and learn habits and routines; all children have an innate creative imagination and an ability to revere. Educators would be wise to enter into an alliance with this fourfold natural help.

Imitation and habits

Imitation

We can be moved when we see a little boy imitate his father's walk—slouching, folding his hands behind his back, bending his upper body slightly forward; or when we see a girl change the diapers of her doll with exactly the same gestures her mother uses when she is changing the baby's diapers, even including the familiar talk that goes with it. I myself feel caught when I suddenly observe in a meeting that I have taken on the same posture as the person who is sitting opposite me—relaxed, hands folded behind my head, leaning backward. Which of us started this? When I observe how someone has imitated the voice modulations and the expletives of a colleague, I again become conscious how powerful the impulse to imitate is and how that power can restrict someone's freedom. It is a kind of magic. We, both children and adults, are being directed in our movements and behavior in a way that is beyond our conscious awareness.

Indeed, it is magic. *Imitation is being moved.* The capacity to imitate is the capacity to let oneself be directed, guided, or moved. When we are imitating, our will is completely surrendered to the will of another person. Earlier in this chapter, we have learned that it is not the brain, the nervous system, or the muscular system that makes us move and teaches the child to walk—it is the I that moves us. How can it be that, instead of the I, another person makes me move? This is exactly what happens to children during their first seven years. As adults, we sometimes experience that this magic still works in us—this might then come to us as a shock.

How does imitation work? Children who imitate open themselves to their environment, full of surrender and trust. Then a gesture, a word, a tone, a mood happens; one could say something is sounding. It resonates within the child, and this moves the child. The young child is not in the position to choose whether to move or not. When children are not sleeping or crying, they imitate. Children move with everything they see,

212

hear, feel, or taste. The inner world of the child resonates with all soul experiences. This can be compared with a lute—when it is well tuned, the strings that are not touched by the musician will vibrate with the strings that are played. It is essential that the instrument is well tuned. This also holds true for children. Children resonate with everything for which their instruments are tuned. Children differ somewhat in this respect; each child has a physical instrument that somewhat differs from others. This determines to a large extent what each specific child will imitate and what not, but this is subject to change. By imitating, the physical instrument develops and changes, and this, in turn, will affect what can be imitated next. However, the natural disposition of the child will remain a restrictive factor. Children who are born with a disposition for music will more easily imitate lullabies and other songs from their mother than children without such a disposition.

What happens to the sounds, the gestures, or the moods that children imitate? Some of them appear again, such as in the examples of the boy and of the girl with which this section started. Those two children were moved and they expressed this movement outwardly in their actions. This is not always so. The resonating often remains an inner process; the astral body first takes up the sound and timbre and starts to resonate. It then passes it on to the ether body, especially to the tone ether. Then the ether body starts to move along with the soul movements. This activates formative forces in the ether body, especially ether forces of the tone ether, which is also called the chemical ether. These affect the chemical processes in the body. When children hear the wind whispering in the willows or when they hear the birds sing, the processes in the liver and other organs progress differently. When this happens frequently and is not a one-time occurrence, the structure and composition of the physical body will change. Only during the first seven years of childhood will imitation have such far-reaching effects. Children not only learn to move—inwardly and outwardly—by imitating, but they also build and rebuild, tune and give timbre to their bodily instrument. Later in life, we may recognize remnants of this, for instance when a close friend does something foolish and I turn red with shame. I imitate my friend's shame.

So far, I have discussed the instrumental aspect of the imitation process, how it works. There is also another aspect—intention. Why is it that one child learns to speak the mother tongue faultlessly, whereas another child muddles for years, for instance with the regular and irregular verbs? Why is it that children can speak a children's language, which does not imitate the way adults speak? Something similar occurs

213

in the area of music; adults and children do not hear the same way. All of this stems from the fact that children cannot imitate what they do not perceive. The more the twelve senses are developed, the better the child imitates. But what children do not perceive in the outer world cannot resound in their inner world, even when their physical instrument, their body, is capable of doing this.

What is the purpose of imitation? What does it do to children when, growing up in an artistic environment, they learn to imitate colors and sounds; when, growing up among craftspeople, they learn to imitate technical skills; or when, in a religious environment, they learn to pray? This often does not become clear till later in life, when we notice that we are making good use of what we have learned during childhood. Of course we can say that we have chosen our life's path and our profession because of the way we were raised. But it is also possible and often surprisingly to the point, to turn this the other way around. We may find that we are able to accomplish something later in life (in the profession we have chosen, or otherwise) because we had developed certain abilities during childhood—for instance, if our profession requires the capacity to listen to people and we were raised in a family where music played an important role. I see this as the intentional aspect of imitation. Imitation always brings something new, something out of the future; some intention is there, which is initially hidden but may reveal itself later. What makes this happen? Who is directing this? Where does the force come from that knows the future and brings from there the capacities the children will need in later life? I assume that this is the higher I of the child, especially the spirit-self (see page 32). Caregivers are invited to look together with the higher I of the child when they ask themselves the question: What does this child intend to experience and imitate? Of course, it is not easy to find an answer. It can be of help to look at the child's special dispositions and to observe what this particular child brings into the family that is different.

As parents, we do a lot to support healthy imitation when we provide good conditions and good content. The conditions are good when the child can live in an atmosphere of trust and confidence. Children who feel insecure do not imitate. Children imitate naturally in an atmosphere of trust, openness, and connectedness. We provide good content when we offer what is worth imitating. This does not mean that everything has to be rosy, harmonious, and warm. It does mean, however, that gestures are true and fit the situation—black when it should be black. The warranty of quality is truthfulness. Imitation is neither good nor bad; it is just there. It is given by nature; it is instinctive. Animals follow the impulses from their body and also imitate what they see their parents do. In humans, imitation enables the children to grow beyond the dictates of the body's instincts. The adults around the child are given the opportunity to provide either situations that are worth imitating or situations that are not. Both ways, imitation is very powerful: it can ruin children's behavior or it can help them realize their own potentials.

Summary

Acting out of imitation is a means of educating the individual will. Imitation has an instrumental aspect—the child is moved magically. The conditions are trust and well-developed perceptive abilities. Imitation has also an intentional aspect—something new is generated in the child.

Young children cannot distinguish between what they would like to imitate (what is worth it) and what they would rather not imitate (what is not worth it); they cannot imitate selectively but imitate everything they can perceive.

Habits

What is frequently imitated can become a habit or a routine.

As with imitation, habits and routines are types of motivation for action. However, unlike imitation, they are much more connected to the inner world of the child.

How do children acquire habits and routines? How did we—adults—acquire them? How do we learn certain routines and how can we undo them? What is the purpose of having them?

We can find an answer to the question: what is the purpose of habits and routines? when we try to imagine what life would be like if there were neither habits nor routines. Freed from day-to-day duties and conventions, we would experience an intense feeling of being on vacation. No longer the alarm clock, brushing our teeth, the traditional breakfast, the usual place at the table; no longer the "don't forget to take your snack with you" and the habitual goodbye kiss. Nothing would have to be done and nothing would run by itself. At any moment I could decide, out of the fullness of the moment and out of my presence of mind, what my next action, feeling, or thought would be. I would not be able to write, because that is routine; I would encounter severe difficulties speaking, because much of that is also routine. I would take my steps with much hesitation, because I would miss the security of the routine.

215

What at first looked like tremendous freedom soon confronts us with chaos in which we would feel completely helpless. We become aware that life is almost entirely based on routines—habitual actions, habitual emotional reactions, and habitual thought patterns. Routines make life secure and familiar—this is the way we do it here. Routines are *the* expression of education and culture. In a foreign country, we might experience that we do not know how to behave and how not to draw attention. "They have given me only a spoon next to my plate. Does that mean that I have to eat the whole meal with a spoon? Or is the spoon just for the soup, and am I supposed to eat the main course with my fingers? I have not noticed the soup as yet; will they serve that later during the meal?" The child might notice the power of habits when he or she spends some days with another family. It is an exciting adventure to learn to manage when you don't know the conventions.

Habits provide us with a supply of actions and reactions that we can use. Our will can either make use of them, or decide not to. Habits are the treaded paths of thinking, feeling, and willing; we can always walk these paths again even when they are seemingly forgotten. When I return after twenty-some years to the house where I grew up, my body knows exactly how to turn and what to hold onto going down the stairs to the cellar; only the proportions have changed considerably—the stairs are very small and my legs very long.

Habits are akin to memories. Memories are located in our ether body. This is also the place where habits work. Together they constitute the safe place of behavioral patterns with which a person can come along in society. Parents gradually have to let their toddlers leave the safe place of their physical protection and care, but they can provide the children with "a safe place" of habits and routines so that the children will be able to manage within the wide world.

The disposition or the constitution of the child sets the limits for what he or she is able to imitate; the same holds true for habits. Each child has areas in which habits develop easily and other areas in which they just do not want to come. The child with a disposition for movement might easily learn to walk, run, draw, and write. The child with a disposition for digestion might easily learn table manners. One child might feel connected to rituals and conventions, whereas another child might feel connected to honesty and harmony. There are as many dispositions and indispositions to habits as there are parts of the ether body. Observing the habit patterns of young children teaches us about the ether body of these children.

Children can acquire habits through imitation. This is one way, which is rather unconscious. Caregivers may want to draw the child's conscious attention to certain activities in order that these will become habitual. Getting dressed, tying a bow, having good table manners, wiping the feet, giving a hand, and many more activities—they all must be learned with more or less consciousness. Caregivers may be motivated to teach children these activities, but the children themselves may also be motivated to learn them—because, for instance, they want to be "grown up." The children themselves need to want to be involved, to bring in a certain degree of attention, and at least to be awake. Rewards, verbal or otherwise, can accelerate the learning process. This method of education comes very close to what is known as conditioning. Caregivers should be conscious of their motives when teaching children a habit. Some self-reflection can help to see whether the acquisition of a certain habit might be good or bad *for the child*. Often it is not the content of the habit that makes it good or bad, but the motivation to teach the habit makes it good or bad. For example: if adults want to teach children to stroke an animal after they have hurt it, they should reflect on what their own motivation is.

What can caregivers do to help children to unlearn bad habits? We probably know from our own experience, and through experience with our children, how easy it is to acquire bad habits. How to dispose of them? Because habits are located in the ether body, it is obvious that replacing them is not a simple task. Soul movements can relatively easily adjust to circumstances. Habits are located in a deeper layer of the body, and we are less conscious of them than we are of our soul movements. We can do two things in dealing with habits that we want to let go of—ignore them, or bury them. Normally developed and well brought-up children have many habits at their disposal, besides the undesirable ones. It is possible to appeal to the other habits and ignore—as much as possible—the bad habit, avoiding paying attention and giving nourishment to the undesirable habit. The other way is to teach children a new habit that is located in exactly the same spot of the habit body where the bad habit had nestled in. Then a new pattern of behavior can bury the old one. It is not possible to erase habits; this is not how memory works. But it is possible to bury them. This is a process that requires time and attention—a project of at least four weeks of consequently trying to acquire the new habit. Sometimes grandma or other people, who are relative outsiders to the child but who are very important to him or her, can accomplish the same thing in a much shorter time period. However, the question is then: will the result last when the child has returned to his or her day-to-day situation?

Some adults and children may be inclined to let their habits fossilize. Habits do have the possibility of becoming straitjackets. Habits should not rule human behavior as if they were the law. They need to remain the expression of a culture—of family tradition, school tradition, and so on. Because reality is subject to change, conventions and routines must follow the change. It is sometimes beneficial to do things differently, such as having a different place at the table. If, however, there are only a few well-rooted habits in day-to-day family life, then it is important not to change the place at the table where each family member sits at mealtimes.

Summary

Imitation and habits are educators of the will. In what way are they similar and in what way are they different?

Habits help children literally to cultivate their own will, to bring their will into the culture they live in. Imitation helps children to dispose of habits, and to replace them with actions that fit the situation of the moment. Habits provide the resistance we need to avoid continuous imitation. Imitation is a powerful agent for preventing the fossilizing of habits. Habits have an affinity to the past—"this is the way we do it" means "this is the way we always did it." Imitation has the charm of the future, of the unexpected. Habits provide security—I know what I have; imitation is dangerous—whom am I imitating?

Imitation and habits also work together in the same direction; imitation helps to acquire a specific behavioral pattern and lets it grow into a habit. Habits live in the ether body. Imitation reflects the movements of the astral body. The entire human body (all its four members) is involved in imitation as well as in habits. This is obvious—no member of the human body can function by itself; the other members always join in, even when only passively.

Reverence and imagination

Reverence

Every child has an innate faculty for reverence. When we bring moments of reverence back to our minds, we can observe at first glance that this is not primarily an issue of educating the will. Reverence is not in the first place connected to activity; it makes us go inward. In a mood of reverence, we do not run, we do not chat. We are very much within ourselves and experience the relativity of our existence. Reverence shows us the

218

right proportions between ourselves and something else—a phenomenon, a being, nature, an admired person, or God. Reverence does not humiliate; I may feel myself very small but not without value. Reverence shows me my modest place in a larger context full of meaning; reverence increases the awareness of my value as a human being by showing where being human can lead. Reverence has nothing to do with power. Power creates powerlessness; reverence creates confirmation. Reverence connects us with the reality of the creative forces in the world; reverence for nature connects us with the magnitude of the created world. That is to say: the world created by God.

Can we also have reverence for what is created by human beings? Can we revere a painting, a violin sonata, a complex machine, or a new software program with almost unlimited possibilities? Can we expect children to revere other human beings, such as their parents and teachers?

I think that we need to decide for ourselves in which situations we want to speak of reverence and in which situations it would be more appropriate to use other terms, such as admiration and respect. I myself choose to apply the concept of reverence only to the healthy relation that human beings maintain with their divine origin. Another person might play an important role in my relation to the divine origin, as an example or as a mediator. A work of art could also play into this relationship, when it gives me more than just esthetic satisfaction. Reverence—together with its corresponding mood of piety—is the bridge over which we have access to being human, to our origin, and to the purpose of our existence. Who would want to take this bridge away from children? As habits provide a safe place in the physical world, so can reverence also constitute a foundation of our existence, on the level of morality. Reverence is a healthy antidote against self-conceit, but also against low self-esteem and defeatism. Reverence brings us closer to the all-human, rather than to being an individual; imagination brings us closer to our individuality.

Is reverence in danger of becoming extinct these days? It is obvious that respect and admiration are more prevailing. What is left for children to revere? There is not much to experience that manifests the divine source of creation. A waste-generating society and reality TV do not teach reverence. Morality has been replaced by rules and agreements, and children are taught that it is efficient when we stick to the rules and keep the agreements; without that, the human species might become endangered. Considering all this, we might be astonished and delighted to observe the reverence with which the toddler allows a ladybug to walk over his or her hand. In the Dutch language, this insect bears the name "little animal of our dear Lord." Obviously, over and again, new generations of children are born with the faculty of reverence. It is as if they experience: in heaven we knew that it had to be, and here on earth we have it in reality.

How do we teach reverence? Or, how can we prevent ourselves from hindering children from developing their innate faculty of reverence? It is obvious that we cannot teach reverence; we can only set the example and call on imitation to help. It is a privilege when children can experience people in their environment who know their place in the whole and can look up with reverence to powers greater than they are. An atmosphere of reverence is the best climate for reverence to grow. When idolizing or adoration threaten to take the place of reverence in the child, caregivers might try to bring the child into situations in which he or she can again experience true reverence, such as in nature, in meeting a wise person, or in hearing a profound story.

It is important to know the physiological region in which reverence works. Reverence has to do with secrets of the creative and created world, of the human being as the image of God. Thus we are talking about the physical body and the physical world of animals, plants, and minerals in nature. The physical body is the oldest member of our body. It contains the most wisdom; by comparison, the ether body is just a youngster. The physical body is the most holy, because it has experienced everything that has happened in the development of humanity.[19] This entire wisdom has been transformed to serviceability. There is a physical body available for each new life. At their physical birth, children enter into the world in a holy way. Over the years, they become less and less holy and more and more human. There remains, however, a bridge to the origin and purpose of being human—reverence.

Imagination

It requires creative courage to allow opposites such as reverence and imagination to co-exist within one being. The Creator did have this courage when He created the human being. Imagination changes everything, turns things upside down, finds a way out of dead-end situations, adapts reality to our wishes, brings movement in what has become stuck, and brings a smile to sincerity. When children develop their imaginative play, they create a pretend world that is simultaneously true and not true. They receive powers of creation. A wooden block is a boat, and when little brother comes too close it is a red traffic light. Children manipulate reality in a magical way. At the same time, they keenly watch the line between their imaginary world and the reality of the adult world. Pretend raisins you have to pay for with pretend money, but real raisins you eat right away. When an adult walks through the space of the pretend castle, the child complains, "you cannot walk there; that is my castle." Yet when the adult comes and puts the pretend castle away in a pretend box because it is time to eat, the child might say simply "Why are you doing that? You know that it is not real!"

What is the relation between imagination and reality, between imagination and making something up, between imagination and lying? What source do children access when imagination is born in them?

Around the age of four, imagination blossoms in children. Before that, everything is reality; there is no distinction between the toddler and the environment. Toddler's toys are material to practice with. They are to pound with, to make noise with, to put into and take out of a box. Older preschoolers lose part of their creative imagination. Toys must be real—a toy car must have wheels and extras; a doll must have real hair and clothes that can be taken off and put on again.

In normal situations, children keep some of their power of imagination. With this, children can make up imaginary games—"I am the mother and you are the child." In elementary school, children can mobilize their powers of imagination to deal with difficult situations and to digest exciting or scary experiences, by playing them out in imaginative games. Often, through the medium of imagination, children can digest experiences that otherwise are too real and allow these experiences to be part of their inner world. This is not always possible; there are events that children cannot digest. They will drop out and ignore these events, or they will place their imaginary world above reality. Then they will experience their own reality as more real than the actual facts. This can be a protection for a while, but in the long run it causes problems. Because other people no longer fit in the fantasy-world of the child, the child may end up in loneliness and confusion.

Around the age of four, children develop their rhythmic middle region, the domain of the life processes (see chapter 3). This is the area of metamorphosis—taking in, metabolizing, and recreating. The life processes are working creatively within the body, and during this phase of development in which children are submerged in the life processes, children make those processes visible in their drawings and in their imaginary games. Imagination is not yet a soul faculty or mental capacity at this age. Imagination is still the exuberance of healthy life forces. By

221

nature, they will not go beyond their limits. Children do not lose themselves in fantasy. Imagination is as yet the manifestation of life forces working within the physical body. For healthy children, this is something they can go by to check—"taste"—whether things still tally. When the child loses the reality check of connection with the physical body, fantastic stories may be made up that no longer have the pretend quality, even when the child still tries to believe these stories. It is unusual for children younger than seven to make up such fantastic stories; they are rather a phenomenon of the older child.

The adult's distinction between fantasy and reality does not exist for young children. For them there is only one reality, which is an actual, created, marvelous, and varied reality. It takes a lot of effort for children to involve their contemplative head forces in the perception of adult reality. Only in the mirror of mental pictures would they be able to perceive reality the way adults do. But with children this mirror is not yet finished. To gauge true reality, adults use as their point of reference "can I make a mental picture of it?" whereas children have as their point of reference "does it fit my physical body?" This leads to a different concept of true and not true than is common in the world of adults. For children, something is true when the reality that they experience is measured against their physical body by their sense of life. I will give an example: Nancy takes a piece of candy out of the jar; father has noticed it; Nancy denies it. Is she lying? No, says Nancy, Lucy my doll did it because she was so hungry. Father might answer that Nancy is lying and that this is not nice. A difficult situation! The father will of course prevail; however, is that correct? The point is that the imagination of young children uses a gauge that is different from the one adults use in their reality. Most children are eager to step into reality as it is perceived by the mental picturing of adults. Many children can already be approached on this level at the age of five. But imagination points in another direction—that of the artist who does not trust his or her eyes but recreates reality through metamorphosis. Actually, this is the only road to independence and to finding personal answers to personal questions.

Do caregivers have to agree with whatever children create as their reality? No, but they have to develop a feeling for the distinction between imagination and making something up. Sometimes children need to be protected against their own obtrusive fantasy, if it goes too far. The life forces, which are the source of imagination, are the activity of beings that live in our organs. These are the elemental beings I spoke of in the second chapter. If imagination does not manifest itself in the child's play but enters the child's consciousness, these beings can also enter the child's consciousness. There they can manifest themselves as kind beings, but

222

also as scary apparitions. This can frighten children. It is helpful for children to speak about them, draw them, and play them out. Through this process, these beings can find a place in the real "pretend" world, where they belong.

Imagination is magic, as is imitation. In imitation, the magic comes from outside; in imagination, the magic comes from inside. In imagination, children show something that is extremely personal. They show how and to what degree they are able to create their own new reality. Here we meet the child's I. Children that use their power to imagine are practicing the faculty to create a new world, a world that is better than the existing one.

Imagination requires involvement. Involvement is the force with which children want to meet the world, with which they take everything in with their eyes, with which they meet other people, or with which they digest their food. Long live imagination!

Summary

Reverence leads children toward morality in their actions. It educates the will because it places the child in a larger perspective. It helps children to stay connected with their origin; thus it points to the past. Reverence is based on the physical body, which is the most wise and holy part of the human being. Reverence makes the child more healthy, even at the level of the physical body.

Imagination dissolves the past and introduces the future. Children who develop their imagination create their own reality. That reality keeps its "pretend" character as long as the children do not lose contact with the reality. Imagination is connected with our most human part, the I. Imagination educates the I-organization.

Figures 53 and 54 present diagrams in which arrows indicate the direction in which reverence, imitation, habits, and imagination work. In figure 53, the arrow pointing down indicates forces that work out of the future, or that enable the future to come. They enter the body through the head and continue down into the metabolic-limb organization. The arrow pointing up indicates forces that work from the past and make the past visible in the present. They enter through the limbs and continue into the nerve-sense organization. In figure 54, there are also arrows that start where the upper pole or the lower pole of the child are depicted in the drawing. These arrows indicate forces that are a reversal and metamorphosis of forces represented by arrows coming from the opposite direction, from outside the body. These forces "die" at the end of their course in the body, to be reborn as the forces indicated by the arrows that start where these regions are depicted, representing either the upper pole or the lower pole. I will discuss this further in the next section of the chapter.

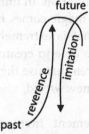

Fig. 53 *Reverence and imitation are human potentials that enable children to have access to the past and to the future.*

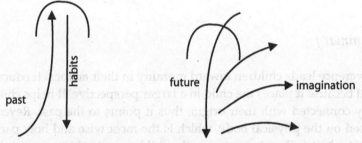

Fig. 54 *Habits form the child and work into the will; starting in the head as a metamorphosis of forces from the past—that came from below/outside—they make the past manifest in the child. Imagination is a force that awakens the child and creates culture; it originates in the future, enters the child from above/outside, goes through a metamorphosis in the lower pole, and works upward to become manifest in the acting, feeling, and willing of the child, creating the future in the outer world. (These statements are made from the earthly standpoint of the here and now.*

The arrows in figures 53 and 54 indicate four processes in child-development. Two arrows—representing *reverence* and *habits*—have a connection to the past (reverence directly, habits indirectly), whereas the other two arrows—representing *imagination* and *imitation*—have a connection to the future (imitation directly, imagination indirectly). In the discussion of these four processes in child-development, I have indicated the member of the human body that is the home base of each of these four helpers of will-education—*reverence*, physical body; *habits*, ether body; *imitation*, astral body; *imagination*, I-organization. We need to be aware, however, that all four processes work in all four members of the human body.

Forces working through
architecture, sculpture, music, and speech

We can deepen our understanding of the physiological laws underlying child-development when we become aware of the connections that exist between the physical body and architecture, the ether body and sculpture, the astral body and music, and the I-organization and speech. See figure 55.

The laws behind the formation of the physical body are the same as those behind architecture. They govern the use of space and gravity. One main concern of architecture is, for instance, how weight can be absorbed. In the inner structuring of bones (the femur, for instance) we encounter these laws and see how the capacity to bear weight is maximized with a minimum of substance.

The laws behind the formative forces of the ether body are the same as the laws behind sculpture. Sculptors look at how the ether body works, to learn about working with the materials they want to use. I have described these formative forces in the second chapter, in discussing the form of plants. We meet these forces in surfaces, boundaries, fullness, and surface tension. In human physiology, we encounter this in the way organs are formed and also in the way the muscles can be seen in the human build.

The laws behind the forces with which the astral body, through the ether body, forms the physical body are the same as the laws behind the formative forces of music. Music works with intervals and proportions; the relation between tones is the essence of music. Metaphorically speaking, "it's like music" when the proportion between upper arm and lower arm is harmonious, or when the angle that the neck of the femur makes with the vertical is exactly right.

The laws behind the activity with which the I-organization, through the astral and ether bodies, influences the form of the physical body are the same as those behind speech. The essence of speech is that sounds, intonations, vowels, and consonants deliberately put themselves in the service of that which wants to be spoken. When speech becomes an art, language is much more than just a tool for passing on information. The human being is able to speak in such a way that a sentence is an artistic creation of form and sound, through which ideas can become manifest in the sense world. Divine speaking created the human form. The human appearance in the sense world is the expression of an idea, of a spiritual reality; it is the manifestation of the I.

225

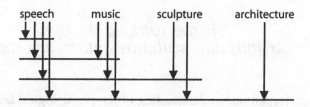

Fig. 55 The formative forces of speech affect all four members of the human body, working from the I-organization, through the astral and ether bodies, into the physical body. Musical forces affect the astral body directly, and through this, they work also in the ether body and in the physical body. Sculptural forces affect the ether body directly, and through this, they work on the physical body. Architectural forces affect the physical body directly.

We will see that the formative forces of speech and music are more related to the future whereas the sculptural and architectural forces are more related to the past. We will also see how the working of these forces undergo specific changes as the ether body, the astral body, and the I-organization are born successively. These changes manifest in the change of teeth, the change of voice, and reaching adulthood, respectively.[20]

During the first seven years, all formative forces put themselves in the service of the ether body. We could also say that the ether body opens itself up for the other formative forces. Through the ether body, they sculpt the physical body during the first seven years. The ether body works from within the head. The head works formatively on the substance of the physical body, provides boundaries and gives structure to it. The ether body works with the architectural and sculptural forces from the head downward. The forces of music and speech, coming from the outside, join the architectural and sculptural forces in the head, and there they take on the character of sculptural forces. See figure 56.

When the physical body is born, the architectural design is already completed. The ether body continues the work with sculptural and musical formative activities and with those that involve the forces behind speech. This can last for only seven years, because then the physical material substance must have been brought entirely into its proper form. If the sculptural forces from the head continued to work after these seven years, they would cause great damage. They would slowly harden the body and turn it into a statue, hard as the enamel of the teeth. To prevent this from hap-

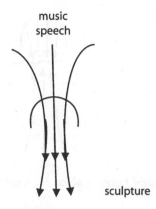

music
speech

sculpture

pening in the child, forces are mobilized that arise from inside and work

Fig. 56 In the first seven years, the forces of speech and music join the sculptural and architectural forces.

from below upward. These are the ether forces from the metabolism, and they counteract the hardening effect of the forces from the head. This saves the physical body and keeps the ether body in flux. These freshly awakened forces also have a sculptural and architectonic character, but they do not work formatively on the body; they are used for creative activities such as modeling, painting, writing, and drawing.

This process can be compared to when a carpenter is asked to make all the furniture for a newly built house. He does the job in the house and accomplishes it within one year. All supplies have been used, but the tools are still there. The carpenter has broadened his skills and experience, and he is available for a new job offer. If no job offer comes, the carpenter may become depressed or may start to remodel the carpentry shop. Anyhow, the recommendations by the owner of the furnished house will increase the chance that a new job offer will come soon.

In the field of tension between the forces from above and the forces from below coming from outside, the permanent teeth are born. The tooth enamel is the hardest bone in the human body. The teeth give a picture of the ether body, namely of the battle between the two opposing forces from above and from below/outside. The forces of the upper pole are potentially dangerous during the time of the change of teeth, whereas the forces of the lower pole have a healing character. See figure 57.

227

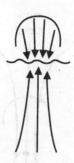

Fig. 57 The sculptural forces at about the time of the change of teeth.

In the first seven years, education can help the outcome of the battle between the opposing forces to be positive for the child's development, by stimulating the forces of the lower pole. These forces develop when children use their limbs and have an active metabolism. That is why these forces cannot yet work before physical birth. Exercising metabolism and movement stimulate these forces, which oppose the hardening forces from the head. Thus healthy nutrition and a healthy motor development support tooth development as well as the birth of the ether body. Once the ether body is born, these forces become available for learning.

In the first seven years children take in the forces—coming from outside—that work through music and speech, from above through their senses. In the head, these forces take on the character of sculptural forces that work formatively upon the physical body. The education of the child can also help the outcome of the battle—fought between the forces from above and from below/outside, as mentioned above—to be positive for the child's development by supporting the forces behind music and speech.

Where do we find these forces behind music and speech? We find them first of all in music, singing, and spoken language. Children are formed by the melody of the mother tongue, the peculiarities of the dialect, the nursery rhymes, the children's songs, and the music they hear.

We may also speak metaphorically of music and language. Music is an issue of proportions. Therefore the proportions of all that surrounds children (such as buildings, rooms, plants, or flowers) contain a musical quality. Also the waves that roll onto the beach are music.

Speech is an issue of forms. The forms of the created world speak a language. A pyrite crystal tells a different story from that of a boulder in the river, and a birch tree speaks to me differently from the way the oak tree does. Each form, including the human form, is the result of the power of the creative word. When God created the world, He spoke it.

228

Adam named everything. When we speak, we do something that is, in principle, similar, though on a different level. Therefore we have to watch our words, especially when we educate children.

In the first seven years, the forces of music and speech do not work freely into the physiology of the child. They are safely kept within the etheric sculptural activities. The musical forces begin to work directly into the physiology of the child at the age of seven, and the forces of speech do the same at the age of fourteen. When they begin to work directly into the physiology of the child, they do not encounter ether forces anymore, but their own forces. This I will explain.

In the organs of the human body, the musical forces manifest not only as structure and proportion, but particularly as digestion. They are present in the caustic quality of gastric juice and in the dissolving activity of the digestive enzymes. Through the seven life processes, they serve the body and are harmless as long as they destroy food substance. If they go beyond this, they become dangerous. The stomach becomes damaged when it is exposed directly to the working of gastric juices, and people immediately become very ill when the pancreas becomes directly exposed to the working of pancreatic enzymes. The working of these forces, belonging to the organs, can be a potential threat not only for the body but also for the soul. The musical astral forces, which are set free to work in the physiology of the child at the age of seven, vibrate the organs and loosen the organ forces from the organs. Up till then, the child was not conscious of their presence, because these forces were safely kept inside the organs; the child was innocent. From the age of seven, children can become conscious of aggressive, corrosive, unreliable, and cunning forces inside themselves. Children lose their innocence. Aggression and venom become available to the soul and to the will; when children want to, they can now lie, hit, or betray. Toddlers are also capable of misbehavior. They can exclude other children or ridicule them. These are, however, different types of vices that originate more in the upper pole. This type of mischief has to do with isolation and separation. After the age of seven, children have to learn to cope with the forces coming from the organs, from the lower pole. They experience these forces in their own souls. They are conscious of them and can be asked to take responsibility for behavior such as anger or aggression. This is physiology, not a moral judgment.

It belongs to being human that we meet these forces as children and that we have to learn to deal with them. Already during childhood we all have to learn to tame our own wild beasts. Caregivers know that this is not easy. It is hard work, and it does not happen by itself.

This second battle is the battle between the musical astral forces coming from outside and the astral forces coming from the inner organs. In this battle, the therapy comes from above whereas the danger threatens from below. The battle ends with the change of voice at the start of puberty. See figure 58.

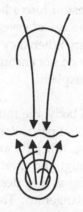

Fig. 58 The astral musical forces when the voice changes.

After puberty, the child lands on earth, the earth as it became after the expulsion from paradise. The child becomes male or female; it must be so after paradise. For fourteen years the balancing healing forces could oppose the potentially destructive forces. Then comes the time that children on their own have to discover the risks of this new situation with its potential of other types of evil. Music, however, can remain a great teacher. When children have learned to play a musical instrument, they are prepared for dealing with puberty.

Summary

The sculptural forces that work from the head downward have their origin in the past. They give a picture of the human being as he or she was before birth. The forces of movement from the lower pole, which originate in the will and are activated in the child after birth, open up the future for the child. The battle between these two opposing forces prepares the child for thinking—the ether body can be born.

The musical forces that enter the human organism through the head originate in eternity. For seven years they help to form the body. After

230

that, they sound through the child with healing harmony and with magic power to tame the wild forces coming from the organs (one could think of Mozart's *The Magic Flute*). The organ forces are freed from the metabolic organs that they have served—unnoticed—for seven years. They are potentially destructive for human existence, as well as the source of healthy energy and vital will power. The battle between these two opposing forces prepares the child for willing—the astral body can be born, and the child comes down to earth.

I will not write about the third battlefield that has to do with the forces of speech and the attainment of adulthood, since this is too far removed from the subject of this book. I will, however, still write a few lines about the time aspect of the births of the ether and astral bodies.

The birth of the ether body. The sculptural forces, which work from the past as they form the child, bring along the danger of isolating and hardening the child if they do not go through a metamorphosis. The metamorphosis occurs when the child is occupied with creative activities, such as drawing or building. Creative activities connect to the future, since they are akin to creative forces. As human beings, we encounter the results of our deeds; the reality of our actions is in the future. The past is active as long as the body is formed and "invented." The future becomes active when children start to act. See figure 59.

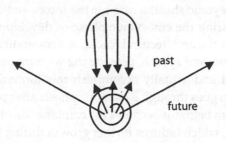

Fig. 59 Past and future at the birth of the ether body

The birth of the astral body. From the age of seven onward, the musical forces create the future in the child's body. They awaken the organ forces that have been inserted into the organs in the past. These organ forces are potentially dangerous for the child, and they need to be tamed and controlled. See figure 60.

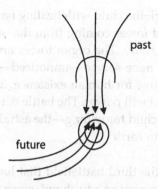

Fig. 60 Past and future at the birth of the astral body

The architectural forces and the forces behind speech

The sculptural and musical forces are the most important ones during the first seven years of childhood. Yet I will discuss briefly the architectural forces and the forces behind speech too, in order to give a picture of the entire developmental process.

The architectural forces. The architectural forces provide the human being with the blueprint of the physical body. Heredity provides a model, and this is what the human being starts with at birth. During childhood, the human being adjusts and adapts this model to his or her needs by remodeling it. The embryonic sheaths care for the forces and substances of the physical body during the embryonic phase of development. This is also the time in which the architectural forces, in cooperation with the forces of sculpture, music, and speech, provide the wisdom needed to form the body of the child and actually accomplish this formation too. This tremendous wisdom goes through a metamorphosis after physical birth and starts to work from below. It becomes the combination of forces of growth and regeneration, which induces further growth during youth and which keeps adults as healthy as possible. These forces enter the human body through the arms and the legs, through the lower pole. On their way from below upward, they come under the influence of the forces from the head, which form and quiet them. Because of the influence of the head forces, the wisdom from the past can now work formatively in the human being as sculptural forces. As sculptural forces, they now work from the head; yet their origin is in the periphery. In the upper pole, the centripetal direction of the formative forces that enter the body from below—which form the human being—is reoriented to come downward. See figure 61.

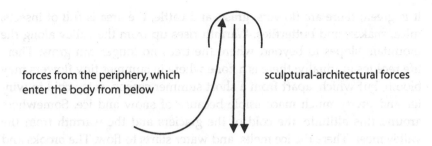

forces from the periphery, which
enter the body from below

sculptural-architectural forces

Fig. 61 The forces coming from the periphery work mainly before physical birth, after which they start to enter the body from below. Metamorphosed into architectural and sculptural forces, they then work from above downward.

The forces behind speech. Through the senses, the musical forces and the forces of speech make the human being move. Forces of will work magically into this. They call upon the human being to appear, be heard, be visible, and act. Earlier I described how music makes us move, and we touched on this also in the sections on the senses of tone and movement. The forces of speech are involved in the formation of the physical body during the first seven years. They enter the body from above. During the second seven-year period they assist the astral body in tuning and forming the ether body. From the age of fourteen onward, the forces of speech assist the forces of the I-organization for seven years. We become really human because we are formed by speech, and—after these forces have changed direction in the lower pole—we act and perform deeds which are subject to moral judgment. The fact that we acquire the capacity to speak indicates that the human body has an innate relationship to the forces of speech. When we reach adulthood, the downward direction of the forces of speech—which enter the body from above—changes to a centrifugal direction. In the lower pole, human actions arise from the unconscious plan of action that we brought with us from before birth. We saw this in the sections about the sense of movement and about learning to walk.

I will now give two examples to help in understanding the metamorphosis of centripetal forces that become architectural and sculptural forces, and of the forces of speech and music that become centrifugal forces. One example is taken from nature, and the other is taken from the human realm.

The first example. From the peaks of high mountains, always covered with ice and snow, glaciers descend slowly as rivers of ice. Below in the valley it is green; there are flowers, grass, and cattle; the area is full of insects, mice, snakes, and butterflies. Warmth rises up from the valley along the mountain slopes to beyond where the trees no longer can grow. There life recedes gradually; there is a zone where in summer tiny flowers may bloom, but which, apart from a short summer season, is icy cold in winter and pretty much inaccessible because of snow and ice. Somewhere around this altitude, the cold of the glaciers and the warmth from the valley meet. There the ice melts, and water starts to flow. The brooks and creeks aim toward the valley, transporting fertile soil downward; they polish the rocks, create the landscape, and make the valley fertile.

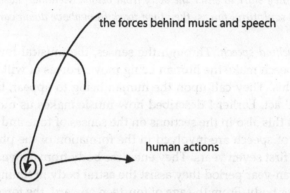

Fig. 62 After they have accomplished their task in forming the human body, the forces of speech change into forces through which human beings connect to their surroundings.

Through this picture, I realize that the source of the life-bringing water is in the cold pole. In the cold pole, the aspect of life that manifests so exuberantly in the warm valley is hidden. On the other hand, the bare rock of the mountains clearly shows the aspect of life that has to do with aging and dying, with too much form, whereas this aspect is more hidden in the valley. In fall and winter, we see this aspect also appear in the valley. Death belongs to life. The life span of a butterfly is a few days, for a tree it can be a few centuries, and for a landscape it can be a few millennia; yet an end always comes.

The second example. A civil engineer dreams of building a bridge over the Rhine river. As a boy, he was already interested in building and construction. He invented a method to increase the stiffness of a long board over a creek by supporting the transverse board with other boards placed under it in a certain way. In college, he learned many other methods to make something capable of bearing weight. He admired the bridges he saw over famous rivers—the bridges over the Seine River in Paris, over the river Thames in London, and over the Rhine River in Cologne. Biologists taught him about the geniality of creation, how, for instance, tall grasses become very sturdy with not much substance for building material. In his mind, he developed a clear picture of the blueprints he would make if he were ever asked to build such a bridge. He familiarized himself with all the places along the Rhine where a bridge could be built. In his profession, he was involved in the construction of many bridges over land for highway crossings and the like. He gained experience in dealing with new materials, with the government, and with contractors. He encountered pressure groups who considered the impact of his constructions negative for the environment and for people. In that way, he learned to look for alternatives that were better for the people and for the environment. Shortly before retirement an opportunity came to make his dream come true. He no longer had the strength to take it on alone, so he signed the contract jointly with a younger colleague. He taught his colleague all the wisdom and experience he had conquered and collected, and together they accomplished the job and built this bridge over the Rhine River!

From this story, I learn that the forces from above, which want to make something visible, have to be taught by the wisdom of the forces from below. In realizing an idea, we encounter factual reality. The dialogue between idea and reality purifies the forces from above and can give human actions a quality of service.

Summary of this chapter

In this chapter we looked at various ways of relating the members of the human body to the time aspect of past and future.

We discussed four helpers with the education of the will. Imitation magically moves the astral body. Habits imprint the ether body with regular patterns of behavior. Habits may lead to inflexibility, and imitation can then offer a way out of that. As humans we know what reverence is, because we have been created in the image of God, and our physical body is a token of that. Imagination is creative power of the I, and it can put everything in a new light.

The laws behind architecture, sculpture, music, and speech have an inner relationship with the physical body, the ether body, the astral body, and the I-organization respectively. The architectural forces play a role before physical birth, and the forces of speech play a role from adulthood onward. The birth of the ether body occurs in the field of sculptural forces from the past (which enter through the head) and sculptural forces that children newly develop in this life (in the lower pole). The birth of the astral body occurs in the field of musical forces that enter through the senses and open up the future, and musical forces from the lower pole (the organs) that connect the child to the past.

6 Helpers with Individualization

In this chapter, I will discuss some processes children can make use of when they want to bring their individualities to expression in their own bodies. The fifth chapter described what helps children to become a human being, to bring forth in the newly received physical body what is generally human, and to incorporate what they have brought with them as fruits from experiences in previous incarnations. In this sixth chapter, I will pay attention to how the future deals with this past.

We were already looking at the connection between the past and the future at the end of the fifth chapter, for instance in the sections about imitation and imagination; we cannot separate these time aspects completely. In the fourth chapter, I also touched on aspects that would fit in this sixth chapter, when I described how the twelve gates of the sentient soul give the child twelve possible ways to learn to know their new earthly reality. These twelve gates are opportunities for encounters through which the child's destiny can manifest itself.

In this chapter, I will discuss:

1) the traditional children's diseases, with the theme: a transformation of heredity
2) naughtiness and curiosity, with the theme: lose yourself to find yourself
3) forgetting and remembering, with the theme: seed formation and germination.

Children's diseases—transforming heredity

Health is maintaining equilibrium between dissolving and coagulating. The human body can do both. The process of dissolving culminates in the lower pole, exemplified in the working of the digestive juices. The process of coagulating culminates in the upper pole, exemplified in the formation of the skull bones. Both processes can become too strong and then they become diseases which typically belong to childhood and old age, respectively. During childhood, we see the occurrence of inflammatory diseases with pus formation, and in old age we see the occurrence of rheumatism with scleroses. These two processes have an interrelationship; an intensive process of sclerosis often calls for a fever as a counter process.

The body the child receives at birth is a temporary dwelling. It is a model with which the child starts to work, especially during the first seven years. It can happen that the child is content with his or her provisional dwelling, because it fits exactly. Then the child will make his or her house identical with the model given at birth. It may also be that the child is not content with the model, but that he or she does not have the forces to remodel it. The provisional dwelling will then be maintained, and when the child turns seven, he or she will live in a house that does not fit properly. The house will remain irritating, too large, or too small. Most of the time, however, children accept their provisional dwellings gladly, but then remodel them according to their individual needs at various stages of their childhood.

All diseases that come with fever can help with this remodeling. The traditional children's diseases (such as measles, mumps, rubella, chickenpox, diphtheria, and whooping cough) are special, because they remodel a specific part of the house. This is not so with influenza. Influenza, colds, bronchitis, and middle-ear infections are related to the circumstances in which the child lives. They help to dissolve the impressions and experiences the child has not digested. In doing so, they may also contribute to remodeling. In contrast, the traditional children's diseases are not caused by the outer world; they are caused by the inner world of the child. When the child experiences a traditional children's disease, those parts of the hereditary model of the body that do not fit the child can be dissolved and replaced by what the child needs. I will give two examples of these traditional children's diseases.

Chickenpox. This is an itchy disease. It is tremendously contagious; it is as if it blows through closed windows and doors. It is a harmless disease, but very irritating. The rash with blisters and scabs is tremendously itchy, and it makes the child restless and unhappy. It can affect the skin and the mucous membranes; if there is no inflammation, the rash will not leave scars. There are seldom complications. The disease remains at the outside of the body, and after a few days (at most two weeks) the child is healthy again.

Mumps. There is no rash, but the uppermost digestive glands—which produce the saliva—are inflamed. Even thinking about eating hurts. This

238

is the main reason why children with mumps usually lose weight. Fever and feeling sick are not the primary concerns; the issue is that the child does not want to eat. One does not easily recognize the child when he or she has mumps; one mainly sees a child with thick eyelids and inflated cheeks like those of a hamster. It can happen that both cheeks are inflated simultaneously, but usually it is first one cheek and then the other. This, of course, will extend the duration of the illness for another week. Most often there are no complications. If there are, they affect the pancreas and/or the genital glands. These organs have a central position in the functioning of the inner world of the human body. The pancreas is essential for the digestive process and for sugar metabolism. The genital glands are essential for procreation and for the full development of one's male or female form.

I do not intend to give a full description of chickenpox and mumps, but I want to show that these two diseases—caused by viruses—each have a different working area. The field of action of chickenpox is at the very outside of the human form, there where we can be touched and irritated. The field of action of mumps is inside the body, there where we transform the outer world and take care of our inner world.

Each traditional children's disease has its specific field of action, which determines how far-reaching the disease can become. When a vital organ is the working area of the disease, the process of remodeling the hereditary house is risky. The risk consists of complications that occur when the remodeling goes out of control. The effects of complications can be very serious, and children might carry some of these effects with them throughout their entire life or even die of them. So it is quite understandable that humanity started to use the technology of immunization when this became available. Immunization against the traditional children's diseases has become a cornerstone of health care. I do not want to present arguments either for or against immunization for these diseases. I only want to describe the tremendous tasks that children's diseases have.

What happens when the child goes through a traditional children's disease? Such a child is no longer master of his or her house. The management of the physiological processes is temporarily given over. The new management is in fact invited by the child. This is done through imitation. In this respect, imitation is becoming infected. Being receptive includes being susceptible to infectious diseases. Children who are susceptible to contagious diseases are good imitators. The virus is not contagious, but rather the disease is. The disease can only infect children who are open for it. This has to do with the confidence I wrote about in the fifth chapter (page 214). This trust, however, should not be blind. The child was and is the patron who commissioned a certain task for a short time. The child and his or her caregivers need to follow the work of the contractor with vigilance and assess whether it develops according to plan and when it is time to finish it up.

I see this as *the* way to understand and prevent complications. We should not distract the child, not disturb the process, but be vigilant. With the child, or on behalf of the child, the caregiver has to be available to monitor the process of illness with vigilance and confidence and ask for medical help when desired or needed. The caregiver can use simple home health care techniques when, for instance, the rash does not develop as it should or when the child becomes confused through a fever. Guided by the medical profession, the caregiver can help with more intensive measures when, for instance, the child develops pneumonia or other serious complications. This attitude is no different from the basic attitude in education. Every development bears risks; that is nature. We can learn to develop this basic attitude very well by guiding children as they go through traditional children's diseases.

Who is it whom the child invites as a contractor? To answer this question, I need to say something about the beings who live in diseases.

From an earthly point of view, we may speak about beings who live in diseases, because on earth we differentiate between health and illness. In the spiritual world this differentiation is non-existent. In the spiritual world, specific spiritual beings manage qualities and faculties. There are specific spiritual beings who oversee the formation and functioning of the human body. When children need help with the remodeling of the "perception organization," the "gland organization," or another area of their bodies, they can ask for the wisdom of these spiritual beings. These beings are able to break down that part of the body that needs to be remodeled. In doing so, they enable the child to begin with the building-up phase of the remodeling. This part of the work children want to do themselves. When I described the seven life processes, we saw how children learn to build up their bodies by watching the breaking down of the nutrients. So, also, children learn to build up their bodies in their own way by watching the breakdown process enacted by these spiritual beings. The real issue of children's diseases is that the child wants to transform as much of the inherited body as he or she has the forces to manage. Remodeling too little is an opportunity lost; remodeling too much invites complications.

When children go through traditional children's diseases in the first seven years, the remodeling includes the physical body. This means that the remodeled part of the body carries the memory of the disease process in all its four members. Thus, in the example of chickenpox, not only the skin is healed (physical body), but also the life processes in the skin have changed (ether body), as well as the vulnerability of the child (astral body), and the wholeness of the child's stature (I-organization). I do not know whether the effects of a traditional children's disease are the same when they come at a later age. I doubt it. Once a member of the body is born and has matured, it is less apt to be transformed than before.

Usually a child is not susceptible to all childhood diseases. Children can only imitate something they have a connection with. The constitution and disposition of the child and the properties of his or her ether and astral bodies determine what can be imitated and what not. This is different for each child. Also, for humanity as a whole, this has been different throughout the ages. For instance, humans are no longer as susceptible to the plague as they were in the Middle Ages, as far as we know. We could say that the being that belongs to the plague has receded. Our constitution and disposition are partly determined by experiences and occurrences in previous incarnations, a subject that falls outside the scope of this book. Reading about this subject (see suggestions on pages 269–271) can deepen one's understanding of the task of children's diseases.

What can we do for those children who with or without immunization do not go through specific children's diseases? Compared to what the traditional children's diseases can accomplish, we cannot do much. The remodeling has to be postponed until the next incarnation. However, we *can* be of help on three levels:

1) to provide opportunity for development in those specific areas where the traditional children's disease would have worked;
2) to educate those soul qualities that belong to the specific area; and
3) to work wisely with other illnesses that naturally come to the child and are accompanied by fever.

Regarding 1. When we know which area of the body would have been worked through by a specific children's disease, we can take the resolve not to be in the way when children are exercising this area.

The working area of *chickenpox* is vulnerability, sensitivity. This is also the field of action of the senses and of the capacity of empathy. When we are working with children who have never had chickenpox, we may help them to use their senses well and let their souls be touched by sense

241

impressions. We must be more accepting of these children during the phases when they emotionally overreact. We can then mirror to them the actual proportions of their reactions and overreactions. This way children can use as best they can the "perception organization" of the hereditary body, without its having been remodeled by the chickenpox.

The working area of *mumps* is the digestive process in its aspect of nurturing the physical body. In this area, we can help children to eat what they can digest, not more and not less. Through this, these children develop a good sense for taking care of their bodies. In a similar way, we are helping children when we support them to take care of their clothing and toiletries properly. When the caregivers of a child who has not had the mumps are negligent in the areas of nutrition, clothing, or any aspect of the child's body care, this will be more harmful to the child than if he or she had had the mumps.

For each traditional children's disease, we can find the area in which the child can work to compensate, to an extent, for the absence of that disease. We as caregivers can help by giving the child the opportunities to do so.

Regarding 2. The actual cause of susceptibility for a specific children's disease is a one-sidedness in a previous incarnation. In one way or another, the human being was then too much occupied with him- or herself and too little with others. It may have been a one-sidedness in the area of thinking, compassion, willing, or caring for the physical and social environment. This one-sidedness gives the impulse to do better in the next incarnation by going through the necessary traditional children's disease *and* maintaining the resolve to transform this one-sidedness. Even when the specific children's disease does not occur, the resolve can be kept. This is why we need to know which one-sidedness belongs to each specific disease. In each of the traditional children's diseases, the central theme is that the child seeks to act and think in harmony with the given situation and with other human beings. When caregivers take up this theme both at home and in school, they help support the work that the traditional diseases are meant to accomplish.

Regarding 3. Nature comes up with new diseases that give rashes, as we try to eradicate the existing ones. Since rubella is generally prevented from appearing, many different kinds of viruses have appeared that try to bring about what rubella would have accomplished. Whooping cough has been generally eliminated, and now another virus has appeared that gives a pseudo whooping cough that can barely be distinguished from the genuine one. Many children have a fever for a day or so "without cause" or have "the flu" for a couple of days each month. Nature is trying to find other ways to give the beings behind the traditional children's diseases access to the children. These new illness processes, however, are less distinct and less structured than the traditional ones and, for that reason, also less predictable. These replacement illnesses may linger on for a long time or need several recurrences to accomplish what the traditional disease would have accomplished. The caregivers—including the babysitter and the playgroup supervisor—must consciously guide these illness processes with confidence, vigilance, and courage. We will find this courage more easily when we are aware that these vague illnesses may be replacing the traditional children's diseases that had the important task of helping the child to remodel his or her hereditary body.

Naughtiness and curiosity

It may seem rather unusual to consider naughtiness and curiosity as virtues. When we penetrate the matter, however, we will see that these two are capacities that keep each other in balance. Children need them to become themselves in a healthy way.

Naughtiness

What is naughtiness? Do we apply this concept when a one-year-old child halfway through eating the bowl of porridge throws the spoon willfully on the floor and observes this with interest? Or when a two-year-old child does not cooperate when being dressed? Or when a three-year-old child never puts the toys away? Or when a five-year-old child pushes another child out of the way on purpose so that he or she falls over?

There are numerous situations in which children do something that caregivers consider annoying, aggravating, clumsy, foolish, or bad. But not everything children do that goes against the grain is naughtiness. Naughtiness presupposes a certain degree of consciousness. Naughtiness goes together with pleasure; children experience it as something fantastic! "Johnny, we are going to feed the ducks; come here, and I will put on your coat." Habitually Johnny turns towards his mother, but then suddenly he stops, starts to beam, and turns around to walk away from his mother. The mother is surprised. "Come Johnny, you wanted to go out and feed the ducks." If Johnny would have the consciousness of an adult, he would answer "Yes that is true, but I have just discovered that I am able to do something that goes against your expectations." Johnny does not give this answer because he does not know it. He only knows that this first anti-authoritative deed gives him a thrill. Was Johnny up till now a submissive child? No, absolutely not. As with most toddlers, he could be obstinate, annoying, and moody. When that happened, it was unpleasant for him and for everyone else. It was as if thunderclouds had entered the room and darkened everything, including Johnny. And now: no thundercloud! A naughty sun sheds quite another light on the situation. Now he is enjoying the event. First they were on their way to the ducks, and now mother is standing there with Johnny's coat in her hands while he is walking away to do other things. Naughtiness creates an unexpected situation with a tension that is created by the child. It is a risky adventure, because Johnny does not know how mommy will react. The tension could go high. Will she start threatening punishment, or will she start to laugh and break the tension? It could be that then Johnny will let himself be dressed and off to the ducks they would go. But often this will not go so smoothly. Mommy may not be able to laugh, or Johnny does not let himself be distracted and digs in his heels. Where is the fun?

Obviously there is something very special in naughtiness. Children place themselves against the normal course of events and go their own way with pleasure. This has no purpose when the person who sets the course of the events is not present. If you are alone in your room, it does not make sense to be naughty. Drawing on the wallpaper may be an act of revenge; it could also be naughtiness if the child can make a mental picture of his parents and imagine their surprise at seeing it. More or less consciously, the child creates with pleasure a field of tension in which he or she becomes distinct from the environment. Children will only do this as long as they can be sure that this distinction will be temporary. They need to know that the harmony will be there again. There we touch on another field of tension. For children the way the tension will be released is as important as the initial creation of the tension through naughtiness. Mutual respect between caregiver and child is a necessity. If adults always laugh about naughtiness or always like it, there would be no resolution. If adults always fight against naughtiness, they may win but there would be no pleasure. Naughtiness is a game, yet it is a serious game with two parties. Neither of the parties has to win, but the game needs to be played. The game has no definite rules. Over time the adults and the children will come up with new ways of playing the game. Johnny might abruptly go for his coat, or mommy might find the excuse that there was after all not enough bread to share with the ducks. If Johnny were an older child, his mother might say that she just remembered that she had something to do before they could feed the ducks. The essence is that both parties play the game earnestly and that the resolution can come from either side. In this way, rules for the game will develop. These rules will be different for different players. Johnny will display another type of naughtiness toward his dad than toward his mom. Naughtiness and the rules of the game can be the beginning of living as an art. In conclusion, I need to emphasize that I am writing about pure naughtiness and not about other kinds of serious trouble-making such as laziness, or unacceptable or aggressive behavior.

Physiology

What do children exercise when they are naughty, and which physiological processes are involved? I will first give the answer and then try to explain it. The answer is that children are exercising the process of sleeping and being awake.

It may sound rather strange, but each child has to *learn* to sleep and to be awake. Only here on earth can we learn to alternate sleeping and being awake. It is the same with breathing. Children learn to practice perception in a rhythmical process that we call breathing. When discussing the life process of breathing in the third chapter, I described how all processes of perception are based on the rhythm of directing oneself to the outer world followed by directing oneself inwardly, on the rhythm of exhaling and inhaling. The human body is full of rhythms. *Breathing* is the collective term for all rhythms involved in perception, which are the rhythms that are directed toward the upper pole. Another group of rhythms is included in the collective terms *sleeping* and *being awake*. These rhythms have to do with the connection between the ether body and the astral body, and they have the middle region (between the upper and lower pole) as their working area.[21]

Naughtiness belongs to the group of rhythms that are included in the concepts of sleeping and being awake. First I will discuss sleeping and being awake, and then I will come back to naughtiness.

When sleeping, we humans are divided into two parts: the physical and ether bodies are lying in the bed, whereas the astral body and the I-organization are in the spiritual world. When we are awake, all four members of our bodies are connected again. When we are asleep, the tired body recuperates, whereas the soul—within the spiritual world—is listening to our plans and purposes, to what we intend to accomplish in

245

this present incarnation. When we are awake, we collect experiences. It belongs to being human that, during the day, we will often act against our own plans and purposes, as well as against the social, earthly, and cosmic order. This has to do with the complex plan of the spiritual world that humanity develop freedom of choice.[22] For this purpose, the human being must experience the potential absence of freedom. During the day, we can be below the level of freedom when—awake—we have forgotten what we intended to do with our lives. During the night we can be above the level of freedom when—asleep—we are taken up by the cosmic order and divine wisdom and compare our deeds of the day with the divine plan and our own pre-birth intentions. Placing sleeping and being awake in this light makes it obvious that children cannot do this yet. When awake, children are not yet on their own on earth. Children are given three times seven years (the I is born around the age of twenty-one) to acquire this condition. Nor can children's deeds be considered earthly deeds. Children act, but they do not take the consequences of their deeds with them into the night-process or, stated otherwise, they do not take them along as something that belongs to them (see below).

Young children act on the basis of impulses from their inner world (wishes and desires) and also of expectations and conventions from their environment (family and school). The life processes have the task of taking in and digesting the impressions of the outer world in order that children can make them their own. The theme of sleeping and being awake has to do with these activities of the life processes.

Naughtiness can be a first exercise in waking up. With naughtiness, the child turns away from the order of which he or she was a part. It is a first step toward freedom and individuality. It is the beginning of "I do what I think is appropriate now, I choose it, and I am willing to examine the consequences with the higher reality during the night." It is only a start. Not before the age of fourteen will children at night be called upon to take responsibility for their deeds. At that age, the astral body is born and therewith it is free from the physical and ether bodies at night. Thus children are given fourteen years to prepare.

The force by which children turn away from the established order I will call antipathy. It means—I do not connect to you and your intentions, and I will loosen myself from them. Antipathy is not the same as dislike. In the example of Johnny and the ducks, Johnny likes to feed the ducks, but for a moment he wants to decide for himself. "I am my own boss," says the naughty child. We need the force of antipathy to find ourselves. Only when children turn away can they discover what they themselves want, such as putting on a coat or not. In this way, they gradually become conscious of their own will. The mental image arises *after* the deed through the force of antipathy. Johnny does not think: no, I don't want my coat on. He does something, and by doing this, he may discover that there is such a thing as: with or without coat, yes or no, inside or outside the house. Antipathy is a prerequisite for acquiring the capacity to make mental pictures through thinking.

Curiosity

Since antipathy is such a powerful help for the human being to attain freedom of choice, it is likely that there is also a force of sympathy to balance naughtiness. Sympathy is the name I give to the attitude of turning toward something, the will to connect. In this discourse, sympathy is different from liking, just as antipathy is not the same as disliking. There is not such a thing as turning toward something and connecting, when there has not been a separation. The young child does not turn to his or her mother with sympathy (in the sense I am using this concept). Children are connected with their mothers, and they experience this connection as a matter of course. Thus, initially, children cannot practice sympathy with people near to them such as parents and siblings. Yet, there is another part of the world where nature has made the child separate. This is the sense world. We human beings are not naturally connected to the sense world. For us adults, the separation we experience between the sense world and ourselves is, however, essential for our consciously relating to the sense world. The one-year-old child cannot yet experience this abyss, this being separated from the sense world. Therefore this child cannot yet actively perceive. As long as children are naturally part of their environment and as long as they do not yet experience a differentiation between the sense world and themselves, there is no consciousness of separation and no active perception of the sense world. As children develop the faculty of perception, the separation between them and the sense world gradually becomes a reality. When the separation is completed, the children can build a bridge over the abyss on their own accord. Then they start exploring.

When we observe a toddler or preschooler concentrating on a bug or a leaf, we witness a child bridging the abyss between him- or herself and the sense world. Children are hungry for all that newly appears in their field of attention. Initially this curiosity is still fleeting. But rather soon, young children can watch a spoon, a piece of wood, or their toes for minutes. One is inclined to say: what is so special about these things? they are so common! The child would say: no, for me they are brand-new; they are just created and I cannot get enough of them in wonder and curiosity.

Physiology

Curiosity goes through a development over the years. Initially the drive to bridge the abyss is so strong that everything needs to be touched and put into the mouth. For toddlers, the drive has become less strong even when touching remains important. Touching is the most important sense for children, as we have seen. It is, however, important to teach children not to touch everything with their hands, but rather with their eyes; yet touching, when appropriate, should be stimulated. The perception picture is made with the help of the senses (of touch, smell, taste, etc.) and the more perfect it is, the more perfect the picture is that the child will internalize. The senses that are directed toward the body will move toward the background in the course of the first seven years even without our intervention, and the use of the higher senses will become more important.

There are children in whom the impulse of curiosity is too strong, and there are children in whom it is too weak. Too much curiosity is a problem. Often these children are restless and run after whatever their eyes see. We can help them by restricting the possibilities of receiving sense impressions and by strengthening the force of antipathy.

When children have too little curiosity, we face the question: can we stimulate curiosity? I think that we can do this only in an indirect way. When the weakness has to do with the child's constitution, we may have to work with movement development. Curiosity is turning toward something, connecting with it, and moving toward it. Children's movement development follows the same direction. We can stimulate the movement development and motivate the children to enjoy movement. Then we may hope that curiosity will come along. We still need to take care that the process does not go too far or too fast; children should not make movements for which they are not yet ready. The phase of development and the disposition of the individual child determine the degree of readiness.

There are also children who have become apathetic and have lost the impulse of curiosity, for instance, because every initiative they have tried has been undermined. A discussion on ways to help children in this situation lies beyond the scope of this book.

Most adults have forgotten the mood of their early genuine curiosity. We should try to remember this mood—when did we last see a natural phenomenon, a flower, or a piece of art whose existence we had not dreamt of? I remember the mood of seeing for the first time a *sparassis crispa*, a mushroom in the shape of a sponge. I was amazed, and it absorbed all my attention. I have had the same experience time and again when I have observed an ant hill; it goes beyond my power of imagination that there can be so much chaos and such strict order at the same time. When we try to connect to this mood again, we may be better able to live with curious, investigating, exploring children. There is more going on than just perception. There is breathing out, and falling asleep in the perception. The thing that attracts the child's interest pulls the child toward it with the force of sleep. Children can be so absorbed in what has caught their interest that they do not even hear when they are spoken to. They also become very tired from genuine interest.

When children practice interest in the sense world, they can develop interest in their fellow human beings and in world events later in life. Through the force of sympathy that works in curiosity, children acquire the skill of observing things actively, of seeing things with engagement, and of creating their own imaginative pictures of what they have perceived.[23] This capacity is quite different from the capacity of making mental pictures through thinking out of the force of antipathy.

Summary

By turning away from something, by being naughty, children learn to let go of security for a moment and to find themselves. This is the force of antipathy. Waking up, they break away from the cosmic order and create their own thought world. By turning toward something, by being curious, children learn to unite with the surrounding world without losing themselves in it. This is the force of sympathy. Falling asleep, they build a bridge between themselves and the world, and they will come back with a true picture of reality.

During childhood, naughtiness and curiosity are the child's companions. At a later age, we call them non-conformity and interest. When they balance one another out, they create a base that is ideal for the development of a free human being.

There are many stories and poems about children who run away from home to explore the world. This theme combines the phenomena of curiosity and naughtiness. These stories contain much of what I have described, and we may even enjoy them more since we have learned more about naughtiness and curiosity.

Forgetting and remembering

When we imagine how life would be without the capacities of remembering and forgetting, we realize the great importance of these two soul faculties. If we could not remember, we would be absorbed by the events of each moment. Without memory, life experiences cannot build up the inner framework of the personality. Without memory, we can learn no more than our instincts tell us at each moment. We would live on the unconscious level of being conditioned. Yet, if we were not able to forget, life would be even more hopeless. If we compare a life without the capacity of remembering with a life without the capacity of forgetting, the absence of memory would have the advantage that we would not remember our problems and difficulties. Without the capacity to forget, however, our souls would be overwhelmed by the continuing presence of all the pictures and images we ever encountered or created. I think that a human being could not bear this even for a day.

When we focus on memory, we enter an area that is directly connected to the core of our being human. Instead of asking, "who are you?" we could as well ask, "what all lives in your memory?" I need to discuss this subject, because the way we deal with the faculties of remembering and forgetting is even more existentially connected with the theme of "becoming who we are" than subjects such as children's diseases and naughtiness. There is much literature on this subject, so I will focus on what is needed to understand the physiological aspect. I will discuss the picture character of memory, the development of memory, dangers to which the faculty of memory is exposed, the physiology of forgetting (which is like a process of seed formation) and of remembering (which is like a germination process), and finally, the conditions for a healthy development of memory.

The picture character of memory

What kind of reality does memory give us? There is no doubt that memory gives us some kind of reality. People who suffer from obsessive memory pictures will affirm that these are not just appearances. Whoever has sought in vain for a missing part of his or her memory, realizes that he or she has lost something real. Of course there is an essential difference between the rose that we see and smell and the rose that we remember—between the party we are participating in and the party we remember. The rose and the party we remember do not need to be less real than the ones we experience at a particular moment. The memory of something can be more full and beautiful or more vague and shallow than our original experiences. The memory picture is a picture of the original situation. Still, it is not like a copy or a photograph; it leads a new and genuine existence, while at the same time keeping the relation with the original perception or experience.

We can compare memory pictures to the physical body. The appearance of our physical body at a particular moment bears the memory of our life up till that moment. Scars of wounds, rough hands of bricklayers, smooth hands of surgeons, wrinkles caused by the cheerful person's laughing and smiling, the frowning mouth of those who feel wronged, these all are memories of the past. Each has a direct relation to the situation that brought it into being. Each is a picture of that situation, rather than the situation itself. When we extend our scope and include the previous life and the next life, we can extend the example. The outer form of my head is a memory of my previous life, of the things I did at that time. What I do in this life is the germ for the shape of my head in the next incarnation. Therefore all we do has a futuristic character. An extract of all our deeds remains. Our will forces are not entirely used up in our deeds; a part of them is saved. When we resolve (consciously or unconsciously) to do a better job next time, such a resolve will shape the future. After death, we carry these resolves and other "germs" with us on our journey toward the next incarnation. Then a picture of this situation is made. This picture forms the upper pole of our bodies in the next incarnation. This memory picture is very accurate. Rudolf Steiner stated that we do not yet have the maturity to understand this process thoroughly; we would misuse it.

A process of tremendous metamorphosis in the time between death and rebirth transforms the experiences of the previous life into a memory picture in the following incarnation. What happens within one and the same life can be compared to this, on a simpler scale. Within one and the same life, it is our individual human power of transformation that makes the memory picture of a situation we have experienced.

The development of memory

In the past, memory was different from the way it is now, and in the future it will be different again. The development of memory in the history of humanity can be likened to memory development of children today. Children begin earthly life without memory. In the important first years of their lives, they learn to walk, to speak, and to think, mainly through imitation. This learning process occurs under the guidance not of the children themselves, not of their parents and educators, but under the guidance of the Christ (see chapter 5). Growing up, children will not remember this phase. Memory starts to develop when children begin to be conscious of the differentiation between themselves and the world, between the I and everything else. Initially the faculty of remembering is bound to external objects such as furniture in the house, objects in the near surroundings, the daily trip to the grocery store, or whatever serves as a marker. The child's consciousness connects to these objects and not to the individual inner experiences. This phase lasts till about age four.

Then memory begins to work differently— it is more free on the one hand, more restricted on the other. Children can let go of the necessity to connect with outer markers, and they can connect to inner experiences. This also has a restrictive effect. Instead of being part of the outer environment and finding memory markers everywhere, children now have to find connections in their inner world. Now memory becomes based on what is living in their souls as feelings and moods aroused by what they have experienced either in the moment or repeatedly. This is the phase of rhymes and poems, which the children never can get enough of and which lay the foundation for the type of memory that is based on sentiments, throughout life.

At about the age of seven, the third phase sets in—personalized memory. Children become able to form memory pictures of past experiences; this is more or less independent of the occasion and of what their soul experienced in the original situation. They no longer need physical markers or recollection of the mood of a situation to remember a fact. This type of memory is required when the child enters the school system in which more and more abstract concepts and pictures have to be understood and memorized. This third type of memory continues to develop and becomes what adults experience as their normal memory. The first two memory types remain, but in the background. Our contemporary faculty of memory is not the last phase in human memory development; this becomes obvious when we compare the development of memory to the development of human consciousness.

In ancient times, before the Flood, human beings did not have a personal consciousness. Their actions, feelings, and thoughts were inspired by guiding spiritual beings. No one would say, "let me think for a moment"; spiritual beings were thinking in each person. All human souls were open to the cosmos; there was no independence, no freedom. Everybody could remember everything, because the cosmos kept the memories and they were accessible to all human beings.

In the second phase, the collective storage of memories was still accessible to anyone, but most people needed help to make this connection. This help was given by mural paintings, dolmens, and other physical markers. Those markers assisted the collective memory of (large) groups of people.

The next phase is the development of "rhythmic memory." The history of a tribe, a nation, or the whole of humanity was put into verses that were passed on from one generation to the next in melodious recitation. When people wanted to create pictures of their history, they could memorize these numerous lines in a state of mind that was neither asleep nor awake.

Only after a large part of the so-called Greek civilization had passed, at about the time that the Christ walked on earth in a physical body, did some people start to become aware that they themselves could have a say over what they would think and remember. This development announced the end of the soul's clairvoyance and the open connection of the ether body with the cosmos. Now people have to make an effort to learn to memorize.

After the Middle Ages, remembrance of the divine origin of thinking and of memory disappeared. People became proud of their independent world of thought. They, however, no longer realized how shallow and dull their world of thought had become compared to the previously accessible cosmic wisdom, because the memory of the existence of this great wisdom had been extinguished. At present, where we are oblivious to cosmic intelligence, we are on the summit of independent thinking and personal memory. This phase is necessary for humanity in order to attain freedom. Thinking had to adapt itself to the functioning of the physical brain, and memory had to restrict itself to copying earthly reality. Humanity could only disengage itself from the guidance of the spiritual world by losing itself—in itself, in the observation of the sense world, and in acute scientific thinking.

Still, this will not be the end. The time will come in which we no longer experience our thoughts and memories as personally and individually as we do now. This is related to the way the ether body is connected to the physical body, especially in the region of the head. In times long past, clairvoyance was common because the human ether body was much larger than the physical body, especially in the region of the head. Therefore, divine spiritual beings could send thoughts into human ether bodies. (In the second, third, and fifth chapters, I mentioned that the ether body is the thought body.) Personalization (individualization) of thinking and memory occurred as the human ether body was shrinking and attaining the same form as the physical body, eventually overlapping it exactly. This tight connection between the physical body and the ether body will loosen again in the region of the head. Through this it will become easier again for us to find access to the spiritual world, and we will no longer feel so strongly the necessity to check our thoughts against the structure of the physical body and against the reality of the sense world. Thoughts and memory pictures can again become more spiritual, but also more prone to fantasy. The only way to prevent unrealistic fantasy is to hold on to what we gained through our present stage of consciousness. We must retain the exactness of our thinking and the connectedness of our thoughts and memories to earthly reality. Educating our thinking with the help of natural science and educating ourselves with the help of spiritual science will provide the security we need to practice our new incipient faculties, which will enable us to think in communion with spiritual reality out of our own inner forces.

At the time the Christ entered into a physical body on earth, the conditions for these new faculties were created. Since the Christ came down to earth, died on the cross on Good Friday, united Himself with the earth on Black Saturday, and was resurrected on Easter Sunday, the human physical body has been transformed. Since that moment, the human physical body has in itself the possibility to turn toward the spirit in freedom and to decide in freedom to live in loving compassion with fellow human beings. This is the saving grace for our faculty of memory. Our widened memory can then be Christian when, in our compassion, we realize that each human being is created as an image of God. This will not lead to a more or less unconscious feeling of "we and they" or to sentimental charity, but to the deliberate choice to use the faculty of memory in a Christian way. This will prevent thoughts and memory pictures from becoming unreal and fantastic, because they will reflect factual situations. We will have the will power to accept only those thoughts and to form only those memory pictures that truly fit the specific situation and are beneficial for that situation. This potential still lies in the future. The time will come when the Christ will not only teach us to walk, speak, and think, but when He will also educate our faculty of memory. At present, we can already start teaching our children to be careful with the use of their memory, as well as to involve others in their perceptions, experiences, and opinion forming.

Dangers to which the memory faculty is exposed

To threaten the memory is to threaten the I. Therefore I want to discuss some dangers to which memory is exposed, as they may affect child development. When we are aware of the dangers, we can try to avoid them.

When our consciousness is not clear, we are not able to check our memory pictures against reality. In the transitions from being awake to falling asleep and from sleeping to waking up, our consciousness is not clear. In this phase, we are not bothered by outer sense impressions and therefore memory pictures can rise up from inside. Activating memory in such a situation bears the risk that we cannot control these pictures. This can be frightening, especially for children, and may be a reason why a child does not want to go to sleep. We can try to help the children by letting them fall asleep more quickly. When the transition between being awake and sleeping is not extended, this twilight period is shortened, and fear has less opportunity to develop. For adults also, it is sometimes difficult to place memory pictures properly and not become confused by memory fragments that arise out of a trance-like or dream-like situation. Yet, adults can consciously decide whether a memory picture actually belongs to them, if it is based on factual reality, and whether they can consciously work with it.

Another danger can come from the way we train memory. Learning to memorize facts or lines by heart bears the risk that segments become stuck in our memory. These segments rise up from our memory, separated from their context. As they separate from the whole, they also separate from the I. Then they can become obsessive. The danger is that human beings start to act as automatons, motivated by these memory fragments. This does not mean that we should not ask children to memorize lines or facts by heart. Such memorizing can increase the wealth in our souls. The issue is that we should prevent the memorized material from losing its connection with the original and genuine context.

A third danger is the externalization of memory. This is especially encouraged in our time. We are sure that we need external memory support. We start to write everything down and end with computerized data-management. When we realize that libraries and data files have taken over what belongs to the task of our faculty of memory, we can realize the effect of this externalizing of memory on our personal development. Everything that is recorded with the help of an external memory support has lost the opportunity to go through a metamorphosis. A true memory picture has the characteristic that it will not remain the same. It will grow along with new memory pictures. Through this constant evolving, our memories can always be current and alive. Externalized memory (such as data files and books) cannot go through this metamorphosis; we all know this problem. When we teach children to externalize their memory, we should also teach them that the context of a fact is as important as the fact itself, and we should also stimulate their creative capacities when they involve themselves with facts.

Physiology of forgetting and remembering

Forgetting is like the process of seed formation; remembering is like the process of germination.

When we want to perceive something, we turn our gaze outward; when we want to remember something, we turn inward. Both processes require an inner activity; at least it should be so in our present time. We should not give ourselves up to impressions from outside or to an involuntary stream of memories from inside. Between these two, we have acquired a free space, in which our souls can experience themselves at rest; it is within this space that we can be masters of our perceptions and memory pictures. In ancient times, human beings did not have this free space. In our time we can have it, in spite of the abundance of outside stimuli and the memory pictures involuntarily rising up from inside. When we are healthy, we can maintain this free space. Children cannot do that yet. Young children do not have the capacity to resist impressions from the outside nor demands from the inside, from the metabolic system. This is the normal situation for young children, and it does not affect them as much as it would adults. Babies are barely conscious of sense impressions (which are building up the child's body instead of being mirrored), or of metabolic activity (which is determining the child's sleeping, being awake, crying, or drinking rather than becoming memory pictures). Infants are in a state of awake unconsciousness. They need to be "awake" off and on to eat, but they are basically unconscious of all the activities and processes occurring in their bodies. Infants do not know about the sense world, nor about the world of memories.

This situation changes gradually over time. Throughout life, the soul's relation with, on the one hand, the sense world and, on the other hand, the world of memories is subject to change, but the first three years are crucial for the potential of change. Why? Because toward the outside as well as toward the inside, boundaries are being created. The creative power of the sense world—which worked in the infant without restrictions—is receding behind the perceivable objects, and the children are only able to see (smell, taste, hear, touch) the sense perceptible qualities of objects. Now they perceive only the outside of things. The inside—that which belongs to the object as a creative force, as spiritual principle—is now hiding. This is the first veil, the veil before the sense world. This veil is woven by learning to use the senses, to look with the physical eyes.

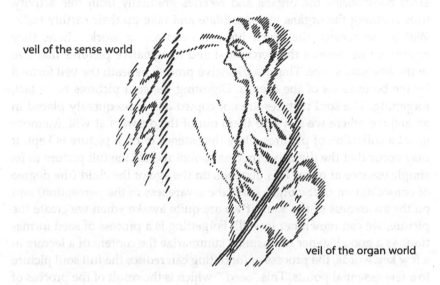

veil of the sense world

veil of the organ world

Fig. 63 During childhood, two veils are woven before the soul. Because of the veil in front of the sense world, we develop sense perception. Because of the veil in front of the organ world, we develop the faculty of memory. In between these two veils a free space for the soul is created. (From Rudolf Steiner, Menschenwerden, Weltenseele und Weltengeist, GA 205 Dornach 1987.)

Parallel to the development described above, another process occurs within the body. The maturing organs increasingly become organs that serve the earthly processes such as digestion, metabolism, and excretion. Through this, they consolidate, contract, and cloak themselves in boundaries. This is meant functionally rather than physically. (Obviously babies already have physical organs with physical boundaries.) Earlier I described this process as maturation of the physical organ under the influence of the ether body. I will give blood formation as an example. At the time of physical birth, the liver and the spleen still form blood. Later, this activity is concentrated in the bone marrow, which we consider the organ of blood formation. I could also describe this receding, this consolidating, in the following way—a veil comes over the world of the organs; the organ world receives a boundary and a surface. We could look at the diaphragm as a picture of the surface of the organ world. Below the diaphragm, we have our unconscious, subconscious world.

Thus, we see two boundaries arise and in between a free space where the soul can exist. Various factors work together to accomplish this. The ether body forms the organs and recedes gradually from this activity, thus enabling the organs to consolidate and take up their earthly tasks. Within the organs, the seven life processes are at work. There, they reduce to the essence the perceptual and imaginative pictures that live in the free soul space. This is a digestive process beneath the veil formed by the boundaries of the organs. Digesting the soul pictures is, in fact, forgetting. The soul pictures are not copied and subsequently placed in an archive where we can take them out of the drawers at will. Memory is not a collection of pictures. Only the essence of each picture is kept. It may occur that the digestive process cannot reduce the full picture to its simple essence at once. This depends on the age of the child (the degree of consolidation of the organs and the awareness of the perception) and on the awareness of the soul (if we are quite awake when we create the picture, we can remember it well). Forgetting is a process of seed formation. As a good listener can usually summarize the content of a lecture in a few key words, the process of forgetting can reduce the full soul picture to a few essential points. This "seed," which is the result of the process of forgetting, can now wait until the day memory might want to take it up again and recreate a full picture.

While waiting, this seed is still active. What we have forgotten is as important as what we remember. Pictures that are truly forgotten start to work. They find a place in the background of memory, they connect with other experiences, and they become part of the whole of one's life experiences. When they are not disturbed (i.e. when the child does not try to remember them), the life processes can use these seeds to make them part of the child's ether body. Then they will contribute to a healthy state further on in life! Thus we need the faculty of forgetting, not only to keep the free space of our souls clean but also to keep our bodies healthy. We experience our personalities on the basis of the whole of our life experiences (of which the forgotten ones are an integral and essential part). This is a prerequisite for the I to experience its continuity and integrity. Forgetting—we can hardly overvalue it!

It belongs to being a free human being that we can pull up memories at will. How does this process occur? Who brings the seed-of-the-forgotten to life? Who starts the germination process? Who recreates the full memory picture out of the hieroglyphs of what has been forgotten? In nature, seed must fall on fertile soil to germinate. Warmth, humidity, and light bring it to life. A new plant grows out of it, identical to the mother plant that produced the seed. This process we also find within the human being, because the human being reflects the cosmos. What I have described as the power of imagination is a description of the physiology of calling up memory pictures. As long as the picture has not yet been forgotten completely, we can activate it by imitation. We need imagination when the picture has been forgotten completely. Imagination creates a new picture. It is similar to the original picture, but it has gone through a metamorphosis if the process went well. The seed has been taken up by the "forgetfulness-organization" of the child and has become part of the child. When it is called to life again, it germinates and grows in a different soil. We may think about the familiar experience that after years we suddenly understand a situation that had been incomprehensible until then. This can only happen when the situation truly has been forgotten; it does not occur when we have kept it as an active memory picture.

Conditions for developing healthy memory

There are a number of conditions for an undisturbed memory development in children.

Young children do not relate to facts; facts do not mean a thing to them. Their souls can only work with pictures, which are simultaneously the child's reality as well as pictures of it. Pictures are open and can grow; this is different with intellectual statements. When I use the word "picture," I do not mean a fairy tale shown on TV or stories depicted in comic books. What I do mean is the pictures children can make in themselves when adults speaking to them are vividly and imaginatively picturing to themselves what they are talking about.

Memory development occurs in phases, and proper education will make use of this. In the first phase, children need physical objects to support their memory. In the second phase, children need to sing, to repeat, to create the mood through which memory can be activated. Only in the third phase can children begin to practice picturing events in their own souls. Memory and imagination are closely related. When we stimulate children to have imagination (in their games, for instance) and be creative, and when we accept and value their pretend world during their first seven years, we also help them to have a good memory when later they go to school.

Children do not need to understand everything; it is even better when they don't. A picture or an imagination that is incomprehensible to them has the power to germinate. In the unconscious regions of memory, it finds a place among other life experiences. If we were to explain everything on a level that could be understood by children, we would make it difficult for them to understand anything on a higher level later in life. It is essential for children to have the opportunity to ask questions; yet they do not need answers on the level of their understanding. Mysteries are interesting because we do not have an answer.

We help preschool children when, once or twice a day, we lead them to concentrate quietly on an observation, a picture, or an imagination. This is a relief especially for children with an inner unrest. If children have these moments, then at least a few pictures a day can take the orderly route to the unconscious. This brings order below the diaphragm.

Summary

Forgetting and remembering, reducing soul pictures to the essence and unfolding them again, are two human faculties that are related to the fact that, at present, we can experience the I as being free. We are able to forget when the veil in front of the sense world causes us to meet the sense world exclusively through sense perception, and when the veil in front of the organs prevents the forces that work in the organs from working in the soul in an uncontrolled manner. Memory as a process is closely related to imagination. Memories go through a metamorphosis between the moment they are imprinted in the organs and the moment they are called upon again to enter consciousness. Through this metamorphosis, they remain current. The processes of forgetting and remembering occur to a great extent unconsciously.

In the future, we must learn to be aware of them and guide these processes consciously, just as we now guide walking, speaking, and thinking.

Summary of the chapter

Children are given a great deal of help to become who they are as human beings. Children's diseases help them to adapt certain parts of their hereditary bodies to their own specific needs. Naughtiness and curiosity help children to learn the most important thing they have to learn—the rhythm between being awake and sleeping. Naughtiness makes children turn away from their surroundings and makes them aware of themselves and the world. Through their interest and curiosity, children turn toward their environment, which they learn to know and understand by temporarily falling asleep in it.

Forgetting and remembering are the conditions for acquiring a free soul space between the sense impressions of the outer world and the organ forces of the inner world. Forgetting is like seed formation in nature—a perceptual or imaginative picture is reduced to its essentials. Remembering is like the growing of a plant from seed. The power of imagination initiates this germination process in the child. These three are helpers that enable children not only to strive to be human, but also to become who they want and need to be.

Epilogue

I am interested to know how you, the reader of this book, arrived at this page. Did you go immediately from the Introduction to the end of the book to see how it comes out? Did you read through the book page by page? Has it been easy for you to find your way and did you find the trail again after you lost it for a while? Did you enjoy vistas now and then? Was the climb rewarded and the descent easier than expected? Did you read a section here or there, as a long-distance trail can be hiked bit by bit without connecting all of the segments in their sequence? Of course, I hope that you have enjoyed your journey. I also hope that you will give me feedback by letting me know the shortcomings and errors of this travel guide. If this book has helped you to value the uniqueness of the first seven years of childhood, it has fulfilled its purpose.

Please send any questions or comments to me at:

Het Kindertherapeuticum
Homeruslaan 22
Utrecht NL 3581 MG
The Netherlands

Fax: + 31 30 258 1014

E-mail: schoorel@kindertherapeuticum.nl

Glossary

Anthroposophy

A path of consciousness development presented by Rudolf Steiner, as well as his indications on how to find, walk, and stay on this path.

Rudolf Steiner

An initiate of the highest rank. He lived in the German-speaking part of Europe 1861–1925. His task was to bring out into the open much of the spiritual knowledge that had been strictly guarded in esoteric circles. He taught a method of acquiring higher states of consciousness and he showed in various areas of science how the healthy development of human civilization requires that we expand our consciousness and develop a living thinking that is connected to the warmth of the heart. He wrote a few books, mostly between 1898 and 1912. Near the end of his life, he wrote, in collaboration with his physician, a booklet on the principles of medicine, and he published part of his autobiography as well as a collection of 185 aphorisms that give the essence of Anthroposophy. Most of these books have been translated into English. He gave lectures all over Europe (many of which have been translated into English) and inspired initiatives in the areas of farming, education, medicine, and caring for people with developmental disabilities, to name a few. He stressed the importance of awareness of reincarnation for building social organisms and for engaging in human services such as education and medicine.

Creation

The author of this book considers the resistance to acknowledging the fact that the earth and humanity have been created by divine spiritual beings as an important, necessary, but also temporary phase in Western science; this phase started at about the end of the 15th century. As science since then has uncovered, for instance, how intricate the biochemical and other physiological processes in the human body are (to mention only one example in one field of science), it seems at present more appropriate to research the existence and working of spiritual beings than to hold on to the rather naive hypothesis that the cosmos, the earth, and all that belongs to it has developed by mere chance.

Spiritual beings I have named them according to the Christian tradition. The readers of this book who are raised in other religious traditions are invited to substitute these names with the nomenclature they are familiar with. The same applies to the pictorial images of the Old Testament of the Bible that I have used, such as Adam, Paradise, the Fall, and the Flood. Early Christianity distinguished three times three ranks of spiritual beings placed between God and the human being. The three lowest ranks—from above downward—are here named the Archai, Archangels, and Angels. Other religions have different names for them. These beings are more highly developed than human beings. They all have their specific tasks in the cosmos. Artists used to depict these beings with wings, to indicate that they are not subject to the laws of the physical world, such as gravity.

The Christ The Christian name for the Being Who encompasses all of humanity, and Who is the archetype of the ideal, fully developed human being, beyond racial, religious, denominational, and any other differentiation. He is one of the highest spiritual beings, and represents the all-human, accessible to every human being. He has a special connection to the Earth, and knows what love, sacrifice, and suffering are.

Eurythmy A specific way of moving the body and the limbs, developed by Rudolf Steiner. In this artistic and fluid way of moving, we can trace elements of sign language, body language, mime, drama, and dance, but eurythmy goes beyond all of them. Eurythmy can be done just for pleasure, as a means of education, for therapeutic purposes, or on the stage as a performing art. Generally it is practiced in a group. When people are practicing eurythmy, they give expression to that which makes them move, and thus they transform their movements into gestures. The gestures are not made arbitrarily; they follow the laws of the etheric world (discussed in the second and third chapters). These gestures bring sounds (tones) to visibility. These sounds or tones (originating in the Logos) can be music or spoken language. In eurythmy, the formative forces behind music and speech (discussed in the fifth chapter) are made visible through the posture and the movements of the physical body.

Notes

1. The plant is an etheric formation and does not have an incarnated astral body. The plant's astral body affects the plant from the outside; it does not contribute to plant formation from the inside.

2. When I use the words magnesium, fluoride, and calcium, I am referring to the forces and processes that have created magnesium, fluoride, and calcium as material substances. I am not referring to the properties of these physical-chemical substances or the effects they have in nature. An example from the plant world: carbon can be understood as condensed sunlight. The plant condenses sunlight and carbon dioxide to carbon through a process of assimilation.

3. In the lower jaw, the eyeteeth erupt when the child is around the age of ten; soon after this occurrence the first molars erupt. In the upper jaw, the first molars erupt when the child is ten; the eyeteeth erupt half a year later. It is interesting to observe this sequential difference.

4. The hormones of the adrenal glands also have other effects, especially on a psychological level.

5. Michaela Glöckler has brought this theme (of the differences between the male and female ether bodies) to the fore.

6. Rudolf Steiner compared the human skeleton to a sonata. I assume that he was indicating that we look at the "movement organization" as a musical composition. See Rudolf Steiner, *Balance in Teaching* (Spring Valley, NY: Mercury Press, 1982) and Armin Huseman, *The Harmony of the Human Body* (Edinburgh: Floris, 1994).

7. This is different when we consider the planets. It is quite possible to relate specific organs to specific planets and their activities. We can relate the planets also to specific areas of the soul (such as memory and wisdom).

8. The physical body of animals is also lifted out of gravity, actually in a much more perfect way than in human beings. Look, for instance,

at butterflies, squirrels, or wolves. Animals do not need to conquer this levity; nature gives it to them.

9. The sense of color gives the complementary color in the after-image. We can consciously work with the phenomenon of the after-image. If we do this, we can train ourselves to work with images from the ether world, with imaginations.

10. The designation "imprints of cosmic wisdom" refers to the situation that the body of each human being retains imprints of the developmental process of humankind, of the history of humanity. Rudolf Steiner described the human being as a micro-cosmos in his books *An Outline of Esoteric Science* (Gt. Barrington, MA: Anthroposophic Press, 1997) and *Cosmic Memory* (Blauvelt, NY: Garber, 1987).

11. In this phase it obviously bothers children when they must consciously pay attention to their movements.

12. Sign language is symbolic and rather abstract. Eurythmy is real, living language made visible.

13. We need to distinguish these gestures from sign language, which can serve as a substitute for spoken language.

14. Children who are deaf go through a language development which is different from that of children who can hear. Children who are deaf also come into a "language-stream" that develops into language of the deaf.

15. We may not put this the other way round. Children who have no problems with movement development can have speech problems.

16. The child is ready for elementary school when his or her ether body is born. The way memory functions is one of the factors that indicates this readiness.

17. There are children to whom everything comes easily. They do not need to exert themselves and still understand everything. It is most likely that these children have a sense of thought that is functioning extremely well. Yet this asset could make it more difficult for them to learn to think. They may face problems later in life, when they need

to think for themselves, because they have not learned to activate their will in thought activity.

18. See Rudolf Steiner, *An Outline of Esoteric Science.*

19. In the development of humanity and of the earth, the physical body has been brought to development first. See Rudolf Steiner, *An Outline of Esoteric Science* and *Cosmic Memory.*

20. Rudolf Steiner speaks about these directions of forces in *Balance in Teaching* (Spring Valley, NY: Mercury Press, 1982). The concepts he developed in these lectures seem incongruent with other statements he has made. I have tried to come to a synthesis.

21. There is a third group of rhythms; this is connected with the meta-bolic-limb pole. These rhythms span the events from birth to death. The laws governing a person's successive reincarnations belong to this group of rhythms. In human physiology, this type of rhythm affects the relation between life forces and death forces.

22. In *Cosmic Memory*, Rudolf Steiner describes the task of humanity: to introduce in the cosmos a new capacity—to be free. This process contains a tremendous risk, because it requires the existence of evil, in order that human beings can freely choose between good and evil.

23. We do not receive a picture passively, merely as a result of chemical and optic processes in the eye. We need to be active to create a picture of the reality; this then can be called an imagination. Children look with big eyes and create their pictures of the sense world. Rudolf Steiner distinguishes this common imagination from the imagination that is an initial step toward clairvoyance.

For Further Reading

For books by Rudolf Steiner, the GA number refers to the volume
of the complete works of Rudolf Steiner published in German.

Bockemühl, Jochen. *Toward a Phenomenology of the Etheric World*. New York:
Anthroposophic Press, 1985.

Glöckler, Michaela and Wolfgang Göbel. *A Guide to Child Health*
[Kindersprechstunde]. Edinburgh: Floris Books, 2003.

Holtzapfel, Walter. *Children's Illnesses*. Spring Valley, NY: Mercury Press,
1989.

Husemann, Armin J. *The Harmony of the Human Body: Musical Principles in
Human Physiology* [Der musikalische Bau des Menschen]. Edinburgh:
Floris Books, 1994.

Köhler, Henning. *Working with Anxious, Nervous and Depressed Children: A
Spiritual Perspective to Guide Parents*. Fair Oaks, CA: AWSNA, 2002.

König, Karl. *The First Three Years of the Child*. Spring Valley, NY: Anthroposophic
Press, 1969.

Lievegoed, B.C.J. *Phases of Childhood*. Edinburgh: Floris Books. 1997.

Marti, Ernst. *The Four Ethers*. Roselle, IL: Schaumburg Publications, 1984.

Pikler, Emmi. An extract of *Peaceful Babies—Contented Mothers* is published in
"Emmi Pikler 1902–1984" *Sensory Awareness Bulletin* 14, Winter 1994.
Sensory Awareness Foundation, 955 Vernal Avenue, Mill Valley, CA
94941.

Soesman, Albert. *Our Twelve Senses: Wellsprings of the Soul*. Stroud, England:
Hawthorn Press, 1990.

Steiner, Rudolf. *Anthroposophy: A Fragment* [Anthroposophie, ein Fragment
GA 45]. Hudson, NY: Anthroposophic Press, 1996.

————. *Balance in Teaching* [Meditativ erarbeitete Menschenkunde GA 302a].
Spring Valley, NY: Mercury Press, 1982 (3rd revised printing 1990).

————. *Cosmic Memory: Prehistory of Earth and Man* [Aus der Akasha-Chronik
GA 11]. Blauvelt, NY: Garber Communications Inc., 1987.

————. *Foundations of Human Experience* (also published in English under the
title *Study of Man*) [Allgemeine Menschenkunde als Grundlage der
Pädagogik GA 293]. Hudson, NY: Anthroposophic Press, 1996.

————. *Harmony of the Creative Word: The Human Being and the Elemental,
Animal, Plant and Mineral Kingdoms* (also published under the
title *Man as Symphony of the Creative Word*) [Der Mensch als
Zusammenklang des schaffenden, bildenden und gestaltenden
Weltenwortes GA 230]. London: Rudolf Steiner Press, 2001.

————. *An Outline of Esoteric Science* [Geheimwissenschaft im Umriss GA 13]. Great Barrington, MA: Anthroposophic Press, 1997.

————. *A Psychology of Body, Soul and Spirit* (also published in English under the title *Anthroposophy, Psychosophy, Pneumatosophy*) [Anthroposophie, Psychosophie, Pneumatosophie GA 115]. Hudson, NY: Anthroposophic Press, 1999.

————. *The Riddle of Humanity* [Kosmische und menschliche Geschichte. Das Rätsel des Menschen GA 170]. London: Rudolf Steiner press, 1990.

————. *The Spiritual Guidance of the Individual and Humanity* [Die geistige Führung des Menschen und der Menschheit GA 15]. Hudson, NY: Anthroposophic Press, 1992.

————. *The Spiritual Hierarchies and their Reflection in the Physical World: Zodiac, Planets, Cosmos* [Geistige Hierarchien und ihre Widerspiegelung in der physischen Welt, Tierkreis, Planeten, Kosmos, GA 110]. Spring Valley, NY: Anthroposophic Press, 1970.

————. *Spiritual Science as a Foundation for Social Forms* [Die zwölf Sinne des Menschen, (Sonderdruck aus Geisteswissenschaft als Erkenntnis der Grundimpulse sozialer Gestaltung) GA 199]. Spring Valley, NY/ London: Anthroposophic Press/Rudolf Steiner Press, 1986.

————. *Theosophy* [Theosophie GA 9]. Hudson, NY: Anthroposophic Press, 1994.

————. *The Waking of the Human Soul and the Forming of Destiny* [Gehen—Sprechen—Denken, lecture given in Prague Apr 28, 1923, GA 224]. Toronto: Steiner Book Centre, 1970.

Strauss, Michaela. *Understanding Children's Drawings*. London: Rudolf Steiner Press, 1988.

Wachsmuth, Günther. *The Etheric Formative Forces in Cosmos, Earth and Man*. London: Anthroposophical Publishing Co., 1932.

The following works in Dutch and German were also given as references in the original Dutch edition.

Georg von Armin, *Zum heilpädagogischen Kurs Rudolf Steiners*, Stuttgart 1981

R.A.E. Bilo e.a., *Kind in ontwikkeling. Een Handreiking bij de observatie van jonge kinderen*, Utrecht 1995[2]

Christhilde Blume, *Kleinkinderzeichnungen—Spiegel der Entwicklung*, Stuttgart 1976

Jochen Bockemühl, *Elementen en ethersoorten*, Driebergen 1992

F.J.J. Buytendijk, *Algemene theorie der menselijke houding en beweging*, Utrecht/ Antwerpen 1979[9]

Gregg Furth, *Tekeningen, beeldtaal van het onbewuste*, Rotterdam 1991

Norbert Glas, *Kinderkrankheiten als Entwicklungsstufen des Menschen*, Wien—Leipzig—Bern 1937

Thomas Göbel, *Erdengeist und Landschaftsseele*, Dornach 1994

———. *Die Quellen der Kunst. Lebendige Sinne und Phantasie als Schlüssel zur Architektur*, Dornach 1982.

———. 'Über den Nerven-Sinnesprozeß', in: *Der Heilmittelbegriff bei Rudolf Steiner*, Dornach 1980

Britta Holle, *De motorische ontwikkeling van normale en geretardeerde kinderen*, Lisse 1980[2]

Friedrich A. Kipp, *Die Evolution des Menschen im Hinblick auf seine lange Jugendzeit*, Stuttgart 1991[2]

Rita Kohnstamm, *Kleine ontwikkelingspsychologie. Deel 1. Het jonge kind*, Houten 1996[4]

Karl König, *Sinnesentwicklung und Leibeserfahrung, Heilpädagogische Gesichtspunkte zur Sinneslehre Rudolf Steiners*, Stuttgart 1978[2]

Christof Lindenau, *Der übende Mensch. Anthroposophie-Studium als Ausgangspunkt moderner Geistesschulung*, Stuttgart 1981[2]

Olaf Oltmann, *Das Aetherische Christuswirken*, Dornach 1991

Wilhelm Pelikan, *Heilpflanzenkunde. Der Mensch und die Heilpflanzen*, Dornach. Deel 1 1985[5], deel 2 1982[3], deel 3 1984[2]

Emmi Pikler, *Friedliche Babys—zufriedene Mütter. Pädagogische Ratschläge einer Kinderärtzin*, Freiburg—Basel—Wien 1987[3]

Hermann Poppelbaum, *Entwicklung, Vererbung und Abstammung*, Dornach 1961

Edmond Schoorel (red.), *Leren, op weg naar een antroposofische leertheorie*, Driebergen 1995

Rudolf Steiner, *Die menschliche Seele in ihrem Zusammenhang mit göttlich-geistigen Individualitäten*, GA 224.

———. *Zur Sinneslehre. Themen aus dem Gesamtwerk, Band 3*, Stuttgart 1990

Baruch Luke Urieli, en Hans Müller-Wiedemann. *Übungswege zur Erfahrung des Aetherischen*, Dornach 1995

F.G. Verhulst, *Ontwikkeling van het kind*, Assen 1997

Lucie Wassink en Edmond Schoorel, *Kindertekeningen*, Driebergen 1996

Frank Wijnbergh, *De twee stromen*, Schoorl 1995

Frits Wilmar, *Kinderziekten in het licht der anthroposophie*, Den Haag z.j.

———. *Vorgeburtliche Menschwerdung*, Stuttgart 1979

Index